C000230471

Anyone can experience trauma and be (My brother and friend Josh has written treatment of how trauma 'rewires' the of life of the PTSD victim is masterful person, but takes the reader on a journey victim's family, friends, pastors, chaplains, mental health professionals, the Holy Spirit and Scripture. Josh's writings reinforce the notion that it does take a village to encourage, energize and experience the joy of a person's recovery from the effects of trauma.

Mike Higgins
Retired US Army Chaplain
Colonel with experience in hospitals, FORSCOM, and the Pentagon
Pastor, South City Church (PCA), St Louis, Missouri

Holler provides an illuminating account of the grief and tensions resulting from his service as a Marine. He argues that many of the difficulties that veterans face when returning from deployments arise from the radical disparities between the values and traditions of the military and society. Whereas veteran suicides are often attributed to PTSD, Holler suggests that the isolation and lack of communal support are more decisive. Since the book applies Biblical analysis to military disciplines, it offers invaluable insights for Christians concerned with understanding and assisting veterans struggling with grief and loss of identity.

Mark R. Amstutz
Professor Emeritus, Wheaton College, Wheaton, Illinois
CDR, U.S. Naval Reserve (r)

One word leaps out to the reader of *Redeeming Warriors* – Honesty. Josh Holler presents a candidly engrossing account of the veteran's struggle with suicide ideation. His evaluation of Marine Corps ethos, returning from combat, and subsequent caregiving is accurate without hyperbolic accusation, while showing Jesus as the grace solution. Well-written, this book is an essential read for those who have served in the military or desirous of helping the vet appropriately reengage civilian culture. It's an excellent resource for all intent on assisting with the healing process of those who have faithfully served and now endure the rigors of reintegration.

Richard Townes
Retired Marine and US Navy Chaplain,
Pastor, Bethel Lutheran Church, Howard City, Mississippi

Josh Holler's book is an intriguing blend of raw military stories and relevant spiritual truth. Additionally, he tackles the serious issue of Veteran suicides with compassion, wisdom, creativity and empathy. He offers hope for Vets struggling with life itself as he provides a positive path forward for them. This is a great book for someone thinking about joining the military, too. It will open their eyes to the life of a Warrior.

Douglas E. Lee
Chaplain (BG), US Army (Ret)

Josh Holler gives an excellent perspective on how the trauma of war, the comradery among enlisted warriors, and the grief of suicide intersect with the good news of the Gospel. Pastors who are not veterans should read this book to understand the veteran's mindset and how to minister to our warriors returning from a war which is often forgotten here in the safety of the USA. I wish I could have read *Redeeming Warriors* before I deployed with the 821st TC BN in 2011. I think I would have been a better chaplain if I had done so.

J. Alan Branch
Professor, Christian Ethics, Midwestern Baptist Theological Seminary,
Kansas City, Missouri

In *Redeeming Warriors*, Marine Corps veteran and pastor Josh Holler offers a deeply thoughtful and incisive response to veteran suicide. Rather than limiting his scope to PTSD-related loss, his expansive view is more holistic, considering the breadth and depth of experiences military members face throughout their service. Having known nine veterans who took their own lives, Holler's approach is as compassionate as it is brave, and as forthright as it is nuanced. I recommend this valuable resource for military and civilian readers alike.

Jocelyn Green
Co-author of *The 5 Love Languages Military Edition*
and *Stories of Faith and Courage from the War in Iraq & Afghanistan*

One of the very best books ever written on the critical subject of veteran suicide! *Redeeming Warriors* provides a powerful 'translation' of the gospel to provide a path to redemption and reconciliation for our veterans. This trailblazing book applies not just to veterans; but to many other areas where modern culture and technology slams head-on into human frailty and the deep need for God in our lives. Using a framework of 'Creation, Fall, Redemption, and Consummation,' Josh Holler shows us the road to reconciliation with God, for everyone who is lost in these traumatic, tumultuous times.

One of the truly unique and powerful contributions of this book is to lead the way to 'vertical' and 'horizontal' reconciliation. Vertical reconciliation refers to our innate, deep seated need for peace with God the Creator. The horizontal aspect of reconciliation is the role of our salvation and relationship with God, in all other aspects of our lives. This horizontal reconciliation is one of the great challenges. The author demonstrates that factors like sleep deprivation and Facebook have 'more to do with veteran suicide than combat or PTSD does.' One of the most powerful and useful observations in this brilliant work is that 'the problem isn't with "them" (veterans) as much as it is with "us" (society as a whole).'

Redeeming Warriors gives us hope for healing not just our veterans, but also (and most importantly) healing our culture and our society with the redeeming power of the gospel. Thus, 'the worst parts of our culture will be subverted, and the best parts will be redeemed. First, a redemption back to Christ, second, a redemption with each other that comes as a result of the first. This is what it means to redeem warriors.'

A hearty 'Well done,' Josh! You are a true, redeeming warrior pathfinder, blazing a trail for healing and redemption in our veterans and our world at large, with the gospel of Christ!

Lt Col Dave Grossman (retired)
Author of *On Killing, On Combat, On Spiritual Combat,*
and *Bulletproof Marriage: A 90-Day Devotional*

Veteran suicide is one of the most painful realities facing today's military community and families. Josh Holler's Redeeming Warriors is an important resource for greater understanding and empathy. May it equip many to minister with compassion to those at risk and to walk alongside those who have suffered loss.

Albert Y. Hsu
Senior editor, IVP Press
Author of *Grieving a Suicide:*
A Loved One's Search for Comfort, Answers, and Hope

We lose 8,000 veterans each year. Right now, a Marine with whom I served has been missing for months. It's assumed he's taken his own life and has yet to be found. The moral injury inflicted on our veterans wreaks havoc on them and their families as they resume 'normal life'. Josh Holler is no stranger to this, but he notes that this brokenness is not isolated to our military veterans, as the recent tragic suicides of several well-known pastors sadly illustrate. Josh helpfully examines the issues, considers the situation, and suggests practical ways to help those at risk—and he does so from a biblical foundation. Read and share this book.

Lt Col Karl Johnson, USMC (Ret.)
Director, C.S. Lewis Institute, Chicago
Senior Advisor, Ravi Zacharias Intl. Ministries

Having also served in Southern Iraq with Multinational Division (South East) in 2007, we can identify with much of the military culture described in this compelling mix of applied theology and wise counsel. Drawing many parallels with the military, Josh Holler applies the truth of the gospel of Jesus Christ with engaging clarity and penetrating analysis. His first-hand accounts of life as a US Marine draw us into a strange and unique culture that both captivates and repels in equal measure but forms the basis for timeless truths to be examined and applied. A deep concern for military veterans underpins the author's longing for all men and women to be reconciled with their Creator through saving faith in Jesus Christ.

Colonel John Lewis
UK Force Support Commander – MND(SE) - 2006/7

REDEEMING
WARRIORS

VETERAN SUICIDE, GRIEVING, AND THE FIGHT FOR FAITH

JOSHUA D. HOLLER

Scripture quotations are from *The Holy Bible, English Standard Version*, copyright © 2001 by Crossway Bibles, a publishing ministry of Good News Publishers. Used by permission. All rights reserved. esv Text Edition: 2011.

Copyright © Joshua D. Holler 2020

paperback ISBN 978-1-5271-0586-7
epub ISBN 978-1-5271-0661-1
mobi ISBN 978-1-5271-0662-8

10 9 8 7 6 5 4 3 2 1

Published in 2020
by
Christian Focus Publications Ltd,
Geanies House, Fearn, Ross-shire,
IV20 1TW, Great Britain.

www.christianfocus.com

Cover design by
Pete Barnsley

Printed and bound by
Bell & Bain, Glasgow

All rights reserved. No part of this publication may be reproduced, stored in a retrieval system, or transmitted, in any form, by any means, electronic, mechanical, photocopying, recording or otherwise without the prior permission of the publisher or a licence permitting restricted copying. In the U.K. such licences are issued by the Copyright Licensing Agency, 4 Battlebridge Lane, London SE1 2HX. www.cla.co.uk

CONTENTS

For Lance Corporal Nickoli David Diamond

February 10th, 1988 – June 3rd, 2013

ACKNOWLEDGEMENTS

Writing *Redeeming Warriors* was the fastest and longest piece of writing I have done to date. In March of 2017, while still a full year and half from finishing seminary, I began writing. It was one of the few times that I *felt* the hand of God was upon me in a providential way, blessing me with clarity and speed. In less than a month, I finished a 70,000-word draft between classes, papers, being a dad, a husband, working, and sleeping occasionally. The draft remained untouched until a contract was in hand and the tedious and needed refining work began. This book would not have been possible without the help of two people, in particular, Jay Yosef and Dr. Robert A. Peterson, theologian and writer. Monthly I would funnel the chapters their way and elicit their feedback, suggestions, and sometimes pointed corrections. Without them, my writing would not possess the same quality, unity and form. I am also indebted to the training of the pastors and professors at Covenant Theological Seminary. In particular, my dear friend, fellow veteran and pastor Andrew Martin assisted me in listening, processing and articulating the applications of the gospel into a military culture on our long runs. This present work is apologetics, theology and counseling as best as I know how. Among my frequent trips to Midwestern

Baptist Theological Seminary came long conversations with a former teammate and friend, Kyle Patton. Kyle helped me to articulate my arguments and think through the complexities of our disparate communities and the peculiar social environment we live in. I most certainly would not have been able to make it through this long process if not for my wife's faithful encouragement. As a helpmate, there is no better. Lastly, this book would not be possible without the grace of God who blessed and protected me while I waded through waves of grief, depression and processing the deaths of my brothers in arms. May glory be to our great God, alone.

INTRODUCTION

During my time in seminary I read a book called *Translating the Message* by Lamin Sanneh. The book was heady, dry, slow-going, and in general, a tough read. And yet, it is perhaps the single most influential work that lies behind this current book. At a bird's eye view, Sanneh's thesis is that wherever Christian missionaries have gone, they have *not* destroyed culture through aggressive practices (a common misconception), but rather, the reverse is true. While horrific practices like 'foot binding' in China or Sati (burning widows alive with their deceased husbands) in India have been subverted, the best aspects of any given culture haven't been destroyed, but preserved and redeemed. How could this be? In part, this is to credit the essence of the Christian message which is meant to be translated. Jesus' earthly ministry in first century Palestine was likely in Aramaic. Yet the New Testament was written in Greek. Why? Because the message of Christianity bears with it the presupposition that it is translatable. It is translatable because it is a transcendent message that is true for all times and all places, and in particular, for *all* cultures.

When it comes to the military culture of our day, I see many noteworthy and admirable cultural features, artifacts, and rituals. But it also has many barriers that have made it resistant to the Christian message. This is ironic, because on the one hand the military borrows many Christian truths, while simultaneously distancing themselves from where those truths are derived. My two greatest concerns are 1) the alarming rate at which veterans are taking their own lives and 2) the disengagement of our military culture. I believe firmly that reaching active-duty, reserve service members and veterans is primarily an issue of the translation of the gospel. The issue of veteran suicide, in my estimation, is not an isolated anomaly of the military. The complexities of the military subculture isolate its members from Christian engagement and increase the same problems everyone else in the West is facing. In other words, veteran suicide (for example) is a greater problem in the military versus its civilian counterpart because of the cultural complexities that exasperate the pressures upon current or prior service members. To be clear, what is taking place in the military is also taking place outside of it. Suicides are on the rise, and for many of the same reasons (as will be discussed in chapters nine and fifteen). Thus, the way forward I propose and hope to demonstrate in translating the gospel is not an isolated suggestion unique to a particular kind of suicide. With some minor adjustments, suggestions can be applied to the broader population.

As for the format of this book, it follows an order. Chapter Two retells the story of my friend Kythe Yund, who took his own life. His story is exemplary and serves as a template for how and why many veteran suicides take place. While there are always exceptions, his story demonstrates many of the key factors behind veteran suicide while simultaneously debunking the misconceptions about suicide always being tied to combat experience and PTSD (though it sometimes is; this will be discussed in chapter sixteen). Chapters Four through Six and Eighteen very intentionally follow a framework of 'Creation, Fall, Redemption, and Consummation,' the outline of the story of Scripture told through the rubric of

Semper Fidelis. The purpose behind this is to emphasize the need for reconciliation. Reconciliation is a word flippantly thrown around (in discussion of race, for example) and can be misunderstood. Reconciliation possesses two dimensions, one vertical and one horizontal.

Vertical reconciliation is the need for the creature to be reconciled to the Creator. This 'being made right' and securing peace with God is the priority (as will be discussed in Chapter Eight). A horizontal reconciliation is what occurs in light of the vertical. While the vertical reconciliation makes us right with God, the horizontal describes the effects and the implications that vertical reconciliation has for our lives. So, while Chapters Four through Six and Eighteen are more neatly focused on this vertical aspect of reconciliation, the intervening chapters examine its horizontal implications. Chapters Seven through Seventeen also seek to unpack the cultural complexities that have made the causes and solutions of veteran suicide difficult to understand.

Throughout the book I have intentionally scaled the language barrier between military culture, particularly the Marine Corps' own dialect, and that of the civilian world. The military speaks another language of acronyms, slang, and borrowed vernacular. The Marine Corps derives many of its terms from Navy nomenclature and customs that have, like other words in the English language, ceased to refer to one thing and now apply to another. I have defined and translated every term and acronym that was necessary to the story without which it would not have been understood. This 'translation' work is necessary, but it is, at best, supplemental to hearing the stories in their context that give meaning to the challenge veterans, active-duty or otherwise, face. I have included a glossary of terms in the back of the book to help readers.

While I will readily admit I am not a psychologist, statistician, medical doctor, or non-profit founder of an organization focusing outreach to veterans, I believe this book has something to offer. It demonstrates that the impulse of our 'solutions' has produced a niched society that is overspecialized and non-communal. Here is one of the sub-theses of this book in terms of horizontal reconciliation: Facebook has more to do with veteran suicide than combat or PTSD does. To riff in the same direction of Sebastian Junger's recent work, *Tribe*, the problem isn't with 'them' (veterans) as much as it is with 'us' (society as a whole). To be more pointed than Junger, our biggest problem doesn't lie within society as much as it rests in the chasm between a holy God and His image-bearing creatures.

1

THE TWENTY-TWO

Lance Corporal Angel R. Ramirez:
June 19, 1979–February 21, 2007

Twenty-two veterans take their lives every day. The word 'tragic' only begins to describe the brokenness of this painful reality. This alarming, oft-cited statistic originates from a 2012 study conducted by the Department of Veterans Affairs. Though some have contested the figure for not counting some high-veteran states like California and Texas, this number reflects a deeply troubling reality. These deaths represent untold stories, unheard cries, and the torment of a void at the center of one's being which longs for an identity, hungers for satisfaction, and yearns for fulfillment.

I have known nine men who took that final step into darkness. Each death was heart-wrenching and shook me when I heard the news. Five of the nine impacted my life more deeply than the others, and, subsequently, their deaths did as well.

My first exposure to veteran suicide came the first week I arrived in the fleet as a Marine. 'The fleet' refers to the unit a Marine is assigned once completing boot camp and any MOS (military occupational specialty) training, which is simply military speak for 'a job.' I joined the Marines to be in the infantry. The infantry's MOS school is known as SOI (the School of Infantry). After SOI, infantry Marines are assigned to respective units as 'boat spaces' (the terminology the Navy and Marine Corps use for 'job openings') are made available. The vocabulary sounds confusing to an outsider, since we aren't actually assigned to a boat, but as the Marine Corps is technically a branch of the Navy, our nomenclature is indebted to our historical roots when both branches were more integrated. Six other Marines and I were assigned to 3rd Battalion, 4th Marine Regiment (3/4 for short—said like 'three-four') in Twentynine Palms, California.

The onslaught of terminology is a lot to take in when listening to a veteran's story. It tires us in details, and zaps our initial interest in listening. Learning another language, though, requires patience and devotion, which thrive best when in relationship with someone. The energy it takes to delve into a veteran's story is worth it, though the learning curve is steep. The best place to start is at the beginning. This starting point allows us to establish the baseline while we listen. It gives us the new normal and subsequently allows us to contrast the departure from normal in context. As one of my history professors said, 'No context, no meaning. Know context, know meaning.' So, where does that take us? For me, it takes the story back to my arrival at Twentynine Palms.

Twentynine Palms may sound nice, but its name is misleading. Twentynine Stumps, the town's nickname (or just 'Stumps'), is more fitting, given its location in a rural desert community. Even the palm trees in this seemingly land-locked island look depressed. Tattoo joints, massage parlors, and barber shops pepper the town, leading one to wonder if the local economy could survive if not for the influx of military servicemen and women living in this isolated place. This was the town we would call 'home' for the next three and a half years.

The unit 3/4 is affectionately dubbed by its rival units the 'bastard children' of Marine infantry regiments. Somewhat analogous to high school football rivals, their 'otherness' is not ascribed because of competition, but by an attachment to a peculiar dishonor. Their colors, the respective flags symbolizing their unit found outside their regimental office, haven't been allowed to return home since the Second World War. At that time they were surrendered, to the enduring shame of the Marines, by Army Lt. Gen. Jonathan Wainwright when Japanese troops invaded the Philippines. Though Wainwright was awarded the Congressional Medal of Honor for his actions before his understandable surrender, Marines do not remember him that way, least among 3/4. The honorable is forgotten, and the last action is all that is recalled. I supposed that's like veteran suicide, too. Having a misfit heritage doesn't necessarily make 3/4 a misfit regiment today, but it does taint their story with a bit of sad irony. They are a regiment without a home, and like many Marines who return home, they never *really* return. Coming home assumes that things are right not only with those returning, but also with the place to which they return. And it's rarely one, let alone both.

Within the first few days of checking into our battalion, being issued our new gear, and settling into the barracks, we met Lance Corporal (LCPL) Ramirez. The rest of the battalion was still deployed, so we were placed in the Remain Behind Element (RBE). Our experience of checking into the fleet differed from the stories we had heard in the School of Infantry, because 3/4 was still deployed and was unexpectedly extended for a few more months in Iraq. Those who remained stateside in the platoon were a mixture of Marines transitioning out of service, others who faced non-judicial punishments, (NJP, for short. The Armed Forces are governed by the Uniform Code of Military Justice, UCMJ, and the lesser sentences passed by the military penal systems are NJPs), and a small fraction who were injured and or were otherwise unable to deploy.

I vividly remember the stare of one Marine who had been terribly injured in battle from his previous deployment. A RPG (rocket-propelled grenade) had exploded near him, leaving

17

him scarred from dozens of shrapnel wounds and without one of his eyes, revealing a hollow, empty socket that was uncomfortable to look upon. His solemn and penetrating gaze scared me, and rightfully so. I had heard stories and seen movies where men who had experienced unspeakable things on the battlefield undesirably possessed the 'thousand-yard' stare. If there's anyone I know who had that haunted gaze, it was he.

I avoided him as much as I possibly could, which seemed easy enough. I didn't want to be around him, and he didn't want to be around us. I couldn't stand the discomfort of being around him. He, on the other hand, along with the other injured Marines, seemed to project a feeling of disdain. They *hated* us, or so it felt. The looks they gave us were alarmingly akin to the look a paralyzed man has watching someone run. Their eyes said with anger, 'They don't know what they have.' In hindsight, I wonder if this is the same way my Marine brothers, though not bearing any outward injury, perceive the civilian population. While my brothers-in-arms have internalized an alienating, non-conveyable experience, civilians are often enamored with the fictitious glory of war stories, blood lust, or are coldly apathetic to war experiences in general.

Ramirez had been medically evacuated from Al Qaim, a city in the western Al-Anbar province of Iraq, and had to return home earlier than expected to recuperate from some illness or injury, of which the specifics remained a mystery. From what we heard, he hadn't been injured in any combat related incident, so his presence home while his unit was off fighting was colored with a shade of shame. This is an unfortunate attitude that is often projected on Marines, and likely other service members, who face circumstances beyond their control. The honor-shame culture of the Marine Corps runs deep, cutting contours and pathways which appear impossible to re-route or redeem. If there is a fight to be had, then they must do what they can to get into it. Whether that's pushing through an illness or injury, even to the neglect of one's family, all must be sacrificed for the sake of maintaining this often-unattainable sense of honor for a battle which may never even come.

Like most other senior infantry Marines, he had deployed multiple times and yet was only a Lance Corporal. This paradox is largely unique to the Marine Infantry, in which men who bear impossible responsibilities are restrained from advancing through the ranks, though they will nearly always occupy a billet (a position) which technically requires a higher rank. To off-set for this idiosyncrasy and to create distance between *boots* (new-joins or 'newbies'), lance-corporals, and the *salty* (experienced) ones, the boots are required to call them by their rank. To call someone a *boot* denotes the very lowest derogatory connotation. No one is dumber than a boot. No one is greener or more inexperienced than a non-deployed boot. No one, except POGs (personnel other than grunts). The term POG refers to any and all Marines who aren't in the infantry, which was yet another tier of distancing the infantry from the non-infantry. A *boot* can eventually graduate from his status by deploying, but a POG is always a POG. When Ramirez demanded we call him by his rank, it struck us as both novel and absurd. No official regulation demands this, but when the hot-tempered Ramirez barked a command, no argument from me or anyone else would attempt to sway him. So, though we hesitated, we quickly and unwillingly adapted to this new rule. Life in the grunts was just the beginning. We had arrived at the fleet, but we hadn't yet earned respect.

'I am the most senior lance-corporal in the battalion, and *you will* do as I say,' he demanded. We believed him. We had no reason not to believe him. The RBE platoon commander who witnessed this engagement spectated with an indifferent nod of agreement. Though I and the others who checked into 3/4 with me were only one rank below Ramirez, there was more distance created between us by his cammies (his uniform) than his rank alone. We had two styles of uniforms issued to us—Woodland, and Desert. A common indication of a 'salty' Lance Corporal is one whose cammies have faded beyond their normal color. The Woodland cammies (dark greens and deep browns) eventually give way to lighter tones, while the Desert cammies lightened eventually to look almost nothing like when they were new. Having new cammies isn't a thing to be excited about in the same way a civilian might be glad he has a new pair of jeans. Cammie color is one of the many *de facto* ways in which the enlisted men in the infantry showed their seniority. The other outward indicator was haircuts. The 'high and tight' or a clean-shaven head was the only authorized haircut for us boots in the infantry. Once you had deployed you could get a lower cut, a 'medium-reg' or even the envied 'low-reg,' which showed the maximum saltiness and minimum compliance to the rules. Ritualistically, the night before the first deployment for boots, their head would be shaved as a reminder; like entering boot camp, it serves as a reminder they haven't earned their stripes yet. Ramirez's rank may have only been one above us, but he had all the external signs to indicate his seniority and saltiness, his faded cammies, his low-reg haircut, and his demand that we call him by his rank.

Jones, one of the Marines with whom I had been in the SOI Guard platoon, quickly became my closest friend. We became acquainted during a four-week delay to fulfill Guard Duty. We repeatedly failed to process our experiences as boots in the fleet and tried a few times to put words to it, though we were isolated socially as boots, and geographically, being in the desert. Everything from boot camp through Guard, SOI, attempts at Marine Recon, was always new and came attached with new, unexplained rules, new *faux pas*, and often contradictory from one stage to the next. This Ramirez Marine was a reminder that even though we had received our Eagle Globe & Anchor, the insignia of the Marine Corps, had completed SOI (specifically the Infantry Training Battalion), and trained in our MOS, we were still very much at the bottom rung of fleet Marines. Our rank was of no consequence. All that mattered was if we had been deployed, and only after being humbled long enough as boots, hopefully we, too, could become salty, hardened Marines. Maybe we would even haunt our subordinates with our own 'thousand-yard stare.' At least that seemed a trait to be desired, back then.

Our assumptions about how life was going to be in the fleet were rapidly taking form, and none by our will or desire. We thought Ramirez was going to be the hammer and we his anvil, and therefore we anticipated a miserable existence being boots under him awaiting the return of the rest of the unit. But this didn't happen. Instead, during morning formation—shock, disbelief, bewilderment— we were informed Ramirez had taken his life the night before. A swarm of thoughts were running through our heads, but fear and an attempt at professionalism restrained them. The first 'working-party' that Jones and I experienced in the fleet was cleaning Ramirez's suicide scene in his barracks room head (the bathroom) where he had hung himself with his skivvy shirt (the drab olive undershirt we wore with our cammies). His funeral would be held in his hometown; he was leaving behind him a wife and kids, and we weren't allowed to participate in his funeral. Grieving, it seemed, wasn't a part of the process of burying a Marine. Perhaps, as boots, we hadn't earned the right to mourn.

The Navy Chaplain, whose presence felt more like an obligation than a calling, came and spoke a few words with the RBE platoon and was gone. He may have spoken to some of the guys in private, but I don't know. Our perception of many of the chaplains from thereafter was a negative one. I knew all of them probably meant well. I was positively impacted by others in my unit later on. But chaplain was a strange position that was discolored with its own distance on a number of levels. Chaplains were Navy; we were Marines. They were officers; we were enlisted. They occasionally showed up to training; we trained. Many had gone straight out of high school to college, while most enlisted join the military right out of high school. The challenge that a chaplain must overcome to serve the men or women he is attached to is a difficult one. And it's not one I had any sympathy for while I was on active duty, nor, do I suspect, most currently enlisted, Marines or veterans.

Within a week of Ramirez taking his life, a Marine from 3/4 from my hometown was killed in action. A color guard and Marines to attend his funeral were quickly assembled and sent to Dodge City, Kansas. The tenor of anguish for those who died in combat in contrast to Ramirez was stark. One died honorably in battle; the other dishonorably by his own hand. At least that's how it seemed at the time. The truth is, I didn't know how I was supposed to perceive it. That's still how most people think of suicide – we're unsure how to categorize it. This is why I think many of us operate with an oversimplified view of it.

The night Ramirez died, Jones and I went for a ride in his car just to get off base and get away as much as we could for the few fleeting hours of 'liberty.' Twentynine Palms isn't close to much that two underage men can do with only a few short hours. Anything interesting either costs too much money (like Vegas, which was about 2.5 hours away) or is too far to drive in our short time. When we left that night, we had no specific destination, but everything particular about what we shared in our thoughts.

That was a seminal night for us both. We shared the feeling of our identity being stripped from us, and we were powerless to stop it and unable fully to put words to it. We had accepted many of the changes that came our way; we both joined the Marines right out of high school, had done boot camp and training through the summer, but the cadence of returning home wasn't there; only the Corps was there. The haircuts, uniforms, the language, culture, where we lived, everything had lost its novel shine, and we realized it that night. On the one hand, we wanted to get away and tell someone, process with someone, 'Who am I, now?' But on the other hand, we felt crippled by fear of reprisal, neglect of duty, and abandoning the oath from which we felt estranged. We would never willingly, shamefully, leave the Marine Corps, but we both wondered if we would leave it *unwillingly*. It was such a sudden, solemn, anticlimactic, and inglorious end for Ramirez. Was this what life was going to be like? Do Marines just die and no one grieves? Does anyone care?

We drove down the hill and through the dark valleys and deserts with their heat fleeting from the onset of the night falling. Not in a mood for Avenged Sevenfold or the other hardcore bands, we settled for the minor tones of a song by Less Than Jake. I remember that song, not because it was formative to us then, but because in hindsight, it was a tragic foreshadowing of the many Marines that I would come to know who would quietly walk into the night and take their own lives.

'This is my all time low'
Somehow it feels so familiar
Somehow it seems so familiar
I feel like letting go
And every second that goes by
I'm screaming out for a second try
Said goodbye, to my best friend
Sometimes there's no one left to tell me the truth

Within a week, the few Marines that I was with were suddenly moved cross-deck to 1/7. Moving cross-deck means moving laterally from one unit to another. Usually going cross-deck occurs when a sister unit deployed, has suffered casualties, and needs replacements. The replacements go with the condition that they will return to their unit once they return home. And just like that, by moving cross-deck we were separated from seeing the effect Ramirez's death had on his friends in RBE. Just as obscurely as we had entered into his life, one afternoon in the barracks he silently departed from us. His story was not one we specially knew, but the pattern was one we would see unfold again and again.

It is horrible to think that some unnamed affliction marred internally one who was decorated from deployments and his service. I did not know that Ramirez's suicide foreshadowed what I would later witness in greater detail with men with whom I had a tighter bond. His death became a bookend to an indefinite time period filled with suicides whose end I and many others don't know. But he was the first. Two weeks in the fleet and a man had killed himself. I would come to know eight more. Eight that had their own stories, torments, voids, longings, dreams, and reasons for taking their lives. Eight men who are no longer with us and whom their brothers terribly miss.

WAYS OF KNOWING

People interact with suicide differently. Some of us know it distantly, like words on a page, and engage it with a sort of cognitive understanding. We understand the logic of suicide—a person kills himself or herself. But this is a one-dimensional way of knowing. It's flat and cold. Others have friends or family members, veterans or not, who have taken their own lives. People in this category understand suicide more truly. It is comparable to being in a car-wreck and surviving, but seeing and feeling the impact of cars colliding, glass shattering, your body being jolted, and re-formulating your life plans in light of the death of the loved one next to you. And there are some who have attempted suicide and grazed their hand over that veil that divides life from death. Too easily, it could have been torn back and their self-demise met. Too easily their hand was filled with an overdose of pills. Too easily the cold muzzle of a gun and the taste of metal was in their mouths, but they didn't pull the trigger. Maybe a blade caressed the skin or made its sharp and gaping cut revealing the life blood that moves through their veins, but they didn't go all the way, or they survived the attempt.

We all interact with suicide with different starting points, different stories, and varying experiences. C. S. Lewis said that there are two ways of knowing: like one standing in a darkened toolshed and seeing a beam of light, filled with dust particles, piercing through a window and onto the floor. When looking *along* the light, you can see by it, illumining the rest of the tool shed from the sun outside. And then we can know by looking *into* the light, by which everything else is concealed by the brightness of the light itself, and you can see nothing but its source—the sun that gives the light. In a similar but distinct way, there are two ways of knowing suicide. Many stand looking along the light; except it isn't light, but darkness. We may stand several feet back or perhaps right next to it, hesitantly testing it by placing our hand in it. Secondly, some have stood immersed in it, having actually died or have come a breath away from death, nearly collapsing under its weight and the false seduction that it offers relief and respite.

No single experience in the arena of self-killing is the same. No single experience is right or wrong. Likely it's filled with mixed motivations and purposes, noble and malicious, honorable and misguided. I don't write to dismiss those who don't understand this on a personal level, rather to invite them to step closer to those who have. This invitation isn't to toy with suicide, or feather its borders, but to look along the light and see that knowing suicide intimately is something we learn about because a day will come when we no longer have to. Suicide offers no solutions, gives no comfort, only brings pain, only increases suffering and damage. Suicide is wrought with lies and self-deception, and should be as vehemently opposed as a man who breaks into a home to kill people in their sleep. Suicide, because of how it is conceived and spoken of, often loses its tragic connotation through euphemistic gloss. But make no mistake—suicide is self-murder.

We live in a society that calls adultery 'an affair,' an addiction 'a disorder,' or self-loathing reflections 'depression.' In this case, suicide is a better term than self-murder. Though murder mars our own personhood, the term 'self-murder' labels the violence but leaves out the story. I reach for a word that can accurately label suicide and carry all its meanings. We feel tension, as we should, when we call suicide 'self-murder.' It is not the way it's supposed to be. There is something both broken and missing from the story. It feels absent of meaning and in some ways it is. And so, as astute readers know, we find the meaning of words not by a dictionary, but by their usage in context. The meaning of a person's life who has taken his/her own life is not, then, summarized by their final and fatal action. Their meaning and worth can be seen through lives that provide the framework of their story. Though we shouldn't distance ourselves from the true self-violence of suicide, we shouldn't define a person's inherent worth and dignity by their final action. Indeed, I believe there is a grand narrative, a grand story that applies to all people everywhere that gives purpose, meaning, and hope to finite human existence. And that is why I am writing for the twenty-two, be they actually twenty-two, or twenty, or twelve. I am writing for them.

I write not as one who holds degrees in psychology, psychiatry, counseling, anthropology or as one who has received accolades from years of working in suicide prevention centers, but as one who has looked along the light, perhaps pressing my hand forward into it, and seeing friends to my right and left that have been taken by suicide. I write, in many respects, a memoir, but I don't hope to offer only my experience, but to offer hope. I wish, as a former Marine who engaged in warrioring, that I can apply the biblical story of redemption in which the atonement for the brokenness of Christ's redeemed people was purchased through blood. He is the warrior King of redemption, who is currently putting His enemies under His feet, and by His death, defeated death. So as a Christian, who loves my brothers-in-arms, I write this so that they can learn to fight the good fight, understand that their yearnings can be satisfied and their emptiness filled. I write to explain that no one is beyond redemption for atrocities committed against others or ourselves. Even in light of the pain we have made our families suffer or the haunt of honor that we sense for experiences we wish we had, there *is* hope.

I want to caution against universalizing one's experience and projecting it upon every veteran or person who has contemplated suicide. Not everything I write will resonate with everyone. Each of the stories of friends who took their own lives comes with a different context and varied circumstances. I discovered that one of the greatest hurdles for veterans wanting to share their story with others is that many too quickly assumed that they either must suffer from PTSD and/or saw killing on the same level of those in previous arenas of war, like the terrible things the Allied Forces in the South Pacific went through in WW2. I want to urge people to enter a person's story on the terms they offer. Be quick to listen, and slow to speak, both in interacting with this book and with the friends and neighbors we have in our lives.

2

A NARRATIVE WE MUST PRIVILEGE

Lance Corporal Kythe Yund:
June 18, 1989–June 17, 2011

I've been under the command of both good and difficult men during my service. I've likewise had many fine young men under my leadership whose stories I was privileged to hear and sometimes enter. One such Marine was Kythe Yund. Interestingly, I didn't know Kythe's first name for the longest time. This is actually a very common thing in the Marines, where people are known by rank and last name. It is still odd to this day to interact with my old Marine buddies and call them by their first names. It feels as wrong as calling one of your old teachers anything other than 'Mr.' or 'Mrs.' But this differs from a teacher-student relationship, in that you're on different levels of authority. There is nevertheless a space created between someone's true identity and the person we come to know. Naming seems more significant than we realize and is something we rarely ponder.

Kythe entered into my life as a boot, and candidly, he was a sarcastic young man with a wry smile that was often too smug for his own good. His own quick sense of humor and wit made him well-liked by many in the platoon, even those senior to him, though Kythe served many punishments because of his sarcasm. The distance between those in the infantry who had deployed and those who hadn't often bleeds over into separation between groups at every level of command, cascading downward from the company, platoon, squad, and team level. One might say it is a type of cliquishness, but differs from high school cliques. Some differences that normally separate people are arbitrary and non-binding in the Marines. Socio-economic status means nothing, which I would say is a good thing; race, which is a buzzword for many people, also means nothing in the infantry. There is no black, brown, white, or yellow; everyone is appropriately reduced and simultaneously promoted to green. I suspect that this contour is also found in other branches of the armed forces. What matters is if you have deployed. A senior Marine on the platoon level isn't someone who has necessarily been in service for years, but someone who has deployed overseas. Nevertheless, Yund's demeanor won him my approval, even though I had to punish him many times.

During my second deployment, I was fortunate to spend many long hours on post with Yund, posts that would last six hours in a rotation. This is one of the primary areas in which men form bonds, and which makes them ache when distance separates them. Yund and I shared an interest in music, playing guitar, Mixed-Martial Arts, and wrestling. In fact, he knew an all-American who wrestled for the University of Minnesota to whom I had lost a close match at a tournament in Colorado, where Kythe had lived for several years. Although Kythe described himself as an agnostic or atheist, his intellectual prowess made him a superb conversationalist. Our differing views on the origins, meaning, morality, and destiny of life made for stimulating times that chewed up hours on post. It was very good for two men with such different views to be forced to find common ground while standing in a metal box for hours on end. There is no room for pompousness in such a scenario, no room to consume the time talking about yourself, but much to be gained by listening, processing, and entering into one another's story. And to a certain degree, Kythe let me do that with him. This wasn't true for all Marines, of course. Perez, another one of my Marines, had poor English and wasn't able to quickly speak or formulate stories. So, whenever he stood on post with Yund, he would pass the time by requesting him to sing. Yund possessed an appealing singing voice—he even performed in some concerts with another Marine named Hood. Perez would request *Hotel California* by the Eagles, and Yund would gladly oblige by singing it, again and again. This song, I later learned, still reminds Perez of Yund every time he hears it.

One of my favorite memories of Yund is when we first met. Telling it makes me laugh out loud. Yund had done something to demand my attention and disapproval. Upon being late to formation, I had assigned him to write out his general orders as well as a short essay on why he shouldn't be late to formation. I gave the task over the weekend, and it was something tedious and painful to do during the few hours of liberty junior Marines like Yund got. I would rather have taken him out to the dirt and made him run until regret was cemented with a mortar of sweat so never to allow the infraction to recur. But like most other Marines, he coveted the weekend, and a tedious task of writing and re-writing general orders was the second-best punishment. When he returned the essay to me at the following Monday morning formation, I read it. He had not planned on my actually reading it, because on the second page, this weekend essay turned into a mouthful of cursings and reasons why the punishment was in his words, 'BS.' We had another formation later that day in which, while standing next to him at parade rest, I informed him that we would be going for a run in full gear after our evening formation. And then Yund did something I never expected—he offered me money not to do it. He actually tried to bribe me! I was shocked, and even offended that he would try such a thing.

Although Yund descended to this low during his first few months in the unit, he still quickly won the affection of most. Months later, while we were deployed, he brought up his attempted bribe in conversation and remarked that Rangel, another Marine in our unit, had accepted the bribe when Yund was on the wrong end of Rangel's punishment. This was absolutely hilarious to me. Rangel had been busted down (demoted) by the command for previous infractions. And though Rangel was technically senior to Yund and me, he acted like someone who wanted respect but didn't want to earn it. Rangel had deployed before us but was a lazy Marine. It fitted Rangel's character to accept a bribe, and, in a weird way, we enjoyed camaraderie in our distaste for him, though this has dissipated over time. When I think of Yund, I don't remember him as a Marine struggling against the Marine Corps' rigid and hierarchical system. I think of him as a young man, gifted in many ways and liked by all.

Kythe's story, however, doesn't end in the way I wanted. Indeed, his story is nothing short of tragic. I had joined the Marines a couple years earlier than he, and after my second deployment, I was transitioning away from active duty, leaving him and many others I knew behind to begin college studies. Receiving a call from Benjamin during my first semester in college the year after coming off duty should have tripped my internal alarm. *Benjamin never calls anyone; he doesn't even have Facebook.* 'Hey, Holler,' he opened the conversation in his deep and serious tone. 'I'm calling because …' 'You're pregnant?' I stupidly blurted out. After about four years in the military many of the other married Marines were finally in a better position to provide for their wives and start a family, and so I assumed this could be a reason for the call. But knowing Benjamin better than that, I should have guessed differently. 'Uh … no,' he hesitantly responded. There was a long pause, and I heard Benjamin draw a deep, calculated breath. 'Yund killed himself,' he said slowly.

I was shocked. And yet I wasn't. On one hand, my mouth and heart became paralyzed, and I could feel an ache begin deep in my chest. Yet, while Benjamin filled me in on some of the details—Yund had shot himself in the head with a shotgun the moment his roommate Hood opened his door in the morning to wake him up. On the other hand, it eerily made sense. It made sense, not that Yund was a weak, depressed, suicidal guy, but a man who had everything stripped from him in a short period of time, leaving him exposed, vulnerable, and struggling to know who he was.

Towards the end of my second deployment, Yund heard terrible news. His wife of less than a year had a stroke, severe enough that she suffered short-term memory loss and could not remember who she was for several weeks. Yund, having to fly home from Iraq with only a couple months left in the deployment, was thrust headlong into being not only the financial provider for his wife, but her primary caregiver. He arrived home alone, not to be welcomed warmly by hundreds of friends and family on Victory Field like everyone else. Instead, he had to set aside his counter-insurgency tasks and learn to count, grind, and administer medication, schedule his wife's day, and perform a host of other unfamiliar duties— all as a new father to a beautiful, little girl.

Shortly after returning from our deployment, our company had a routine urine analysis. The 'piss tests,' as they are called, are extremely common, and if they don't assure the command we aren't doing drugs, then they certainly keep anyone from thinking about doing them. But Yund failed his test. Those who knew Yund were startled, but others had failed before, so I and others wondered if he had gotten a hold of some illegal drugs. His test indicated he had used some cocaine, but after hearing the results in more detail and speaking with him, the facts just didn't add up. A normal test result for someone using cocaine is around 2000 nanograms, but Yund was below 150, a number so alarmingly different one had to wonder if he really did use. Moreover, if so, where did he obtain the drug while he was taking care of his wife and newborn around the clock? To this day Yund's friends and I maintain, either the test was a false-positive, or there were trace amounts given through something like a straw in a restaurant. Apparently, this was not an uncommon occurrence in the high-desert town of California where we were stationed, where drug abuse was rampant among the civilian population.

Marines who fail drug tests are treated nearly as badly as Marines who desert their company and go UA (unauthorized absence or what civilians commonly call AWOL). Yund was stripped of his rank and reduced to a private, wearing no insignia, the same rank most Marines hold coming fresh out of boot camp. In a single move the last couple of years of grueling training and deploying to Iraq meant nothing in terms of rank. He was separated from the company on two fronts. First, because he was married, he no longer lived on base in the barracks in close proximity to other Marines. Second, during formations, he was forced to stand under the watchful eye of the Headquarters platoon, instead of the command of the platoon he had deployed with and knew the best. The HQ platoon was composed of a small group of Marines who possessed the gift of administration and could type, proofread, and manage dozens of spreadsheets. It also included those unable to pass the physical requirements to be in a line platoon or those under some sort of disciplinary action, which was likely to lead to their separation from the Marine Corps. In the eyes of most, Yund belonged in the last category, and, as such, was treated terribly. He was harshly ridiculed by our command without a chance for rebuttal and sentenced to a reduction in rank. 'An example' is what they wanted to make of him, but what he became was isolated and alone. They may have intended to make him an 'example,' but what they gained was a case study.

When the training cycle started again for the next deployment in seven months, Yund lost nearly everything. His friends couldn't be a part of his life in the same way, the unit continued its mission, and just when he had nothing left, his wife abruptly left him, taking their daughter with her. Yund moved in with another Marine off base, and less than a year later, Yund took his life on the morning he was going to have the hearing for his NJP (non-judicial punishment; the military's way of punishment through the means of their own justice system called the UCMJ, the Uniform Code of Military Justice). In my estimation Yund should not be the prime suspect in his murder. No, it is his brothers, even me, who are partially responsible. He was left as no one should be—in isolation, needing his brothers, needing support, needing to be heard. With great regret, I feel that we killed him, and the thought that I had abandoned this young man haunts me to this day. Others, like Benjamin, are tainted with regret and 'what-ifs.' At 3 a.m. the day Yund killed himself, he sent Benjamin a text saying, 'I've always thought of you as a brother—I am going to miss you.' In moments of self-reflection after the unthinkable has happened, a text like that is re-visited again and again to no avail.

WE ALL HAVE A STORY

Every Marine has a story. For that matter, every person on the planet has a story. It is a narrative, a set of events, victories, and defeats in a unique shape that illumines purpose and molds desire. Without the right formation to ground it in the right objectives and give it direction, our personal narrative will seek solvency and hunger for resolution. Unfortunately, our American culture at large teaches us to banish painful feelings to isolated compartments, hidden from one another.

This is not an alien feature of our society. For example, some primarily find their identity in sexual expression, which leads to an incomprehensive and untenable position that is self-defeating, and when put in conversation with others, reveals more than one story in conflict. Advocates for homosexuality, for example, have long said that their sexual identity is immutable like race, yet these same people

35

demand that their gender is mutable and can (and *should*) be changed based on how they feel. The problem is that *you have to privilege a narrative.* No one is without bias, no one is neutral, and not every story fits everyone else's. But are we doomed to subjectivity? Is the Marine struggling with PTSD left to face his challenges without objective truth? What help or assistance is there if there is no objectivity to life? There is one underlying question beneath all the questions: 'Is there a meta-narrative, a grand story that draws all experiences together, explains all stories, illumines brokenness, and is more than a moral guide for self-help, but also the story that redeems and makes people whole?'

THE NARRATIVE WE MUST PRIVILEGE

If a grand-metanarrative does exist, it must possess at least two features. First, it must be coherent, and second, it must correspond to reality. To be coherent refers to internal consistency. Many religions of the world claim to have a premium on a meta-narrative. Islam, for example, contains contradictory mandates within itself that have led many modern Muslims to formulate a doctrine of abrogation, that the so-called 'newer' revelation abrogates the prior. Of course, this reveals its own internal incoherence as a narrative. Likewise, it also fails to correspond to reality. This refers to its ability to make contact with reality as we know and encounter it. We don't accept *The Lord of the Rings* as a true narrative, for example, because, although it may be internally consistent, it doesn't correspond to anything we know in this world. There are no elves, orcs, or ring of power. It simply is a fantasy.

Many people's lives, including my brothers' in the Marine Corps, are a mixture of coherence and incoherence, correspondence and conflict. In part this is because we live in a world that privileges everyone's and no one's narrative. People demand their narrative be called truth, yet live in conflict with themselves and others when diametrically opposed truths clash. This leads to the stubborn fact that many of us simply do not know who we are or into what narrative we are supposed to fit. There is, though, one story that makes sense of everything, a true metanarrative that must be privileged.

The narrative that we must privilege, the story that gives meaning to all stories, is the one found in the pages of the Christian Scriptures. I know what some of my Marine brothers are thinking the moment their eyes cross these words: 'He had to go all religious on me.' I want those who fall into this category to bear with me. If you immediately have a resentment or distaste in your mouth for Christianity, I want you to dig deeper and ask these questions. 'Why do I hate Christianity? Why is it I have such a vehement reaction to it?' I also want to apologize to those who have seen abuses in what they perceived as Christianity, but which wasn't a true expression of it.

My first squad leader in the fleet, William Hyden, whom I admired for his leadership, once shared with me his disdain for Christian leaders in the south, where he was raised. To paraphrase his thoughts, 'It's pretty despicable to have a preacher telling me what I can and can't do, and that I should give money to the church while I'm broke and he's driving his Mercedes and wearing crocodile boots, and living in a six-bedroom house with a four-car garage.' I couldn't agree with him more. There is something inherently wrong with that picture. But to quote C. S. Lewis, again, 'A man does not call a line crooked unless he has some idea of a straight line.' We cannot call someone's behavior *wrong* without an idea of what is *right*. By what standard are we going to objectively say, 'This is wrong' or 'This is right'? What I want to show my Marine brothers is that the narrative we privilege and we fit into is not about taking advantage of others, or about religious abuses that come from the elegant lips of flashy pastors promising fluffy blessings at the expense of their hearers' pocket books.

The narrative we must privilege accounts for our brokenness and the dark places we have traveled and likewise contains a sober invitation to join the fight of the greatest battle we will ever engage in—the harshest fight we will ever face. It is that story I want to unpack with respect to the experiences I know best in the military, that of being an infantry Marine. And so, over the next few chapters, I will make a humble attempt to relate that narrative to the experiences many veterans have faced.

3

THAT HE LAY HIS LIFE DOWN
FOR HIS FRIENDS

Corporal Jason Lee Dunham:
November 10, 1981—April 22, 2004

On April 14, 2004, Lance Corporal Dunham, serving with a sister unit to a unit I would serve in later (named 3/7), and a few other Marines were dispatched to respond to an attack on a friendly convoy carrying their Battalion Commander (BC for short). As squad leader, Dunham located vehicles near the attack that were likely used by the ambushers attempting to flee the scene of the attack. The Marines quickly began intercepting and searching the vehicles for weapons, a sure indication that the enemy insurgents were involved and attempting to hide among the civilian populace, a common tactic of the insurgents in Iraq at the time. As the Marines approached one vehicle that proved to have weapons inside, an insurgent attempted to escape, which escalated to a hand-to-hand fight going to the ground. While Dunham grappled with the insurgent, he managed to release a grenade that also fell to the ground. With only a moment to respond, Dunham did something that was both unthinkable and sacrificial—he jumped on the grenade. Within seconds he used his Kevlar helmet, attempting to absorb the full force of the blast and protect his fellow Marines.

SACRIFICE

Although the explosion mortally wounded Dunham causing damage that he would die from eight days later, his actions were later described as 'an ultimate and selfless act of bravery.' He was posthumously awarded the nation's highest award for bravery in the face of certain death—the Congressional Medal of Honor. My senior Marines recall seeing the site where Dunham was killed as they operated in the same AO (area of operations) after 3/7 returned home. Dunham's actions also earned him a rare honor commonly reserved only to Medal of Honor recipients—having a naval vessel, the USS Dunham, named after him. Dunham's story of valor is one among many told of those who have made that ultimate sacrifice. Sacrifice, we all know on some level, is an act we are to honor, retell, and if the time comes, replicate.

Sacrifice is deeply ingrained into our culture. Thus, sadly, its meaning is often worn smooth. Many people attempting to deflect criticism from their character flaws will invoke their own perceived sacrifice. 'Don't you know how much I've sacrificed for …' — fill in the blank. Everyone wants to be recognized as a sacrificial person, as one who has given something up, whether in marital relationships, sports, careers, or whatever. Sacrifice means something to everyone. And when we hear a story like Dunham's, we soberly remember that some sacrifices are greater than others because their worth is measured by both what was given up and what was achieved. Where does the idea of sacrifice come from? What is this notion and how do we make sense of the idea that losing something for self is gain for others? Is this even a comprehensible idea? Does it make sense? Is it good in its essence?

Uncommon sacrifice is a common feature in the long, illustrious heritage of the United States Marine Corps. This cultural reality is so commonplace that most don't notice it. It's simply a part of the daily rhythm and grind and, subsequently, we place it in the background of our minds. But when a Marine comes home after a deployment or transitions out of the Corps, self-reflection inevitably ensues. When they have often witnessed the ultimate sacrifice of death, it is easy for them to compare every other sacrifice with it. With this as the standard, it is painfully uncommon for service members to acknowledge any sacrifice less than that. What civilians habitually fail to understand is, first, to see how lesser sacrifices relate to the greater and, second, what meaning we bring to sacrifice reveals about our presuppositions.

LIFE-CHANGING TRANSFORMATION

I can still vividly recall one of my first trips home after basic training. The transformation into the life of the Marines starkly contrasted with that of my peers from high school. In part, my friends embodied who I was before entering the service. Though the pattern of our lives had been close, soon after graduation, our trajectories moved miles apart, perhaps never to meet again. Many begin to see about six months into the initial course of their life in the service that they will become very different people in three and half years and more for each subsequent re-enlistment (four-year periods that earn the hash marks on the cuff of the sleeve of the dress uniform).

On that trip home I met with some friends from high school (a couple of them are still dear friends) who were now in their first or second year of college. Excitedly, they showed me where they lived off-campus, the parties they held on the weekends, and more. They gave an informal tour of where they went to class, the girls they were dating, and those they wanted to date. They shared with me the room where they slept, skipped class, or partied through the night and then went to class the next day. I saw the garbage they were putting into their bodies on a regular basis and learned why college kids get fat during their first year of school. You just can't eat pizza for all your meals, sleep in every day, drink beer every night, and expect to stay fit. I don't mention these things to throw stones at them, but to show that our lives were as different as those of people living in different countries. And when I say different countries, I mean it. We had different languages, cultures, sets of rules, etiquette, lifestyles, work rhythms—everything that confronts you when you step off the plane into a place you have never been.

All servicemembers who enter the military right out of high school for active duty give up the years that our culture considers 'the most free.' The culture gap between two people right out of high school, one a Marine and the other a college student, is drastic! This observation is common, but is so common that it goes unnoticed and unstated. One person might wake up at 2 a.m. to arrive at the armory by 3 a.m., to be ready to be at the rifle range at 4 a.m. The other stays up until 2 a.m. partying. One pulls everything out of his/her room once a week for field inspections, the tedious and painful examinations of cleanliness; the other lives in his filthy apartment with beer cans, pizza boxes, and Xbox controllers lying around. My first barracks had mini-fridges. As nice and accommodating as that might be, it served no purpose other than to look good. Had I wanted to use it, I was required to weekly unplug it, defrost it and have the back coils so impeccably clean that a q-tip could be dragged across them revealing no dirt of any kind. These two groups' experiences vary greatly. And it's not just the outward appearance of weekly haircuts, daily shaving, uniform readiness, and hours disbursed in different ways that distinguish the two groups. The Marines, without knowing it, have resigned themselves to never being able to relate to the college students on the same level.

Servicemembers who delay going to college until later struggle to have a point of contact with those who enter college straight from high school. The circumstances lack an intersection so that it is easy for servicemembers to be harsh, irritated, and disgusted with those who 'don't know what they have.' Every veteran who has forgone those years to dedicate themselves to a serious job and carry a rifle for a season has made a sacrifice to serve their country. I am grateful that most of the men I served with don't weaponize this truth and beat non-veterans over the head with it, but quietly acknowledge the places we simply cannot identify with others. It's so ordinary that most Marines would shrug this off and dismiss it as no big deal. And, to a point, I agree with them. The reason for this is because we have been trained to measure the value of a sacrifice according to what has been given up in comparison to those who have given up their very lives. Lacking the ability to relate to our civilian counterparts in our parallel, yet divergent, courses of life is only a scratch on the surface.

The sacrifice of servicemembers deepens, broadens, and hurts when family and distance are added to the equation, and even more when they lack a greater purpose for their sacrifice. Having put some years between my entrance into the service and now, I don't feel the effects of these differences as much. But consider the one who is married while in service and chooses to re-enlist. The long months of separation between husband and wife during a deployment heap stress on already pressured marriages. Add to this the distance between the deployed father and his young children. Add again the pattern of military life where the wife is not only rearing her children but doing so without the consistent fathering pattern present in the malleable lives of their kids. Add yet once more the transient nature of military life which frequently uproots the family from the friends and community to relocate them to another military base, another assignment, another restart to their lives. These cumulative pressures and sacrifices result in tangible differences between them and their peers. Many marriages end in divorce, separation, or long-term strain during military service. The oft-perplexing challenge a veteran, who has given up several years of life to multiple enlistments, will face is to define what their sacrifice achieved. 'For what,' they will ponder, 'did my marriage end?' Seeking an answer and finding none, many are left to stew in bitterness and misplaced pride.

'THANK YOU FOR YOUR SERVICE'

When service people transition back into civilian life, people often thank us for our service or sacrifice. Sure, it's nice, but how are we supposed to respond? Largely, I think the feeling shared by most veterans ranges between not knowing what to say and thinking, 'What sacrifice? What exactly am I being thanked for?' Or even oscillating to the other end of the spectrum, 'You thank me for my service, but you do not know what I've actually given up.' If readers are those who go out of their way to thank servicemembers, I don't want to discourage you from doing so. Instead, I want you to understand when veterans stammer a response, it's not because people don't thank them; they do all the time. It's because veterans, at least the Marines I know, consistently disqualify their contributions and make themselves feel inferior to those who have lost limbs, friends, or have given their lives to save others. Without fail, we compare ourselves to them and see our effort as an act of failure. 'Since I didn't lose someone, I have not given something up,' the internal and paralyzing dialogue goes. I believe this thinking is both noble and destructive. *They have* given something up, but this isn't said so they can feel good about themselves, but so they can quietly acknowledge that not all sacrifices are equal. Like many things, sacrifices exist on a spectrum. Some sacrifices cost little, and some cost a great deal.

Sometime during my second work up (the training cycle that prepares a unit for deployment), our First Sergeant gathered with the company in the field. He gathered us into a 'school circle.' The school circle is kind of like a football huddle, a tight circle of people around one person speaking. Usually, we would 'sit, kneel, bend,' to allow everyone to see and to keep the person speaking from having to shout. First Sergeant Griffith (a sergeant-major now) was-*is*-an intimidating man. Like many who have served in the infantry for more than two enlistments, he appeared much older in the face than he was. The stress of leading in the infantry and bearing impossible duties for years on end, often under incredible physical demands, with little sleep, age people considerably. Though his face appeared older, his chiseled body was the epitome of what we think of when we say, 'He is a Marine.' His many tattoos did nothing to hinder his reputation. Unlike many first-sergeants who appear in the fleet, First Sergeant Griffith was a true infantry Marine. He had enlisted as a Grunt, deployed as a Grunt, had joined the scout snipers somewhere along the way, earning him a fierce reputation that matched his countenance.

THE GREATEST SACRIFICE

Scattered on the ground and against a berm (a raised barrier, usually consisting of dirt that acts as a fortification line), we formed a loose school circle around our revered First Sergeant. During our work up and difficult parts of our training cycle, he would give us these talks that were often well-timed and emboldening to us when we found ourselves physically and mentally beaten down. 'Where are my Bible thumpers?' He asked, his words ringing out with a commanding tone the way a pit bull might growl at someone. With hesitation, I and a few other Marines in the company half-raised our hands. Pausing as he scanned over us sitting among about 120 Marines, he then delivered his follow-up question. 'What does John 15:13 say?' I knew the verse and timidly half-mumbled it aloud: 'Greater love has no man than this, that one lay down his life for his friends.' I wasn't sure if I quoted it with much confidence or volume, and my suspicion was confirmed by what he said next. With his booming voice, he responded, 'Stand up and say it!' I snapped to my feet from sitting on the berm with my rifle and loudly shouted it out, 'Greater love has no man than this, that one lay down his life for his friends!' I sat back down and awaited what came next. After a few quiet moments of scanning over his company and looking many of us squarely in the eye, he proceeded to expound, in his own harsh, pointed, yet elegant way, the honor in sacrifice, the goodness of sacrifice, and the reality that we may be put in a position to make the highest sacrifice—to give up our lives.

The idea of sacrifice presupposes much. It assumes, at bottom, that we, as humans, value some things more than others. We place more stock in a steak dinner than a hot-pocket. We value a career more than a car. We love the story of Desmond Doss from the true story of *Hacksaw Ridge* more than *Dumb and Dumber*. It also assumes that these value-decisions are intuitive to humans and their experience. Sacrifice, though varying in its stripes, is regarded as honorable in nearly all cultures. If we find some small sect of people who do not honor sacrifice, we would view them as the oddity; they would be the exception that proves the rule.

The idea of sacrifice also speaks to something that God wrote on the hearts of all people: that to give oneself up for the sake of another's life is *good*. Where did this idea of *good* come from? If we reject God, as many of my fellow Marines have, we must wrestle with the idea that by valuing sacrifice, by saying it's good, we are assuming that there is a standard of good by which to differentiate good and evil. In fact, the act of soldiering, which is what the Marine Infantry does, assumes this same standard in presupposing some things are worth fighting for, defending, and even dying for. Some causes are worth the cost of sacrificing many lives, while many are not.

Why Jesus and Why Me?

I know some will vehemently reject these next words, so I implore you to wrestle with them to their logical outworking and ask, 'Why do we invoke the words of Jesus Christ from John 15:13 as a standard, as a litmus test, for what the ultimate sacrifice looks like?' Christ was and is the ultimate standard of sacrifice. When He says, 'Greater love has no man than this, that one lay down his life for his friends,' He isn't spouting a generic moralism about sacrifice. Jesus isn't giving a vague illustration as a spiritual guru that we should all love each other. He is, in fact, pointing directly to *His own* sacrifice. That sacrifice to death was not just for a handful of fishermen on a desert strip in first-century Palestine. It was a costly sacrifice for Him, and one which paid the ransom price for everyone who ever lived, the price of death.

'But what does that have to do with me?' you might ask. It's quite simple. The small sacrifices will always be compared to and point to the larger ones. Those larger, more costly sacrifices possess more contours, parallels, and more of the shape of the cross on which Christ died. Even the greatest of human sacrifices, those being the most like death on a cross, still are subordinate and inferior to Christ's own death. And why is that? The value of any sacrifice is measured by both what was given up and what was achieved. When Christ died, it was the God-man, made flesh, who condescended to humanity, who gave His life. When He rose, His death and resurrection were not only greater, but they achieved more than any other death ever could. Who else could have died and defeated death? Who else could remove the sting of our ancient adversary sin? None other than Christ Himself, the Warrior-Redeemer.

And so it goes. Every sacrifice, whether we bend our knee to Christ or reject Him, points to Him and what He accomplished. Every deferred enjoyment of freedom, every delayed time with family, every strained relationship, and all who died for their countrymen and nation, point to Christ. Our response to Him now awaits. What will we do with this death that was so costly that it cost the Creator His life? And what will we do with this sacrifice that achieved a victory over death when He arose from the grave to rescue those belonging to him? We must respond in gratitude resulting in service for Him. But we must also introduce and probe some perplexing questions that have gone unanswered thus far. Why did Christ have to die? How is it that the death of a Jewish carpenter has any bearing on me today? If Christ 'died for me' what does that, then, require of me?

The journey of exploring the need for sacrifice is a sobering one that requires us to respond to the person of Christ and what He meant when He lay down His life for His friends. We must understand that His, like all sacrifices, involves what was given up and what was achieved. To understand why placing a high premium on sacrifice is written on our hearts, we must go back to the beginning of the story, back to the start of a narrative that we must privilege. It is a story which ropes us in, accounts for our suffering and pain, and delves into the soul of suicide. That story, which fills out the meaning of sacrifice, is what we will tell in the following chapters.

4

SEMPER FIDELIS

The Marine Corps famously has a slogan, *semper fidelis*, meaning 'always faithful.' To most, it has little meaning, but among Marines, the phrase invokes a robust sense of identity. It's *'semper fi'* or *'semper'* for short, sometimes used meaningfully, sometimes sarcastically. The use of *semper fidelis* in conversation significantly shifts in its tone and tenor upon leaving service. While on active duty it remains one of thousands of cultural features and facets that flood the everyday language of a Marine. But when one transitions to civilian life, its rarer use elevates its significance. It is in this post-service life of the Corps that its use buoys Marines as a unifying theme in interactions between them. *Semper fidelis* can be wielded in such a way as to display the common bond of something transcendent between two veterans. These two words transcend time and space, but their meaning is not instilled by the Corps itself. Nor is the slogan created simply as a cultural artifact. Rather, it is bestowed by our very Creator. The Creator of all things has revealed Himself in a narrative that we must privilege.

That redemptive narrative that I've spoken of several times is, in fact, a story of faithfulness. *Semper fidelis* ought to invoke deeper sentiments and greater longings than a cultural code word for insiders. It should, and indeed does, draw us toward and into the story of faithfulness. That narrative, which is also filled with much fighting, includes a struggle that began shortly after the beginning of time, when the faithful God made everything. Conversely, that narrative was also lost through unfaithfulness; it is redeemed through Christ's faithfulness that we ourselves might one day be made fully faithful. The story of Scripture and the drama of redemption is a grand performance which could nest neatly under this same designation—*semper fidelis*.

CREATION: A TESTIMONY TO GOD'S FAITHFULNESS

The Word of God begins with a mighty and wondrous display of faithfulness. The one true and living God of the Christian Scriptures made, sovereignly, without assistance, without need, all things. Echoing from eternity and bursting forth into time and space, God faithfully created according to His benevolent character. The perfection and right order of God's creation of all things point to the end when He will set all things right.

Scripture recounts that God's creation was 'very good' (Gen. 1:31). Common usage causes us to lose the meaning of 'good.' We eat a meal and say it tastes 'good.' We are asked how our day is and we say, 'good.' Often calling something good is as boring and routine as brushing our teeth, but sometimes the meaning is far greater. When God looked back on His creation and saw that it was very good, it means that it was *exceedingly* good. It was whole and pure, unblemished and beautiful. This is central in the Bible's creation account because we cannot get far into Genesis without confronting the pinnacle of God's creation—the creation of humanity. We quickly read about the creation of all the creatures, the seas, dry land, plants, fish, birds, etc., but need to slow down as the text zooms in on one wondrous creature among the rest.

50

Then God said, 'Let us make man in our image, after our likeness. And let them have dominion over the fish of the sea and over the birds of the heavens and over the livestock and over all the earth and over every creeping thing that creeps on the earth.' So God created man in his own image, in the image of God he created him; male and female he created them (Gen. 1:26).

WE ARE MADE IN THE IMAGE OF GOD

One of my pet peeves is when Christians say that someone is 'made in the image of God,' and try to define this by using the Latin words '*imago dei.*' This is akin to asking, 'what does it mean to be "always faithful"?' and replying with 'semper fidelis.' We lose the meaning when we use a Latin definition for the word.

The image of God, though, contains many key aspects that help us to apply the narrative of Scripture to our broken lives. Someone who has lost a loved one to suicide as well as those veterans who have considered suicide as a viable option—these are the people who need to read the following words and let them take root in their hearts: You are not an accident.

A PURPOSEFUL CREATION

Because our Creator made us, our lives are neither accidents nor are they our own. This contradicts the narrative society at large tells us. Life is cheapened when it is reduced to chance. We are told that humans are nothing more than the by-product of time + chance + matter. Why does someone who gives this story the highest premium even care? If we are simply the result of the evolution of simple-celled bacteria becoming complex societies of bacteria, what is 'right' or 'wrong'? In fact, if that is true, there is nothing wrong with people using a metal instrument to mechanically manipulate a compressed explosive and insert a projectile into themselves rendering them dead. If life is just an accident, then nothing means anything. But because life is not an accident, everything means something.

God created us, and we are His creatures. Being created means that there is more to life than synapses in the brain firing or chemical reactions dancing to the tune of laws that bind them. We must reject the notion that we can be reduced to nothing more than a set of biochemical processes situated in tissue bags of bone and muscle. If we accept this, then we will believe and act consistently with its foundational claims. We would be resigned to conclude that nothing matters. But all the while, those who insist that nothing matters gradually reveal the inconsistency of their lives when they appeal to meaning to cover their losses. While they suppress the truth that there is meaning to everything, they need the resources of meaningful currency. How can someone declare that life is meaningless without using logic and the ability to construct words? Such activity inadvertently reveals their worth. To describe ourselves as accidents without meaning, we must *assume* meaning, drawing upon the capital of truth and meaning to express our views. The very process of denying meaning points to the existence of a God, who created us and allows us to use words to deny Him. Scripture tells us the truth in Psalm 139:13-14, as David speaks to God:

> For you formed my inward parts; you knitted me together in my mother's womb. I praise you, for I am fearfully and wonderfully made. Wonderful are your works; my soul knows it very well.

If we hold our worldview and beliefs with integrity, we know this Scripture to be true on some level. Even if we reject the truthfulness of the Bible, we sense that this scriptural statement is right. In a meticulous manner and on a level of scale beyond our sight, God formed us and put us together. In our inmost being, we sense that this corresponds to what we know of the world. The story we have been fed and that many religiously believe, that we are only evolutionary by-products, is a leap of faith that is not even consistent with its own terms.

WE ARE MADE TO WORSHIP

Being made in the image of God is immensely deep and important. Although we belong to the created order with other creatures, we are not mere animals of the earth. The biblical story of redemption begins in the beauty of creation and focuses on the distinctiveness of humanity. Though we are not the Creator and instead are among His creatures, we are special. Al Mohler describes what it means for us to be made in the image of God:

> It means among all the creatures we alone are the creature that can consciously know and glorify God. The tiger with its stripes glorifies God but he doesn't know it. The dog chewing on a bone is glorifying God but he hasn't a clue. The cat doing whatever a cat does is glorifying God but he has no consciousness of it. But we alone of all creatures have the ability to know we were made for God's glory.[1]

Mohler rightly focuses on the distinctiveness of humans apart from other animals. The biblical text points to this distinctiveness when it indicates that only humans are given dominion and the mandate to name others. This is not hard to grasp. No ape has ever built a city. No whale has discovered a cure for polio. Only humans innovate, advance technology, contemplate beauty, write poetry, or compose music. Even the exceptions we think of—a parrot imitating sounds, an elephant 'painting,' or other animals doing something special —are not actions originating from the animals themselves,

---

1. Albert Mohler, 'Homosexual 'Marriage': A Tragic Oxymoron - Biblical and Cultural Reflections,' Desiring God, September 25, 2004, https://www. desiringgod.org/messages/homosexual-marriage-a-tragic-oxymoron-biblical-and-cultural-reflections.

but point to the uniqueness of humans having dominion over animals. The other creatures are created and therefore good, but they are not, nor ever will be, image bearers of the living God, capable of knowing Him.

We are made for God's glory. That is, we are created for worship. We are hard-wired for worship, and in fact we are *always* worshiping. Wherever we direct our deep-seated longings, there you will find what, or perhaps whom, we worship. What do you spend your money on? Where do you devote your time? Some will quickly realize that their many hours watching football, or going to the shooting range, or brewing beer reveals something about them that makes them dislike the words they are reading. But I want to be clear— these are not bad things inherently. Sports are a good thing. I would even say going to the shooting range can be good, but our attention given to these hobbies, vocations, and pastimes should be subordinated to the Creator of all things. It means those things, though good, should be used as instruments to give glory to God who fearfully and wonderfully created us in His image as unique, creative, contemplative and desirous to give glory to someone or something.

WE ARE NAMED AND GIVEN THE TASK OF NAMING

We do not often ponder about the significance of what it means to be named. Certain places in life cause us to ponder names more than others. When a couple is expecting a child, especially their firstborn, it isn't uncommon to have many hours spent 'trying names on' for their baby. It's got to be something we like, it can't be the same name as that guy I hated in high school, and, most of all, something that won't get him or her made fun of. We want to like names, but we also find value in passing on a family name. My father's name is Johnnie, which was also his father's. My brother wanted to preserve this name and its uncommon spelling, so he gave his second son 'Johnnie' as a middle name.

Some names create a heritage that is to be valued. Though the meaning of a name is sometimes an afterthought, it is something people like to discover and remember. Joshua, my first name, means 'Yahweh saves,' and I appreciate the meaning of this. Yahweh, the divine name of my covenant Lord attached to the action of what He does—that's meaning I won't forget.

Naming takes an interesting cultural shape for Marines. The rite of passage in becoming a Marine is first to earn the title—Marine—and no longer be called 'recruit' (among other things). In a very real sense, it's more specific than being named, for it's a kind of *re-naming*. No longer is a person 'William who delivers pizza,' but *Marine*. No longer is it 'Brandon who plays in a band,' but *Marine*. In this title, there is both a new identity taken and an old identity shed. I have come to find out that other branches are similar in their respective designations. A time comes in recruit training where finally the drill instructor places the eagle-globe and anchor in our palm and he shouts the command for the first time invoking our new name, 'Marines! About-face!' That is a ceremony in which a rich heritage, a long legacy, and the assumption of faithful duty is placed upon the shoulders of each Marine and focused in a title bestowed in a ceremony and conferred over a lifetime. Marines, as do many others, understand what it means to earn and receive a name.

Scripture's first act of naming comes by the mouth of the Creator, who names the first man 'Adam.' The duty given to Adam is to name all the other creatures. Being named and given the duty to name is a water-mark of what it means to be made in the image of God. God initiates this action and we respond. Among all the other creatures, which are also good, no other has this duty. No other is made in the image of God and described as 'fearfully and wonderfully made.'

WE ARE MADE FOR COMMUNITY, NOT AUTONOMY

We make this observation very quickly in the Scriptures, for the first thing that God says is *not good* in creation is that man was alone (Gen. 2:18). To fill the absence of another, God created the first woman from Adam's own flesh. In fact, it is easy to miss the beauty of the text because the words seem archaic. But God's creation of woman comes *after* Adam has named all the creatures and found no suitable helper. Imagine the process: Adam is in a luscious garden alone, except for all kinds of animals. These different creatures are brought before him and he exercises his God-given authority to name them. Adam names the cow, 'cow.' He goes on to name the sheep, the birds, and so on. But no one is like this first man. No one 'matches' him in the way that all the other creatures match each other. No one fits. So, God, after putting Adam to sleep and creating woman from his own flesh, places not some kind of animal, not another man, but woman, a counterpart, in front of Adam and says to him, 'name *this*.' And poetry follows from Adam's lips:

> This at last is bone of my bones
> and flesh of my flesh;
> she shall be called Woman,
> because she was taken out of Man (Gen. 2:23).

It is not good for man to be alone, and this aspect of being made in God's image is underscored by his need for a suitable helper, a compatible mate, a partner so that each will complement the other.

There is a second clue we are made for community. This is specified in the next mandate given to our first parents. We might call it an order or description of our duty. They are told to be fruitful and multiply. Quickly in the Scriptures God ordains sex for man and woman in relationship with and under God, devoted to each other for life.

Humans are made for community. What this means for us is very practical. A legitimate place for solitude exists. There are times, perhaps even a season, when we need to be alone. In fact, time should be regularly sought to slip away and be alone with our Creator. But it is undeniable that we are community-made beings. How that community functions and how it looks will vary from place to place and culture to culture. But it is no accident that most people live close to one another. Even rural communities, which exist largely dispersed from each other geographically, plan regular times and events to gather with one other.

I grew up on a farm where my first closest neighbor was a ¼ mile away, my second 1 mile, and after that 3.5 miles. The town where I first attended school only had 300 people from the surrounding farms. Solitude and being alone is a part of life in southwest Kansas, which features the vocation of farming. Even so, there are community events of the church opening its doors for meals, the local high school has a Friday night game, and the local cafe invites noon-time meals with those local farmers separated by miles. When people say they want to live alone up in the mountains, it turns out that they are either enamored with the mountains, or are idealizing the solitude beyond what they require. A week of solitude may be refreshing, but two weeks is not automatically twice as refreshing.[2] We quickly experience diminishing returns until we need to return to community to be refreshed.

We Are Made for Relationships
The alarming irony is that those who live in highly populated areas often report feeling alone. We are on Facebook and have over 300 'friends.' We go to the store, see many people, walk by many faces, but talk to no one. The deadly assumption is that

2. I owe this observation to Andy Crouch. See Andy Crouch, *The Tech-Wise Family: Everyday Steps for Putting Technology in Its Proper Place* (Grand Rapids, MI: Baker Books, 2017), Chapter 3.

being near people in our locale automatically means being near to people in relationships. Sadly, social media make our relationships a mile wide and an inch deep. We are meant to be in relationships with others for a reason, not spread thin because of our networks. The tragic nature of being in the military is that there are many with whom I've built strong relationships, but will likely never see again. This is not the fault of our armed services. It is simply the nature of the duty that men and women from all walks of life and many places across the nation come together for a unique season. When the time is up, we ache because we realize that we can never form bonds as tight or as deep as those we formed. The transient, warrior lifestyle is replaced by transient restlessness, while we seek to gain new relationships and retain the old. Nevertheless, it is evident in those aching moments that we are not meant to be alone, but that God designed us for relationship with others, and that is a beautiful expression of His having made us in the image of God.

Creation, in all its glory and its intersection of image bearers, is a reflection of God's faithfulness. Each facet of creation, including its goodness and purposefulness, display God's faithfulness. God is consistent with His character and doesn't betray His original design. As we image bearers of God long for community, God expresses His faithfulness to His design. As a Marine seeks a deep bond with another person after their service, God's faithfulness is once again illuminated in that person. Creation sets the pattern of God's faithfulness and shows that life is not an accident; it is purposeful. Because of that, every veteran, every person on the planet, is worthy of dignity and respect, and has incalculable value. Semper fidelis, when invoked, should draw upon all of this from one Marine to another, one image bearer of God to another. Semper fidelis is woven through the fabric of God's creation and intent for us. It truly is an appropriate way to label the manner in which God created and an important quality of God—*the faithful one.*

5

TO END ALL WARS

The First World War, called 'The Great War,' is also known as by its lesser used title, 'The War to End All Wars.' It gained this designation because never before had so many nations fought in an entangled war with the means to eradicate so many lives so quickly. Large standing armies coupled with new implements of destruction through gas attacks, automatic weapons, armored tanks, and aerial bombings brought a new level of awareness to the terror and destruction of war. Though the Second World War garners more attention than the First, it was The Great War that exposed the Western World to a new level of ghastliness. The title 'To End All Wars,' appropriately labeled a deep-seated desire that stirs all hearts, a desire for peace. War is not supposed to be the norm. Fighting is purposeless unless it is conducted so that one day it will no longer be. When the horrors of war are most realized, so is the craving for peace.

War, fighting, and killing are not the way the world is supposed to be. They are departures from some ancient and elusive reality. This observation was made as far back as Homer's famed *Iliad*. Within its pages, Homer depicts the shield wielded by Achilles, one of the greatest warriors of Greek mythology. His shield reflects the damage and death of many who have fallen in war. But it also reflects images of peace and flourishing. The message Homer conveys is that we interact with these echoes of discord and conflict as those who should contemplate the tension between war and peace. The shield is like finding glorious ruins of a once great city wherein the former glory is not entirely erased, but the damage is unavoidable. As we are drawn into that story, we too deeply desire to be at peace. We see the potential and the way things *could* be, the way they are supposed to be, but are caught in a reality filled with fighting and dying. The world is not the way it is supposed to be. There is a time for fighting, but fighting is the result of something that has been disordered. This chord has been struck in the hearts of humanity. Of the plethora of cultures and religions, it is difficult to find a belief where fighting, conflict, and death exist after death. Among those who believe in an afterlife, there is a fairly universal belief that one day death and war will be no more and will be replaced by peace.

THE FALL

Fighting exists because sin exists. The entrance of sin into creation was not an introduction of a tiny flaw, but an invasion. Creation still remains good, and the image bearers of God still remain such. But something is wrong with the way things are. Sin has left nothing untouched. Humanity's fall, so the narrative of Scripture tells us, refers to the first transgression of our first parents. Sin, often called 'trespass,' means going too far, like trespassing on someone's property. But it's worse than that. Sin can also mean to 'miss the mark,' like missing a target's center. And we're more than just a little off target. The apostle John describes sin as lawlessness, which gets at the heart of the matter. What makes sin lawless is that it contradicts the character of God. It is by revelation of God's character in Scripture, particularly in the creation account in Genesis, that we discover God makes the rules. God prescribes and delivers His statutes. He sets the standard. But sin is deep. Lawlessness is an act of rebellion against God's law, and therefore, His character. Our sinful actions communicate, 'God is like *this.*' So, when I purposely take what is not mine, I'm not simply violating another person by stealing from him, I'm saying something about God that is not true. In essence, I am making a non-verbal confession as an image bearer of God that *I* make the rules, and that God's law is subservient to my way. Our sin reveals that we are always in conflict with the character of God. We are always at war, constantly fighting and without peace while we are in sin.

In world history, fighting does not happen before the fall, but as a *result* of it. Fighting, which is often inevitable, is the imperfect and often necessary means to prevent someone else from making a false confession about God and us. When the Nazis invaded Poland at the start of the Second World War, one group of image bearers were making a corporate confession that they could take from another group its lives, resources, and more for the sake of German Nationalism. This was a false confession. It violated God's law and told a lie about who He is. Sin, at bottom, is the antithesis of what Marines confess when they say, '*semper fidelis.*' It is the epitome of *unfaithfulness* toward the faithful God. Faithfulness assumes fidelity to God's law, His standard. When it is disregarded, it doesn't just make a false statement about God; it makes a false statement about who God says *we* are to be.

When veterans take their own lives, they make a false confession about God. It is false, because it contradicts the value that persons possess. We bear the image of the Creator. Through the unrelenting struggle, the person contemplating suicide has reduced their worth to a problem that can be solved by their own death. The challenges that led a person to this point are many (more on this in chapter 6). But the central point is that sin distorts relationships. Sin mars our relationships with others and ultimately God. We cannot attain our true identity without paying justice for our transgressions and finding reconciliation for our unfaithfulness. Our inner orientation and outward actions must confess that God is faithful and just.

Injustice disturbs and angers us. Even the pettiest of violations can set us off. Imagine waiting in line at the DMV (Department of Motor Vehicles where vehicle tags and driver licences are typically issued. The American equivalent of the Driver and Vehicle Licensing Agency) for over an hour. You arrived early, took a ticket, and waited your turn in a long line of customers. You watched the ticket numbers count up until finally you are one or two numbers away from getting called. But then someone walks in, eyes the counter, and without grabbing a ticket, walks up the moment someone else steps away. This should be *your* time to speak to the clerk, but at the last moment someone cut in and took *your* place. Do you feel disdain for this person? Even though this isn't a grave sin, you nevertheless want to set him right. And many of us would! We would tell that person to get in line, take a number, wait his turn, not letting him get away with what he did. Now imagine that a person walked in, drew a gun, and shot several innocent people. Would we let him get away with that? If, when that person was arrested for this mass shooting, the judge let them go, what would we say about the judge? We would surely say that he was a crooked magistrate. Injustice reveals the conflict between the way things are supposed to be and the fact that our world is plagued by fighting and the desire for peace through justice.

We are born into a world that has been fighting since the fall, and we engage in that fighting on one of two sides. By default, from the outset, we have been fighting *against* God. We are a resistance of fighters rebelling against the Lordship of Jesus Christ. We want our own way, to be masters of our fate, to fulfill our desires, and we do so by rebelling against our Creator. We take what isn't ours, follow what we ought not to, do to others what we would never want done to ourselves. And even though we suppress the truth of God, we invoke standards of rightness and wrongness, that only

God's existence can justify when someone transgresses against us. Yet, *we* are the ones who have broken God's law, willfully remaining insurgents to His justice.

Since the fall, we have been tainted by sin. No part of us, not our reason, emotions, will, or even our bodies have been untouched by sin's effects. Truly our sin is a false confession about who God is and the ways things are supposed to be. The status of our situation before God doesn't look good, either. God is a just judge who *must* punish evil, must do justice according to His character revealed in His law. What does a holy God do with people like us? Is our sin really so bad? If we want to understand the depth of our sin, the injustice of our transgressions, and our false confession of God, then we must look at God. We must get a glimpse of what this holy God looks like next to our sin. But what is holiness?

MARINE 'HOLINESS'

Service members possess a keen sense of holiness and may not even realize it. Scripture defines holiness as 'otherness,' a separateness from other things. When God calls Himself holy, He describes His character and distance from others. Something holy is set apart from everything else. Also central to the meaning of holiness is its orientation; the things to which we orient ourselves. Real holiness results in being both set-apart and being postured correctly toward God. The outward appearance should point toward an inward reality.

Recruits into the Marine Corps arrive at boot camp looking no different from their civilian counterparts. It is always late at night, and even though the airport is right next to the Marine Corps Recruit Training Depot in San Diego (MCRD for short), the recruits are driven around on busses for hours to disorient them. When they arrive, they collectively experience an immediate shock as they look out the windows on the dimly lit yellow footprints and see their drill instructors waiting for them, impatient and angry. The recruits file out of the bus and go through a painful (and in hindsight, rather humorous) gauntlet of learning how to reply to a drill instructor, what to say, what not to say, how to stand, and so forth. Training hasn't officially begun, but learning certainly has.

During that first long night of boot camp, every recruit's head is shaved. All civilian haircuts are removed. Whatever clothes they wore are taken. All marks of recognition of who they were are flattened and nullified. The next three months of basic training build a new, outward identity for recruits until they earn the title 'Marine.' By the time they graduate from boot camp, they look much different than when they arrived. In a tangible way, boot camp draws recruits out to be different, separate from the outside civilian world. In this sense, they are becoming holy-like. On the outside, they have changed drastically. On the inside, the young Marines may still cling to their old identities. They still remember their friends, lifestyle, and social stripes of the old life. But as time marches on, the outward separateness tends to be embraced more fully inwardly.

Often young Marines will use their first leave from boot camp to get tattoos to display visibly that they belong to a new tribe. Whether it is the eagle-globe and anchor on their shoulder, semper fidelis across their back, teufel hunden ('Devil Dog'; the name the Germans gave to Marines at the battle of Belleau Wood during the First World War), or one of many other designations. Though the young Marines are eager to show off their newly inaugurated way of life, senior Marines often regard it with a mix of condescension and disdain. The reason for this is understandable. They have gone through boot camp, but they have much to learn and experience to be a Marine. The sense of 'holiness' will certainly begin to grow after basic training, but it hasn't taken root. By the time Marines have been in for a deployment, enlistment or two, they fully absorb their new identity so that they do not sense the difference with the outside world as much. Rather, they begin to take their new identity for granted. They feel as though they have always been the way they are. The old life is a memory but no longer their baseline for weighing everyday interactions. At this point, the inward starts to match the outward.

INWARD AND OUTWARD

One of the greatest intersections of the inward orientation and outward separation is a military funeral. When a service-member is buried, there is a ritualistic and precise process. The body undergoes specific, tedious, and laborious care, both for them and the Marines who bury their fellow warrior. Licensed vendors must make official military uniforms to be worn. The dress-blues are freshly dry-cleaned. Not an improper crease exists. There are no 'Irish-pennants,' what we call loose and dangling threads. Every ribbon is in its exact arrangement, cover, and alignment. Even the smallest details, like sock color, are completely uniform. The chloroforms, the Marine's dress shoes, are spotless, without a smudge or scuff. The edge of the shoe bears a fresh coat of 'edge dressing,' a black glossy finish spread in an even coat. Preparation extends to the minutest details of shoe laces, which must not be broken and must be laced so the last lace is left over right. Every brass button dividing the blue coat is rotated and oriented with its eagle poised, upright, wings spread, clutching the earth in its talons. Their hats, called covers, are free from scuffs or scratches. Their taut exterior complements the snugness of the uniform with its perfect alignment above the eyeline. Every dress uniform is tailored to fit the exact shape of the Marine. No one's cuff line is too short, coat too baggy, or pants too tight. True to its name, the Marines, dressed for honoring the fallen, are uniform.

When the dress is as impeccable as this, it elevates the sacred sense that the uniform should not, cannot, must not, be denigrated. The uniform is sacred. It is and becomes more than its physical fabric. It embodies a rich heritage and tradition of honor that is now physically manifest in those wearing EGAs (short for 'Eagle, Globe, and Anchor,' the official Marine emblem) on their collars. The friends and family of the fallen loved one, who come to the funeral to grieve and lament, encounter the striking and solemn presence of the Marines there to escort the fallen. They walk in unison. They do not step, turn, or move without purpose. The salute, normally given in quick professionalism, is altered. It is made with a slow and haunting movement. The dead Marine, lying in the casket, looks as though he may snap to attention at an order. A flag draped over the casket is folded until it is deliberately and finally pleated and placed in the parents' hands. The seven rifles snap, aim, and fire three times, giving their 21-gun salute. Finally, with emotion pervading, haunted by the sense of the trumpet, produced so reverently, *Taps* is played. Its long, mellow notes echo a minor chord in our hearts. Its melody lingers and whispers into the sadness that death is not the way it is supposed to be with life.

These Marines, decorated in honors of wars fought, accommodations given, and medals to show their shooting experience, are a picture of holiness. They are not only outwardly 'holy' but inwardly stand toward the fallen differently from every other person present. Their posture is not simply one of separation, but one received in a heritage given to them. Like the other branches of the armed forces, the Marines receive their heritage. Not by birth, but by a kind of adoption. They have been grafted into its history, reborn through the intense weeks of boot camp, and tested by duty and deployment. Though they stand in proximity to the civilians, they do not stand in the same way. It is not a stance of superiority, but an inherited one of holiness and outward separation gained by accepting the inward posture of the Marine Corps' core values—honor, courage, and commitment.

They are 'other.' They stand out in a contrast impossible to miss. Everything from their outward appearance, the fabric of their uniform, to the tradition they embody, everything shows its separateness from the non-military world. Marines in this environment and ceremony are clothed in a vivid picture of holiness in outward separation and inward posturing. Now, with such a faint picture, we can begin to understand that the Marine's holiness is a distant reflection of what Christians are called to be—holy. But we are not.

God's Holiness a Threat

God is holy. God's holiness, however, is not simply a uniform and a tradition. It is not medals, accommodations, rituals, and honors; it is an essential aspect of His character. A holy God is not good news for sinful, fallen image bearers. Our sins, our trespasses against His law desacralize. They are more horrendous than seeing someone throw paint over a Marine in his dress blues burying a fallen comrade. It is the denigration of all denigrations. Our sin is false confession that says God is not holy, when He is. This is bad news for sinners such as us, because God's holiness is integrally woven into His character as a just God. God's justice must punish the wicked. *We* are the wicked. There has not been a day in our lives when we did not violate His law and denigrate His character. Although God's essence remains unblemished by sin, nevertheless our sin insults and offends Him.

We sinners are without any excuse or defense against this. We are born into and have been at war with our Creator, fighting against His character our whole lives. At bottom, we know that at least part of this is true. We know we are fighters. It feels like fighting is in our DNA. It comes naturally. It flows through and fills us so easily that it's only in the still, reflective moments that we can see that fighting should not always be. It is not the way it's supposed to be. Marines are trained to fight. There is no sugar-coating it, no way to say it nicely. Marines are trained to be professional warriors who efficiently kill the enemy. The mission of the Marine Corps Rifle Squad is 'To locate, close with, and destroy the enemy, by fire and maneuver, or repel the enemy assault by fire and close combat.' But we forget. Fighting is conducted so that one day its purpose is fulfilled. There will be a day when no standing army is needed, when no Marine Corps will be around, but that day is not today. The fighting we inevitably prepare for and engage in does two things. First, it points back to the fall, and secondly, it points forward to a need for a resolution that ends all fighting. That includes both the fighting that we have with God in our hearts and its external manifestation.

Fighting, as vainly as we try, does not make us holy before a holy God. Yet we try, in futility to warrior our own way, to forge our own existence, but we remain unsettled and unresolved in this conflict. But will there be an end? Will there be a day when we veterans can set aside fighting inside and outside the uniform? Will there be a moment when we can outwardly end the war we wage against God and inwardly be at peace toward Him? Will there be a day when our relationships can be restored with our family, our estranged loved ones? What can unholy, sinful people like us do before a holy God to be right with Him? I and many fellow veterans are acutely aware of our ugly, sinful desires. And rather than fight against this, we embrace it as our identity. This self-acceptance of our twistedness doesn't need to be re-enforced. But what does it mean when we are told God is just, and He must punish the wicked for our sin against Him? Is there one who can successfully triumph over sin? Can the Holy One make what is unholy, holy? Can a just God punish the wicked, prevail over sin, triumph over the grave, and redeem warriors back to Himself? We explore this new aspect of the meta-narrative in the next chapter.

6

THE WARRIOR REDEEMER

Toward the end of WW2 in the Pacific Theatre, Navy and Marine Forces had decimated the Japanese Empire. At its height, the Japanese controlled territories stretching from northern China to the Solomon Islands, not far from Australia. The war was nearly over, yet there were pockets of resistance on islands on which Japanese soldiers kept fighting, or were standing by for their orders. In fact, several battles were fought that could have been avoided altogether. As E. B. Sledge recalls in his memoir, *With the Old Breed*, some historians and strategists question why the Battle of Peleliu was even fought.[1] Tactically, in hindsight some battles weren't necessary. In fact, some islands were bypassed altogether. Whether this was by strategic decision, because they were overlooked, or because the Japanese positions in some locations were unknown, some Japanese soldiers were left alone for weeks, months, and in at least one instance, years. When soldiers are cut off from communication in the fog of war, they must continue to carry out their orders. Many fighting for Japan fervently believed it would never surrender. When the Japanese forces surrendered on

---

1. E. B. Sledge, *With the Old Breed: At Peleliu and Okinawa* (New York, NY: Presidio Press, 2010), 55.

September 2, 1945, some of those forgotten soldiers kept fighting in disbelief; they were known as 'holdouts.' These holdouts were convinced that what they heard was more Allied propaganda, not that different from their own, like the infamous Tokyo Rose.

Over the ensuing months the Allied Forces combed these islands, sometimes engaging in post-war battles, to notify the surrendered enemy troops that they had surrendered, and the war was over. In one such case where a soldier didn't believe his glorious nation would ever surrender, a Japanese private, named Teruo Nakamura, didn't surrender until December of 1974. He held out for over twenty-nine years! The war had long been over, but the effects of that victory had not yet been fully realized by some Japanese troops. They refused to surrender, despite the fact they had lost. It is absurd that one would keep fighting after formal surrender, but they could not believe they had been defeated, or if they believed it, they chose not to accept its ramifications.

A Bridge over a Great Chasm

We are like the Japanese holdouts. In our state of sin, we have yet to bend the knee to a holy God, whose wrath burns against us. His justice demands reparations, yet we remain at war with Him, long after we have lost, with no chance of victory in our rebellion. The command given in Scripture is to be reconciled with Christ. To be reconciled means to be at peace, in our case, through surrender. How absurd, that we would fight against the Creator, as though we could ever win! We are more foolish than that Japanese soldier who came stumbling out of the mountains after twenty-nine years to finally lay down his weapon. What does this surrender accomplish if God's justice must be satisfied? The holiness or distinctness of God cannot be broken. We cannot breach or bridge God's holiness. We cannot 'reach' God. The only way we can even know God is if He reaches down to us.

God's holiness, His separateness, is part of His very character. His otherness is an impassable chasm between the Creator and His creatures. The only way we can know who God is and what He has done for us is if He comes down to us and crosses the Creator-creature barrier. The question then is: 'Has He done so?' The answer is an emphatic, 'Yes!' Jesus Christ is God made flesh. He is the eternal Son of God, who having always existed, was not created. But He became one of us when He was clothed in an earthly body like ours. His mother, Mary, gave birth to Him. He was born into this world not merely appearing to be human, but was genuinely and fully human and yet still fully God.

Jesus bridges the chasm that separates God and humans, and He Himself becomes God's message to us. He is the Word of God made flesh, the perfect human, the bridge over the chasm between God and us. He is also the answer to this damnable treason we have committed. The Son of God became flesh and lived a perfect life under the law of God. He was perfectly obedient to it, never transgressing, never sinning. His perfect life was lived so that He could rescue those He came to save. This is why Christ became flesh, to be obedient where we have been rebellious and to be crushed where we deserved to be punished.

Bearing the sins of the world was not an easy task. We could not have done it. We can't even bear our own sins. And so, nearly 2,000 years ago on a desert strip in the Middle East, Christ allowed Himself to be taken captive by the Jews and executed by the Romans for His claim to be God. Although He was God, Israel rejected His claim to be the Messiah who would save His people from their sins. He was falsely accused where we have been rightly accused. He was found guilty, though He was innocent. He was beaten, bruised, bloodied, and ridiculed—and just took it. Christ was crucified, absorbing the blows of what appeared to be a final defeat.

Our very word *excruciating* is derived from the word crucifixion. The pain He suffered— a crown of thorns shoved onto His head, His back torn open from whipping, and His face disfigured from blows—was more than most of us could bear. But He endured more. After all this, He carried His weighty cross to the place where He would be violently executed. Nails were driven through His hands and feet. The Romans stood Him upright on a cross that would eventually cause asphyxiation, while He gasped for partial breaths by pressing His feet up on the nails driven through them. If this wasn't enough, when He died, the Romans checked to see if He was dead by thrusting a spear into His side. If He hadn't been dead, this surely would have killed Him. Christ died a painful and bloody death. This seems rather obscure and meaningless unless we recognize that He was God. Fully God and still fully human.

The Death of Death

Jesus's crucifixion looked like sure defeat. The apostles certainly thought it was. His body was put into a tomb so that His death looked final. We would describe this as a defeat for anyone who was shot and killed in battle. But it wasn't a defeat. Three days later Christ burst forth from His grave in resurrection. Because Christ rose from the grave, death was now defeated. This is what John Owen describes as 'the death of death.' Christ tasted death so we would not have to face the second death. All of us will die once, but judgment waits for those who have not been reconciled to Christ Jesus. The second death is eternal separation from God's love. What great warrior from history can defeat death itself but Christ? What great soldier can elude the inevitable end but Christ? The apostle Paul commented on the magnitude of Christ's victory:

O death, where is your victory? O death, where is your sting? The sting of death is sin, and the power of sin is the law. But

thanks be to God, who gives us the victory through our Lord
Jesus Christ (1 Cor. 15:55-57).

In victory Christ now reigns as King over all the earth, sitting
magnificently and sovereignly at the right hand of the Father.
His enemies are being made a footstool *right now*, and the
final enemy is death. This should cause horror to those who
have not surrendered. To be reconciled means to make peace
with God through that surrender. Only through Christ is this
possible. No human effort could do it. In fact, our efforts only
displease God because they are an insult to Christ, who loved
us and gave Himself for us. To claim to reach God through
human effort is to say that Christ died for no purpose. Such
a claim slaps Him in the face (Gal. 2:21). Scripture says 'All
have fallen short of the glory of God,' setting the standard
high, for God's glory is faithful obedience to His law. That is
perfection. Christ attained it, but we cannot.

The world often paints Christianity as a weak person's
religion for those who can't handle the harshness of life and
need a coping mechanism. It is for weak people who need
to believe a fanciful story to reassure them that things will
be all right. This is far from reality. Christianity demands
the highest calling of faithfulness. The reason we hold
in contempt a pastor caught in a scandal is because we
demand that Christians fulfill a higher level of faithfulness.
Christians are called to be like Christ, and who has greater
strength than the warrior King?

Scripture depicts Christ as slaying His enemies by
His powerful word (Rev. 19:11-16). The battle is violently
described as He is seated on His warhorse, and the blood
floods, not splatters. Blood does not merely splash on Jesus's
white robe; it floods as high as a horse's bridle (Rev. 14:20).
After Christ's mighty victory, God calls the birds to feast on
the flesh of fallen enemies. We don't think about this side of
God. We see the gentle, tender Jesus in paintings carrying a
lamb or holding children on His lap. Is Jesus these things?

Of course, but God reveals Himself as so much more. Although some Psalms offer comfort to hurting people, many of them are prayers for the Lord's strength for battle. Here is an example:

> Blessed be the Lord, my rock, who trains my hands for war, and my fingers for battle; he is my steadfast love and my fortress, my stronghold and my deliverer, my shield and he in whom I take refuge, who subdues peoples under me. (Ps. 144:1-2)

God is the holy, righteous, and just One who fights battles, wages war against His enemies, and is *always* victorious. The nations could gather their armies to war against the Almighty and He would crush them. Psalm 91, which vividly depicts both God's might and faithfulness, deserves our attention:

> He who dwells in the shelter of the Most High will abide in the shadow of the Almighty. I will say to the LORD, 'My refuge and my fortress, my God, in whom I trust.' For he will deliver you from the snare of the fowler and from the deadly pestilence. He will cover you with his pinions, and under his wings you will find refuge; his faithfulness is a shield and buckler. You will not fear the terror of the night, nor the arrow that flies by day, nor the pestilence that stalks in darkness, nor the destruction that wastes at noonday. A thousand may fall at your side, ten thousand at your right hand, but it will not come near you. You will only look with your eyes and see the recompense of the wicked. Because you have made the LORD your dwelling place—the Most High, who is my refuge—no evil shall be allowed to befall you, no plague come near your tent. For he will command his angels concerning you to guard you in all your ways. On their hands they will bear you up, lest you strike your foot against a stone. You will tread on the lion and the adder; the young lion and the serpent you will trample underfoot. 'Because he holds fast to me in love, I will deliver him; I will

protect him, because he knows my name. When he calls to me, I will answer him; I will be with him in trouble; I will rescue him and honor him. With long life I will satisfy him and show him my salvation.'

Christ is the warrior King who defeated death. The question we must face is this: 'What will we do with Jesus?' What will do with this Jesus, who not only rescues the weak but rescues the very rebels who hate Him? Will we bend the knee to Him, confessing our wickedness and His righteousness, or will we remain in rebellion? Will we repent of our sins and turn toward the King with a contrite heart, or will we continue to run away? Will we believe in Him with all our heart, soul, mind, and strength? Or will we place our belief in ourselves?

During WW2, Switzerland opted for a stance of neutrality, rejecting an alliance with either the Axis or Allies. This stance of neutrality, though, does not stand up under examination. The posture of neutrality was, by default, a posture that catered to the victor. Additionally, Switzerland controversially maintained economic ties with Germany to ensure its own survival during the war, and much of the gold and art that Germans pillaged from Jews was held secretly behind Switzerland's borders. Neutrality was and is a myth. When it comes to Christ, no one can remain neutral. You cannot forever postpone a decision. To make such a move *is* to make a decision. Not to act, is to act. Even Christ declared, 'Whoever is not with me is against me' (Matt. 12:30).

It is terrifying to stand with a rebellious heart before the King of Glory. The question remains, 'What will you do with Christ?' Will you bend the knee to Him and be reconciled? Or will you run and be crushed when we face His wrath that burns against the wicked?

THE BROTHERHOOD: LA FAMILIA

First Sergeant Griffith had many devices and unique characteristics that influenced his company of Marines. He would constantly ensure we had a knife and a watch on our person with his famous 'knife-checks.' If you didn't have a knife, you would get down and do seventeen pushups (for our unit 1/7). A trail of platoons, companies, and battalions knife-checking each other long after Griffith had moved on was an enduring imprint of our beloved and rugged First Sergeant. Besides his knife-checks and grappling with Marines in the field, getting dirtied and bloodied along with us, he stressed family.

Griffith emphasized family by invoking the Spanish words *la familia*. We were forced to come to grips with fighting together as a family. We were not professionals who *happened* to work the same job, but professionals who shared and entrusted each other's lives with one another. We were not simply hired guns, but a family who protected its own and carried out its business in light of our love for each man in our company. Griffith stressed *la familia* over the familiar language of brotherhood because 'brotherhood' was overused, which flattened and dulled its deeper meaning.

We are a part of a brotherhood, but we didn't always feel that way or even know what it meant. Griffith's wisdom showed itself in understanding that a unit that fights as family fights best. This wisdom is likewise expressed in the fact that no one gets to choose his or her family; you are born into your family. We didn't get to choose who came and went from our unit; it was decided for us. This included even those in our company who made frustrating and stupid mistakes and would be referred to, in sanitized language, as 'dirt-bags.' But even these Marines, though they may have been dirt-bags, were *our* dirt-bags. They were family. Maybe not blood relatives, but this surrogate family, this adopted family, would at times be tighter than kin, closer than blood-brothers, for we were willing to lay down our lives for each other.

This 'warrior wisdom' resembles that of Scripture. The church is described as the family of God. We do not choose who will be our brother and sister; we were adopted into God's family. The adoption language of Scripture isn't just important. It is at the heart and center for our understanding of reconciliation, family, and adoption. Christ reconciled us to God from our war against Him. We are at peace with Him, and that not only means that we are no longer fighting Him. We aren't just war-criminals who have been allowed to walk free; it's much more than that. Perhaps a dated movie that helps us understand the significance of adoption is *Ben-Hur*, starring Charlton Heston.

The story of Judah Ben-Hur is about a Jewish prince living during the time of Christ who is wrongfully accused of a crime and sentenced to slavery as a rower in a Roman war vessel. During one of the battles, after he had been a slave for many years, his ship is sunk, and he saves a high-ranking Roman commander. By saving the commander, he alters the course of his life. In a moving scene, this Roman announces that without an heir of his own, he will make Judah Ben-Hur his son. He places a signet ring on his finger, signifying Ben-Hur's name is as binding as his own. Ben-Hur is clothed in the same outward garments as the Roman commander. His inheritance is now the same as the commander's. He is not merely a freed slave, but a freed slave, adopted as a son, and lavished with the riches of the redeemer. This is a good picture of God's adoption of former rebels, who bow their knee to Christ.

In the Marine Corps, people go through difficult challenges to earn the right of the name 'Marine.' The moment that EGA is placed into our hand, we are grafted into a victorious heritage. We bear the same title that Chesty Puller, Dan Dailey, and John Basilone carried—*we are Marines*. The Christian view of adoption is like this. We were slaves to sin, rebels against God, and hopeless, but by Christ's sacrifice on the cross God reconciled us to Himself. As a result, all who believe now have peace with God through Christ. Our turning from sin and turning to faith in the Son placed us into God's family as His adopted sons or daughters. The best part is this: when the Father puts us into his family based on what Christ did for us, God gives us all the blessings and responsibilities of sonship. That includes God making us as heirs. What will we inherit? The Trinity and the new heavens and new earth! The brotherhood of the Marines pales in comparison to the riches that God showers on His daughters and sons in Christ. The heritage of the Marines, that traces back to November 10th, 1775, is minuscule next to the call of God from before He laid the foundations of the earth. Christ's heritage and the promise of His coming go back to Genesis 3:15, where God said to the serpent, Satan's instrument: 'I will put enmity between you and the woman, and between your offspring and her offspring; he shall bruise your head, and you shall bruise his heel.'

Christ *is* the skull-bruising seed of the woman. He is the righteous Warrior and Redeemer with whom we must deal. The question remains, 'Are we for Christ or against Him?' All respond, but not all respond with a bent knee. Many of us are still holding out, like misguided Japanese 'hold-outs' in WW2, remaining unreconciled to Christ, despite His decisive and complete victory. What will we do with Christ, the One who died for the very enemies who attempt to usurp His throne?

7

A WARRIOR'S NEED TO WORSHIP

Everybody worships something. We worship what we love. Where do you direct your greatest devotion of time and money? This is often the object of your worship. It may not be a god, but it will often occupy the highest place in your mind. For many, their highest affections center on a sports team. For others, it may be a loved one—a girlfriend, wife, maybe your family. It may even be the comfort of a well-paying job, large home, fun friends, and time to pursue hobbies all wrapped up into one. Often what people worship is actually themselves, or a perception of who they want to be. Whether you worship a deity, another person, a sports team, or a combination of things, everyone worships *something*.

This fact is inescapable. All of us seek the satisfaction that the object of our worship promises to deliver. And, though this unique feature of humanity illumines that we have been made in the image of God, it also underscores our bankrupt status. Those objects of worship, when outside of Christ, continually fail to give the return on our investment. So, in large part, we seek satisfaction in the shadows of what our self-made idols promise. *Next time, I will find satisfaction in this. Next time, it will be great. Next time, I'll enjoy this more than any other thing.* There is always a 'next time.' The end of that road isn't the end, but a continuing search for what we cannot attain. In the words of the Rolling Stones, 'I can't get no satisfaction.'

Why is this? Why do we endlessly pursue satisfaction? It's as though we were made to be satisfied. Why do we perpetually demand that these innate desires be satisfied? And why, when we keep coming up empty-handed, do we consistently find despair instead of satisfaction?

THE GOD OF ALCOHOL

I can think of at least two common places servicemembers, especially Marines, direct their misplaced worship. One is in alcohol abuse, and the other is in sexual promiscuity. Marines are proficient at many things, and wherever they display a skill, pride follows. Some pursuits are truly noble; others, while culturally acceptable, are shameful. In the circles I lived in as an infantry marine, drinking was as commonplace as fitness. I don't mean someone relaxing and having a couple of beers, I mean sheer loaded, blitzed, shouting, loud, obnoxious drinking, until passed out, arrested, or drunk. It was odd *not* to have Marines still drunk in the morning formation with the stench of alcohol leaking through their pores. One of my closest friends would drink heavily the night before a PFT (physical fitness test). On nights such as these, I would go to bed earlier than normal and hydrate. Even in my preparation to do well, I was angered by the fact that my friend still managed to beat me in the run portion of the test. On one such occasion I ran a sub-20-minute 3-mile, which isn't bad, and still finished after my drunk friend! He loved his drinking so much that he was motivated by the fear of having his drinking privileges taken away if he was discovered to be drunk. So, by sheer will power, he crushed the PFT.

While reflecting with some of the Marines I served with, we admitted the problem isn't with drinking, but its excessiveness. However, our excessive drinking never revealed why we drank. Sure, we wanted to have a good time, but this didn't get to the heart of the matter. It didn't answer the real, root question, which hid behind 'having a good time.'

One Marine, named Silva, did get to the heart of the matter. I met him when I activated with the reserves after finishing my active duty enlistment. He candidly admitted his reason for drinking was to fill a gaping void in the center of his chest. Occasionally, others would admit they drank to suppress their deep pain. They would drink to forget everything; reflecting on the pain that came by night filled them with paralyzing self-doubt. By no means is drunkenness the greatest enemy or vice, but it is illustrative of a common mask to camouflage our wounds and shortcomings. Lest my Marine friends misunderstand, I do not believe drinking alcohol is a sin; but we should have a problem with excessive drinking. The most troubling part of drunkenness is not its excessiveness, but rather, the abuse of alcohol as a source of comfort and numbing. For many, drinking can become the object of their worship, whether in moderation or excess. It is a matter of the heart. And here are the aspects of our story that need reflection to evaluate our motivations.

Ironically, when people deny the existence of God yet bow before alcoholism or any other vice, they haven't successfully suppressed the truth of God; they've only swapped one for another. It is with religious fervor we bow before our idols. Devoted and enslaved, we bring our affections to worship and sacrifice before a false god that never delivers on our hopes. We try to fill the gap by pouring beer after beer, shot after shot, night after night of being completely wasted, to the point of starting bar fights or throwing up. All of this is a painful example of our need to worship, but it is more than that. It is descriptive of the worship we do every day that it is misdirected.

It's almost laughable when we write down our internal thoughts. After returning from my first deployment,

I wanted nothing more than to numb myself with endless self-medicating, self-intoxicating pursuits. When I would drink, I would think, 'This will make me feel better.' And for a time, it worked. Deep into the night of one drunken stupor, I remember low-crawling through the barracks to steal a pizza out of a Domino's delivery-man's car because I wanted to. I simply wanted what I wanted when I wanted it. Everything was about me. I wanted to steal something, and so I did. I wanted to get drunk and forget about work stress and my feelings of powerlessness as a lance-corporal, so I did. Despite my great efforts to live free, I became more shackled to my desires. Morning came accompanied by a hang-over, and I would swear off drinking for the hundredth time, again finding that the alcohol I consumed only left me emptier than before. The next weekend would come, and I would do it again, returning like a dog to its vomit. We would follow the same routine, only even more outlandishly to make the time pass and forget our pain. We tried yelling at the boots (new Marines fresh out of boot camp), trashing our rooms, throwing wall-lockers over the third floor of the barracks, or picking fights with each other or with our neighboring artillery unit. In a continually faithful but misdirected pursuit, we would chase after a fleeting moment of satisfaction and fulfillment only to be found thirstier, emptier, and even more enslaved.

It took time and friends rooted in faith to reveal that my attempts of fulfillment were really misplaced attempts at worship. We are always worshipping, and we are always creating idols for ourselves. Even concerning the idols that never satisfy, we lie to ourselves that next time, the return on our investment would come. Next time, we will drink and be satisfied. When we devote our attention and emotions toward something, we are, in fact, directing our affections of worship to that thing. When people devote all their time and money to sports, you will often find that their idol, the little-god they have erected, is there as well. Where the heart is, our actions follow. The thing about idols, though, is that they demand sacrifices. We weave excuses to justify our outlandish behavior, and before we realize, we don't just have one idol that clutters the heart, but a pantheon of false gods that live there. They demand our worship, our service, all in the name of fleeting fulfillment, short-lived passions, and empty hope.

SUICIDE AND TRUE WORSHIP

Suicide is often the last of a series of desperate attempts at fulfillment and release from the emptiness idols eventually bring us. Idols abandon us. We are not nourished by our pursuits, but broken a little more each time. The pain of losing loved ones, our brothers who have fallen in battle, and others by their own hand is intensified by our wrongly placed worship. In the end, we find no lasting satisfaction and no joy in the vain pursuit of chasing our fleeting desires. Our need cannot and will not be met outside of Christ, but will ultimately only be fulfilled in Him. This is where a warrior's worship must be directed.

Often when we hear the word 'worship,' we conjure up the wrong images or only one among many right forms. We think of someone with their arms in the air singly loudly and off key with corny music you skip past on the radio. This instantly creates distaste for many with whom I served because of the abuses they experienced from a local church. Perhaps it is because many are made to feel inferior to those in the church, as if churchgoers have figured it out, no longer sin, and are worthier than they. This abuse, however widespread, is dreadfully wrong. Anyone who has been made to feel this way isn't seeing true Christianity, but a gross mischaracterization of it. Right worship is not done on Sundays only; it is done in all aspects of life with all aspects of our being.

Scripture describes our affections toward God in the greatest commandment that we should love God with all our heart, all our soul, all our mind, and all our strength. That is to say, no part of you should be excluded from loving God and where you find your love for God, your heart follows with worship. This love for God is rooted in what Christ, our warrior King, has done by defeating death, and worship naturally follows it. This kind of worship changes us from the inside out, fills the marrow of our affections anew, and directs them toward God. We respond in astonishment that He would defeat death for filthy creatures such as us.

When the heart is made new and our knee is finally bent toward God, right worship becomes possible in all aspects of life. True, life-encompassing worship includes studying in school, working our vocations, shooting at the range, spending time with our families, or enjoying rest in watching sports. God delights in all of these areas of our right worship all of which we enjoy below our love for Him. Here are some questions that reflect the posture of our heart: Whom do I serve when I do 'x'? Am I trying to bring attention to myself or do I desire to please God in this pursuit? If I could no longer do 'x,' would I suffer a complete loss of identity?

Veterans uniquely experience a need to fill the void they feel deep inside. This drive can keep them running away from the truth of God for years. Some burn out quicker than others, and some realize sooner than others that their desperation to find fulfillment only leaves them emptier until they collapse from within. That void, that emptiness, that place of brokenness, can only be made whole and filled by Christ.

Night after night, many of the men I knew futilely chased fulfillment through the wrong means. One night of getting blitzed wasn't enough, so they tried two more nights. Getting drunk on five beers wouldn't work, so they would drink more. Once beer no longer worked, hard alcohol took its place. That did the job, but was often accompanied by vomiting half of the night and sickness in the morning. Their work came under great scrutiny when some of the guys I knew showed up to work drunk. They weren't allowed to drink at night, so they would sneak drinking in throughout the day. Occasionally they would go to the store while they were buzzed and, later, they were going while completely wasted. I recall the stupor of a fellow Marine being so out of his mind drunk he was doing donuts with his car in the parking lot of the PMO (Provost Marshall's Office—what most people know as MPs, military police). When they came out to arrest him, he abandoned his vehicle and ran inside of the barracks to pass out drunk, hiding under his bed. It is almost laughable, if it weren't such a common occurrence. A sign posted at the entrance to the base in Twentynine Palms MCAGCC (Marine Corps Air Ground Combat Center) listed the number of DUIs that occurred in the last year—the highest of any other Marine base. It's no joke, and the consequences are real.

The wrongfully placed pride in drinking doesn't suddenly stop once active duty service ends. If anything, it enhances it. The Marines in many ways actually provide a restraint for much of this, with highly structured days, a strong support system, and dreadful consequences for drunkenness. But Marines create a culture that says they must get drunk. Those coming off active-duty are quickly silhouetted as those who have a problem, as society at large recognizes that someone who drinks thirty beers per night and can't get drunk has a problem. The constraints of the Marine Corps are lifted, and former active duty Marines no longer have their brothers with them. Drinking alone is about as depressing as it gets. It is in those lonely moments that haunting memories of regret are enhanced. Emotions are stronger, depression is more common, and both can quickly turn deadly.

Drinking is one of the lowest hanging fruits to point a finger at when it comes to Marines' outward expression of inward brokenness. It shows a need where someone's desire isn't being met, and he or she attempts to meet it with the medium of alcohol. It reflects some unmet longing that is fleeting and elusive in the long and lonely nights of drinking.

It is with regret that this is not the only place of friction among the men I know. It is not the only desire that goes unmet, or the only pursuit that ends in vain.

THE GOD OF SEX

The Marine Corps, and the military for that matter, is a very sexually broken place. I say that against the pride that I, and many Marines wrongfully have, that our sexual prowess and exploits are simply 'something Marines do' akin to the adage 'boys will be boys.' The complication and confusion in this come from the twisting of something that is truly good. Sex is a good and powerful thing. Christians often get the reputation of being prudish, and to our own shame, that is unfortunate. Sex is a topic we often avoid, and we shouldn't. We give many sermons on what we shouldn't do and come off as legalists. This is sad, for God ordains, creates, and describes the beauty of sex in Scripture.

During my first deployment, I was both surprised (and to my current regret, delighted) in the availability of and openness to share pornographic materials. The joke one of my former team leaders made was that his external hard drive had so much porn on it that it had an S.T.D. We would consume a wide array of pornographic material in all its mediums. A common thing some Marines do before deployment is to purchase types of masturbation devices. Shamefully and ironically, we experienced no shame from each other. The HBO mini-series, *Generation Kill*, is accurate in the way Marines talk and are bent toward sexual exploits. It doesn't take long before the novelty of the varieties and genres of porn become boring. One of my senior Marines was 100% correct when he described the return home for most men. Often the first things we would come to notice was the fat ugly wives and girlfriends that didn't measure up to seven months of pouring porn into our minds. The images we worshiped were more appealing than the flesh and blood standing before us that we had supposedly devoted ourselves to in faithfulness.

Pornography has an alluring grip that is deceptive and poisons us on multiple levels. It often portrays women who are beautiful and have slender figures. This perverts a God-glorifying enjoyment of the opposite sex, for women are image-bearers of God just as men are. But pornography says that their natural beauty is not found in their person, but reduces it to what they are willing to do in the bedroom. Pornography depicts women with an extreme willingness to please their partners, which is then internalized by the user and projected on his actual sexual partner. The relationship a man then has with a woman stems from his expectations of sex. These expectations are often assembled through continual pornographic ingestion which actually distances the user from the personhood in the videos they watch. Sex, which often contains a dimension of emotion, is now reduced to the person's desire to 'get off.' The confusion and problem this creates are especially felt by married Marines, both those who are currently married, and those who will eventually be married. The bonding-hormone, oxytocin, is released in the brain whenever a person has an orgasm. The problem with the release of this hormone while watching pornography is that the person is then bonding to an image, not a person; to a video, not a partner; to a deception, and not a reality.

God created sex and instituted it as something a man and a woman should do—and often! God created the male and female bodies and made them naturally pleasing as perfect complements and counter-parts. Sex is a very good thing, but pornography twists it. What I write about Marines differs little from the larger culture. We have an epidemic of wrongly-placed affections and pursuits of fulfillment in desires that leave many dissatisfied and returning for more to only be increasingly dissatisfied. At rock bottom, though, this isn't a problem of pornography; it is a problem of worship. Sex is one of the many God-ordained, God-created mediums by which we give glory to Him. Sex is something we can thank and give praise to God for. But sex does not glorify God when we abuse it; it then becomes self-worship, enslaving ourselves to our desires, and distorting the intended manner in which sex is to be engaged in.

Only in the person of Christ, our warrior Redeemer, can our sexual brokenness be forgiven and healed. Often, the healing from years of sexual brokenness will take years of sanctification, but people are not without hope. Sex has a very real and good place in life, but it will not ultimately satisfy. Only worship of Christ rooted in thankfulness for His redemption will satisfy. Only Christ can satisfy, fulfill, heal, and redeem in the ultimate sense. Enjoying alcohol has a proper and constrained place in the life of many. Sex is good, and even mandated, to be a part of the life of every married person, but it will not ultimately satisfy, make us whole, or heal our brokenness and remove our shame. Only Christ can do that.

8

'SUFFER IN SILENCE'

'Suffer in silence.' This adage is commonplace in the Marine Corps. More than one Marine I knew who made it through Recon had it tattooed on himself. During my first work up (the time of training 'working up' to a deployment), this was written artistically on a large piece of plywood during a six-week period for helo-training in Yuma. There was no end to its use as it was easily loosed from our lips to apply to any strenuous or difficult task. We used it so often that it began to lose its meaning because we used it to label a situation in satire. *Who needs water? Water is a crutch. Who needs sleep? Sleep is a crutch. Suffer in silence! Oh, you haven't been off from training in two months? Suffer in silence. Tell someone who cares!* But even with our dry and witty deflections, we still approached suffering in silence submissively as though it were an infallible dogma. At any given time, many were in the midst of suffering but held their tongues with fatal allegiance.

Equally commonplace with our dogma of suffering were 'Dear John Letters,' the infamous letters veterans received while deployed, which announced a breakup. Many received these letters or returned home to find their bank accounts emptied, their wife gone and, sometimes, for those who had kids, them too. What buoy did people reach for to keep themselves afloat in trials such as this? You guessed it. Suffer in silence. Physical injuries occur during training and deployments, some being dangerously serious with their sufferers in dire need of time to recover. But the mission goes on—*someone probably has it worse*—we would reason. Many would rather remain injured than be charged with malingering. So, suffer in silence.

SUFFER IN SILENCE?

The tragic bit of suffering in silence is that Marines don't know to what extent it should be applied. Its application is too broad, its reign too dominant. Many of the core traits in the Marine Corps, which comprise its ethos, are transcendent values for inside and outside military service. Pride, Loyalty, and Commitment are the three core values of the First Team, the First Marine Division. Honor, Courage, and Commitment are the three core values of the Marines Corps at large. These traits give veterans an advantage when they manifest them in civilian life after military service is completed. Suffering in silence, though, is a de facto value in the military which is not only at odds with the tenets of honor, courage, and commitment, but a value that often ousts honor for the sake of a twisted loyalty to remaining silent.

At its best, to suffer in silence is a firewall to contain unnecessary complaining and bickering. There is a legitimate place for service members to be quiet about the misery of their circumstances in training and on deployment. Bickering can be divisive, show insubordination against the command, and kill morale. But suffering in silence was never taught with such nuances. Rather, its sweeping claim was laid on the backs of servicemembers who were suffering under a burden they should have shared. Often, the suffering coalesced into a perfect storm for someone whose family showed a systemic pattern of broken relationships, including marriage. Couple this with the pressures of the profession and a disbelief, not just in the God of Scripture, but in any god whatsoever, and suffering in silence has left many isolated and alone. This deadly solitude regresses into a new level of isolation when it turns into a vicious cycle of seeking comfort in vices which leave people thirstier, hungrier, and emptier after the vice fails to alleviate their suffering. The effects of suffering for too long in silence are cumulative and could be compared to missing hours of sleep for months on end. After a time, the outward working of the suffering takes an observable physical toll which leaves a Marine beaten, fatigued, and longing for respite. Through a sinister window, the release through death becomes a viable option which looks increasingly promising.

Sharing in Suffering

Suffering is *not* silent in Scripture. The view of suffering in Scripture is not all that distant from how Marines can learn to suffer in the good fight of faith. The apostle Paul writes in his letter to Timothy (2 Tim. 2:3), 'Share in suffering as a good soldier of Christ Jesus.' But the suffering of the Christian life, in the good fight of faith, is *not* done in silence. To the contrary, suffering is still present! Suffering will undoubtedly afflict the warrior in the fight of faith. It is unavoidable, yet to our relief and joy, that suffering is not alone but is shared. What does it mean to share in the suffering as one enlisted in the ranks under the Lordship of Christ?

At the MCAGCC (Marine Corps Air Ground Combat Center) in Twentynine Palms, California, there is an infamous live fire and maneuver range large enough to accommodate an entire company, plus attachments, to make a coordinated attack. The range is ominously covered in sharp rocks in an upward slant into the nook of the high desert mountains. During the typical work ups to go to Iraq or Afghanistan, companies would get a chance at running this range during what was known as the Mojave Viper, a full battalion, month-long training exercise right before deployment. At the time, the norm was that most units would run the range maybe twice in an enlistment, and would proudly regard it as an accolade of an accomplishment. During my second work up, we ran the range more than sixteen times in various ways. We did it as a company, squad, team, in daytime, in nighttime, without egress, with egress, and on and on. One of the variations of running the range at night (usually after a full day of training) would be to accompany it with a hike back to base in full gear, about four miles away.

There was one peak in our training cycle before our 2009 deployment when we were utterly beat down from the aggressive training. We incessantly ran the range and other exercises over the course of several weeks. There were no weekends off, just training, long hikes, training, and more hikes. When training comes this hard without a chance for some recovery, the body begins to break down. Marines, to their fault, consistently over-train. There's some merit to this. The over-training of the body is testing troops' mental endurance and resiliency. The body will break down long before the mind will, and so this training philosophy of over-training remains despite its obvious disadvantages.

On one occasion, during the peak of this cycle, most of us already had blistered feet after the long weeks of hiking miles between ranges. But there was no respite; instead, breaking any kind of record the Marine Corps might have, we ran range 400 again. Another long hike back to base followed. Our lieutenant (whom I will not name to spare him embarrassment) was fresh out of TBS (The Basic School where all Marine Officers train before going to the fleet) when he arrived at the fleet at the beginning of the training cycle. Our platoon garnered little respect for this man, who in attempts to prove himself, often abused his authority in the face of poor tactical decisions and leadership characterized by micro-managing.

The road between Range 400 and Mainside (the main drag of the MCAGCC) was a straight shot due west. We finished the range sometime around midnight and finally stepped off at about 0200. Training through the night was the norm during this workup. This night was particularly painful because it came at the end of a difficult week. We were weary and wore it visibly. People wear fatigue differently when they've been awake for over 30 hours at the end of a long, dreary training cycle. Not only were we beat, the water Buffalo (the portable water tank we towed from place to place) was gone, and so against regulations and common sense, we stepped off with *empty* canteens and camelbacks. Rather than use the road and simply get us back to the armory so we could finish cleaning our weapons and check in, our Lieutenant (who we nicknamed Pathfinder after this incident) decided to take a more scenic route. Zig zagging through the desert and the MOUT towns (Mobile Operations on Urban Terrain, towns retrofitted with conex railroad boxes made into miniature cities in which Marines can train for urban warfare) and cycling through patrol formations, it was impossible not to compare ourselves to the other platoons. None of the other platoons had been instructed to return to base this way, and no one knew this was our route. Exhausted, we finally crested the ridge after our Lieutenant had gotten us lost to discover we were several miles south of our desired entry point. This was when our platoon sergeant took over, a move of initiative for which we were very thankful.

Tightening up our ranks to a normal marching column, our silence finally broke. It wasn't bickering or self-pity that was vocalized, but a humorous, and mildly insubordinate critique of our 'bonus' journey. Okay, it was a little more than mildly insubordinate. In a single moment of honor, our Lieutenant recognized his mistake and kept his mouth tight-lipped while we laughed about the odd manner in which we made our glorious return. We laughed, we told each other the pain we had in our feet and backs, and quickly located those who ran out of water to disperse what we had remaining. In a real, tangible sense, we had endured several weeks of physical suffering that could have ended in complete loathing, or even a medical emergency, but ended in a tighter bond formed around the toughness of the shared journey. We shared in each other's suffering during that training cycle. Suffering in silence could have ended in anger and bitterness, but sharing in our suffering made us stronger.

MISERY AND SUFFERING

You may be thinking, 'That isn't *real* suffering.' On the one hand, I agree. Some finally returned home from this physically demanding training peak to discover that their marriage was worse off than before, or that their wives had gone to be with a man who could be present. A problem that Marines share is that only the most heart-wrenching, bloody account of POWs being tortured can be correctly labeled as suffering. My intention is not to allow every inconvenience or discomfort to be called suffering, but to help us recognize there is a spectrum of suffering. To disqualify our own pain only leads to silence. That surely is not the answer.

While in boot camp, Marine recruits feel miserable. Upon graduating, they advance to the School of Infantry training, and, once again, know misery. But they graduate with a hope for something better, and the young Marines arrive at the fleet as boots, but then, once again, feel miserable. But their arduous time as boots finally passes, and finally deployed and *then,* the Marine is miserable. To cope, they often relativize their misery, so that it doesn't seem so bad, compared to their most recent misery. Yet as human beings, they are stretched, tried, tested, and, over time, can become brittle like an old rubber band.

Even when our Lieutenant led us miles in the wrong direction, we weren't suffering to the greatest degree, but only saw a snapshot of what the Marine Infantry endures week after week, month after month, year after year, and deployment after deployment. Sometimes the sheer misery of circumstances isn't appreciated until we leave them behind, gain elevation, and can critically reflect on them. Tragically, too many Marines fall prey to believing their miserable circumstances are not worthy of being called suffering. And so, what do they do? They hold their peace and suffer in silence.

Though many would struggle to call their pain suffering, they may be more apt to relate to misery. Marines, especially infantry, share their lot in being miserable. Camaraderie is met in misery, units become tighter, the bonds of brotherhood grow deeper, and the misery is shared by all. You can call it suffering or you can call it misery, but it doesn't make much difference when you're in the midst of it. You simply want to share it with someone else. Even if the sharing of a commonly-felt suffering doesn't alleviate it, there is a ministry brought by presence and acknowledgment that you are not alone. And sometimes that's all it takes—not feeling alone.

The Christian life is filled with suffering, but Christians were never meant to suffer in silence. Our warrior Redeemer, Christ Himself, suffered much and was left alone, except for the intense fellowship of the Father, while fulfilling His task. His solitude, though, is not prescriptive, but descriptive. This is to say, when Jesus was alone in the garden the night He was betrayed, abandoned by His disciples, His solitude was not a good thing. Jesus rebuked His disciples when they could not stay awake for even one hour. They were supposed to be with their Teacher, in support of their Master. Christ before His death, knowing what was coming, was in intense emotional and spiritual agony. He was suffering, even prior to being beaten and crucified. Christ's solitary suffering was not intended to eliminate Christian suffering. Rather, it points to a day when there will be no suffering and, secondly, that the suffering of life is never meant to be alone, rather it is a burden to be carried in community with others.

When I was beaten down from training, drained from days without sleep, I found comfort and camaraderie in my brothers when we voiced our hurts to one another. Breaking the silence didn't take the suffering or misery away. But it did grant a greater measure of endurance in the midst of it. It didn't magically heal the blisters forming on my feet, but it did encourage me. We don't think of what it means to encourage, often, but it means to emplace strength in another person; and we do this often by our presence. This goes back to the beginning of the narrative of Scripture, that man was not made to be alone. Rather his image-bearing nature is expressed rightly in community. Suffering, the Christian life, and fighting the good fight are not meant to be done alone. We are to bear each other's burdens when life is tough and meet people where they are in their suffering, a suffering that should not be done in silence.

THE GOOD FIGHT

A day indeed will come when fighting ceases, and war is no longer waged. That day, though, is not this day, and so fighting continues, war wages on. We come under the Lordship of Christ and end our war with Him. That doesn't suddenly make us pacifists; rather, it enlists us into His ranks. Surrendering to Christ isn't the end of pain in life, nor is it now an easy path to follow. It is the beginning of a long road, a road costly because it was paid for by the highest price, the life of Christ Himself. The reconciliation we experience with Christ is a vertical reconciliation between us and God. As a result our war ends with God, but the spiritual battle of this life begins in a horizontal direction.

The fight of faith is a fight of faithfulness. Christ is the ultimate fulfillment of being *semper fidelis*, and we are the ultimate examples of breaking it. Even after we ended our war with Christ, we showed, and will show, insubordination toward Him. We will face times when we bicker under our load, when we complain that we have been given too much, and in this process, He will bring us gently back to the cross, where again we bend our knee, only to realize that Christ bore it all; and His burden, though too great for us, is not too great for Him. This process of God revealing the pockets of resistance in us is called sanctification. This is the means by which we are set apart more and more to become holy. Like the holiness of God, we will be drawn out, sometimes painfully, from among those we live. As we are faithful, we are sanctified; as we are sinful, we are humbled.

The apostle Paul, who gave up much, describes horrible things that most of us would see as the epitome of suffering, yet he responds in a strange way (2 Cor. 11:24-30):

> Five times I received at the hands of the Jews the forty lashes less one. Three times I was beaten with rods. Once I was stoned. Three times I was shipwrecked; a night and a day I was adrift at sea; on frequent journeys, in danger from rivers, danger from robbers, danger from my own people, danger from Gentiles, danger in the city, danger in the wilderness, danger at sea, danger from false brothers; in toil and hardship, through many a sleepless night, in hunger and thirst, often without food, in cold and exposure. And, apart from other things, there is the daily pressure on me of my anxiety for all the churches. Who is weak, and I am not weak? Who is made to fall, and I am not indignant? If I must boast, I will boast of the things that show my weakness.

Paul's response almost seems nonsensical. If anyone had the right to complain, it should be him. Yet his response baffles us, for he boasts in his weakness. To boast in weakness is so counterintuitive; it is the exact opposite of what the U.S. Military demands and in which most Americans boast. The weakness of Paul, though, is the strength rooted in the Warrior King. It is rooted in the victory over the grave after the defeat of the cross.

A Victorious Fight

To the unchurched, the word 'gospel' is heard just about everywhere and means just about nothing. Elvis Presley sang 'Gospel' music. A talk-show host underscores a claim by saying 'ain't that the gospel truth?' Churches plaster it on their signs, and pastors are heard on the radio speaking about 'the gospel' all the time. But what does it mean?

The word 'gospel' finds its origins in a Greek word that meant, more or less, *good news*. More specifically, at one point of time, it referred to the declaration of victory that was taken from the battlefield to the commander. The good news of victory, the gospel message in Scripture, is the heart of Christianity. The gospel is that Christ went to the cross having lived a perfect life under the law, bore the sins of the world in death, was buried and rose again defeating death. He tasted the first fruits of the resurrection, ascended into heaven, and is seated at the right hand of the Father, reigning as King of Kings and Lord of Lords, and is putting His enemies under His feet. That is the victory message of the gospel. It's the same victory message of reconciliation that says to sinners, 'The battle has been won; bend the knee to Christ.' Gospel proclamation is therefore the victory that is lived and proclaimed boldly in the Christian life that we can share in with Christ.

On June 6, 1944, Allied forces invaded Normandy Beach in France, which marked both the largest amphibious invasion ever, and the beginning of the end of WW2. Most historians agree that the war was lost by the Axis Powers that day. But even despite the successful invasion and victory, there remained eighteen months of intense fighting. D-Day is a picture of the Christian fight. Christ won His victory at the cross. But just because He won, it doesn't mean life is easy for Christians. Those who come under the Lordship of Christ and enlist in His ranks still have intense fighting remaining in their personal lives. There is much misery and suffering to endure. Those that have not yet acknowledged the victory of Christ know nothing of the entire Christian fight.

Because Christ was victorious at the Cross, we no longer have to suffer in silence. Because Christ bore the most miserable of deaths, we know there is a camaraderie with our Lord. Because the gospel message goes out, we know that a final victory means not giving in to miserable circumstances, years of unspoken pain, or any sort of internal brokenness. The final victory belongs to Christ.

Suffering in silence should not be part of anyone's story. Suffering in silence should never be the ethos, the prevailing, or even the minority practice. It should never be accepted or revered. Suffering in silence allows the cumulative weight of life's circumstances to grow heavier the longer we remain silent. I've known too many Marines that have tasted this detestable practice of pseudo-strength in staying tight-lipped. I have seen them exit the Marine Corps and keep this wicked practice in effect. My first deployment to Iraq in 2007-2008 saw not a single Marine killed or wounded. Not one. Every Marine returned home. Nine men who have taken their own lives after their deployments were over, after their service came to an honorable close, attest to what an untenable failure suffering in silence is.

The only hope that can speak into this brokenness is found in the victory achieved by our warrior Redeemer. Christ tasted suffering. Christ set forth and never departed from His word in which He described our need for each other—our need for community. Suffering is, perhaps, inevitable for some. Silence is not.

The good fight of the Christian faith is very difficult and will likely be filled with pockets of suffering. Some will experience it more intensely than others, but all will face trials. The central doctrine of the Marines, *semper fidelis*, is actually the essence of the good fight. The fight of faith is a fight of faithfulness. Though we are not faithful, we can take heart that Christ is. Though we fail, we can be assured that Christ did not. Though we are discouraged, Christ replenishes us with His victory and pours strength back into us. It is because of Christ's faithful victory that we can share in suffering with Him and not be silent. It is because of Christ's victory that the apostle Paul can sign off on his last letter with these words, 'I have fought the good fight, I have finished the race, I have kept the faith' (2 Tim. 4:7). Paul's confidence was in his warrior Redeemer's words, 'I have said these things to you, that in me you may have peace. In the world you will have tribulation. But take heart; I have overcome the world' (John 16:33).

9

COMMUNITY AND ISOLATION

Community. It's one of those words that is carelessly thrown about. Its meaning is worn smooth. Or worse, it's been hollowed out and filled with a new, shallow meaning. But this new meaning lacks the vibrancy and beauty of true community. 'Community' can be seen stamped across dead and dying churches, epitaphs of an older time. It's pasted and attached to governmental programs for reconstruction and outreach. Though they try to use the term as an ally, it feels as warm as an unplanned gathering of people in a hospital waiting room. If there is anything we can still relate to that still resembles what community is supposed to be like, if there is any institution that hasn't been completely dismantled and eroded, community is supposed to be like family.

Community means living in close proximity with common interests. This accurate, though overly broad, definition contains within it a portion of our problem in forming a true community. A group of travelers at an RV park can be called a community, as could baseball fans who form temporary little communities during the games of a World Series. People who work together may not live in the same neighborhood, but they share the majority of their day together in their occupation. Then there are the so-called digital communities of our 'social' media. At our fingertips, we can access and share the best, worst, and most sanitized version of ourselves with the world. We can access all of these faux communities from our distant and compartmentalized homes. These latest digital versions of communities are the most dangerous assaults on the essence of community as we've formed myriads of 'communities' pivoting off many 'common interests.' The more we've traded the physical for the digital, the more disingenuous community becomes, and the more inauthentic we portray ourselves, usually as the most sanitized version of ourselves.

The truth is, though, a biker, academic, or veteran community is not a community in the most meaningful sense. These subcultures are greater than the so-called online communities. An insider to a medical journal can scale the language barrier through their bona fides and jargon, leaving others on the outside, as it should be. I don't speak 'medical-ese,' nor do I desire to. But I do speak 'veteran-ese,' and though I possess the accolades of service and deployment as an insider to the so-called veteran community, it is not a true community. A true community should not be over-specialized and overly-niched. We may enjoy our insider private Facebook groups, but there is an aura of artificiality to them. They miss something profound about real community.

A community should be a complex web of overlapping kinds of people living in a similar space. It should have rich and poor and be ethnically, religiously and recreationally diverse. Obviously, a rural community of farmers who live separated by farmland will function differently than an urban community. But in that similar space, though often pivoting around a dominant economic interest (like farm or oil towns), community in its purest form includes more than one kind of person.

Now imagine this scene. A man awakens for work. He grabs the morning paper off his porch, eats breakfast with his family and skips out the door. While walking to work, he passes his mailman. He is greeted by his neighbors and stops in his local pharmacy for a few items. The pharmacist knows him by name, and they exchange some warm small-talk. He arrives at work, which is walking distance from home. On his trip home, commuting on foot, he stops at the local grocery store and engages with others with nods and smiles to everyone. The scene sounds fanciful, if not cheesy. Why is this? Because this is not the reality of nearly anybody in North America; it's just a dream. Why is that? That is because of the death of the walkable neighborhood.

I'm not sure where we can put the initial blame. Perhaps, at the feet of the automobile. In its inception and onset, it was not invasive into people's lives, but was a novelty. Demand and industrial efficiency fanned this flame. We take for granted the automobile's place in our lives. Similar to the clock, there is almost no part of our lives not affected by our vehicles. City planning notes this first. Especially in America, city planning and zoning have been influenced heavily around our roads and parking places. Our cars are near the top priority for planning and developing a community. Where can we drive them? Where can we park them? Where can we fuel, clean, buy, sell, and scrap them? And though a single car is not large, everything that it needs to function from coast to coast, is. It needs space so we can park it between our homes. We don't share walls with others because we have cars.

Then comes all the other zoning. Factories, for good reasons, can't be built too closely to residential neighborhoods. Restaurants can't occupy the same space as these either, so like things are lumped together with like things. When you take the sum total of space needed for cars, restaurants, churches, homes, and work, and spread them out, you don't have anything that resembles a walkable neighborhood. The result? We commute. This is demonstrated well between our older cities. Let's take New York City, for example, and Phoenix, which intentionally opted for a simple and modernized city grid layout. Both of these places look, feel, and function differently. Geography, though it should play a role for where we go to church, is secondary to what is primary—our car. We commute to work, church, home, and recreation. There the communities rest, spread thin and wide over millions of square miles, commuter communities that share nothing in common. My neighbor only shares with me the fact that he lives next to me. Besides that, he works in a different part of town and takes his kids to a different school and church. He shops at a different grocery store, and why? Because we are overly specialized and spread out over cities that have prioritized the car as the premium factor. Ironically, as these roads and highways make greater connections to everything else, they disconnect us from everything that matters. Our choices are king and community is the serf. With at least one grand exception—college.

College and Community

The undergraduate years at a university often occupy a special place in one's life. They frequently form the tightest bonds, have the best conversations, while people live poor and eat well, live, fail and live in close proximity to many brothers and sisters. It was there many of us met our future wives or husbands. There was something special about all that freedom in that place. What was it? I would submit that the glue that binds those memories together is in the 'verbness' of community. It was where you '*did* community.'

Think about the geographic arrangement of many universities. They have dormitories where students live in close proximity to others. The café or dining commons is within walking distance. Many of the best conversations were on the way to those places. Special moments aren't shared in separate cars where you finally met up, but stride for stride on sidewalks walking to those locations. The post office, recreation, sporting events, nearly everything students do, is within walking distance. Proximity, though we take it for granted, is close to the marrow of community.

This phenomenon is not unique to universities. Many people who live within dorms saw the public failures and letdowns of others. This is perhaps one of the best places to fail. Why? Because the arms of many brothers and sisters functioned like a social web to sharpen each other, work over each other's dysfunctions, and teach us to live, love, laugh, and fail together.

For veterans, that sense of community is even tighter, but more transient. The people they lived with they often fought with and for one another. They often slept head to head, shoulder to shoulder, crammed in the cold and bickering together in the insufferable heat. They bore heavy loads over many miles and many days. They were separated from their family, forcing brothers-in-arms to become closer than family. They bled with and for each other, and, at times, buried the same brother who died for them.

There comes a day when persevering college students become graduates. Likewise, service members become veterans. Though these experiences are different, part of what is lost and shared by both is the community that was formed out of closeness and common cause.

Lack of Shared Experiences

The experiences unique to the Armed Forces contribute to displacing them further outside the shared experiences of everyone else. For example, during WW2, approximately 9% of the populace actively served in the Armed Forces.[1] Not only this, but the entire effort of a nation at war was felt and shared by everyone. Meat, metal, fuel, and rubber were

---

1. Gerald Swick, 'What Percentage of the Population Served in WW2?,' HistoryNet (HistoryNet, February 13, 2019), https://www.historynet.com/what-percentage-of-the-population-served-in-ww2.htm.

rationed. Churches and communities partook in 'metal-drives' to gather up all the scrap metal that could be found. No other time in history ever saw the gears of war turn entire nations toward a singular effort of victory. Contrast this with the entire active duty population of the U.S. as of 2017, which is estimated to be less than 1%.[2] Not only is this percentage smaller, but the shared experience outside of those directly in uniform is significantly disconnected. You can go days, weeks, or even months without talking or hearing about the Iraq War in its latter years. Business carries on as usual. As a result, this singular aspect of a shared experience is increasingly absent.

Isolation doesn't end there, though. At no other time in our history have people been collectively able to specialize in anything. Our hobbies, movies, social media platforms, news outlets, friends, and communities are customized largely to fit our desires. The average Facebook user has a mean of 338 friends.[3] I doubt we find anyone that comes close to having a night out with even 10 different friends per year. If they attend a church, it will have a group for them. Their gaming platform is niched to their favorite games. The movies they watch are largely of a single genre. Even the most watched televised event, the Superbowl, saw its lowest rating of the last nine years,[4] which means that most people don't even share in what is the most shared television event of the year, despite being more attached to TV than ever before. It's not

---

2. Kristen Bialik, '5 Facts about U.S. Veterans,' Pew Research Center (Pew Research Center, November 10, 2017), https://www.pewresearch.org/fact-tank/2017/11/10/the-changing-face-of-americas-veteran-population/.

3. Aaron Smith, 'What People Like and Dislike about Facebook,' Pew Research Center (Pew Research Center, February 3, 2014), https://www.pewresearch.org/fact-tank/2014/02/03/what-people-like-dislike-about-facebook/.

4. Lucy Handley, 'Super Bowl Draws Lowest TV Audience in More than a Decade, Early Data Show,' CNBC (CNBC, February 5, 2019), https://www.cnbc.com/2019/02/05/super-bowl-draws-lowest-tv-audience-in-more-than-a-decade-nielsen.html.

only that the nation doesn't share anything in common with veterans; people don't share much in common with others. Because of city zoning and coding, downtown and walkable neighborhoods are becoming a thing of the past. The American people are isolated and overspecialized. When we look at the rates of depression, we should not be shocked to see that the human heart is hungering to share stories and experiences with others. We are still longing for and needing community and to *do life* together, face to face.

Veterans enter into the service as isolated individuals, and then experience perhaps the closest thing to family and community many ever had or ever will. So, when a veteran leaves the service, the shock is greater. The brotherhood of all of that shared experience makes no point of contact with the outside world. This vicious cycle drives veterans deeper towards depression and isolation. Out of pride, perhaps, we often think that others don't deserve to hear about what it was like in the military. Civilians often misinterpret this self-instilled isolation as a symptom of PTSD. 'Oh, they don't want to talk about it? They must have PTSD.' Rather than remove their false assumption and the haunting sense of trying to gain honor, we let the lie rest as is.

The instruments of soothing isolation and depression yield notoriously bad returns. Alcohol may work for a while, but it leads to greater abuse. Sexual exploits work for a while, but leave you feeling lonelier. If veterans seek help at the VA and mention the pain they are feeling, an over-prescription of pain meds could be easily at their disposal. Macklemore's 2016 song, 'Pharma,' struck a nerve with many servicemembers who recognize the cruel reality that, though their drug addiction was legal, it left them feeling emptier. Some of his lyrics say:

> And these devils they keep on talkin' to me
> They screamin' "open the bottle," I wanna be at peace
> My hand is gripping that throttle, I'm running out of speed

Tryin' close my eyes but I keep sweatin' through these sheets,
through these sheets
Four horsemen, they won't let me forget
I wanna forge a prescription, cause doctor I need some more of it
When morphine and heroine is more of your budget
I said I'd never use a needle, but sure, f**k it
I'm caught up, I'm on one, I'm nauseous
No options, exhausted
This is not what I started
Walkin' carcass, I lost everything I wanted
My blinds drawn, too gone to leave this apartment

My drug dealer was a doctor, doctor
Had the plug from Big Pharma, Pharma
He said that he would heal me, heal me
But he only gave me problems, problems
My drug dealer was a doctor, doctor
Had the plug from Big Pharma, Pharma
I think he trying to kill me, kill me
He tried to kill me for a dollar, dollar.

More, more, more
Re-up, re-up

Death certificate signed the prenup
Ain't no coming back from this Percocet
Actavis, Ambien, Adderall, Xanax binge
Best friends with the thing that's killing me
Enemies with my best friend, there's no healing me
Refilling these, refilling these
They say it's death, death
Institutions and DOCs
So God grant me the serenity to accept the things I cannot change
Courage to change the things I can
And the wisdom to know the difference
And the wisdom to know the difference.[5]

---

5. https://www.azlyrics.com/lyrics/macklemore/drugdealer.html

Commuter communities have collided with cultural barriers of servicemembers re-entering civilian life. Consider the veteran who wants to get a bite to eat and a drink. He lives alone because he's too old to feel included by the average college student. He recognizes that he is different in a complex number of ways and has no desire to live the dormitory life. Setting out on his own, he has arranged his life around his work in one location, school in another, and family in another state. He goes to a restaurant by himself. If he chooses to sit alone at a table, he has the social risk of appearing alone, perhaps even stood up. What do you do with your time while you wait for your food? You can fiddle with the cutlery nervously, pretend to read the menu, or turn to your phone. You turn to your phone and endlessly scroll until food arrives. If you sit at the bar, at least you can pretend to watch the football game and make small-talk with the bartender. This social funneling channels more to the bar than should be there. Because Americans are so poor with their drinking habits, one beer becomes two, which becomes five, which becomes a bad night. A season becomes a habit, and habit begets a lifestyle, and a lifestyle cements many into isolated compartments unable to be liberated when addressing only one issue. If, after a season of wrestling with alcoholism they finally become sober by white-knuckling the fight against abuse, they still haven't dealt with the layers of underlying problems. And besides all that, they are still alone.

If people don't want to risk a high bar tab or social awkwardness, they can buy more alcohol for less and drink at home. There, alone in front of the TV, they sit. Millions of Americans sit, with separated lives, watching some of the same shows and scrolling through their phone malnourished for friendship, longing to know and be known by others.

How Can We Form a Community?

Though many outreaches, non-profits, and ministries are good, many suffer from the complexities of being too niche. It can be helpful for a veteran to be part of a support group with other veterans suffering from depression. For a while. It can be helpful for a recovering alcoholic to be part of Alcoholics Anonymous, or programs like this, but only for a season. Living life in an overly-specialized bubble will bring with it the seeds of its own destruction. One of the beautiful aspects of community that I have only experienced in the body of Christ in the local church is not what is the *same*; it's what is *different*. Though the universal church is bound together by confessing Christ, it is made up of different people. Some of my most rewarding relationships are with people who are wholly other. From the elderly woman in my local church, whose daughter is a missionary in Africa ministering to the deaf, to the various high school students participating in sports, to the friendly and overly extroverted woman, whom I cannot stand, to countless other varieties of people from varied backgrounds and unique stories.

What's beautiful about this? Each of these people allows the best of my character to flourish and its worst aspects to be challenged and sharpened. I can pour myself into and care for the student as I disciple him. The elderly woman lavishes her love and wisdom on me. The loud woman who is testing my patience reveals my impatience and arrogance. I need them. You need them. We were not made to live, love, laugh, and fail with only people who agree with us and look like us. We were made for diversity that comes out of a unity in Christ. Veterans yearn for reunions to see their old comrades. Why? Because it was in that community the best and worst parts of their character were shown. It was where they were deeply known and knew others. Yet, after the laughs end and they part ways to go back home to their solitary lives, an emptiness swells that longs to make that community last longer.

If you don't recognize your need for Christ, you will never appreciate your need for the community which is expressed in the local church. Is it possible to create and facilitate this type of genuine community within a local church?

GEOGRAPHY MATTERS

Our overly consumeristic and specialized pallets for everything, including churches, neglects some basic criteria for choosing a church. Geography should play some role in selecting a church body. This isn't the first consideration. The first is this: Do they preach the Word of God? And central to that is a more critical point: Is the gospel preached? There may be a church next door to you that you should avoid. If it doesn't regularly teach and preach God's Word and herald the gospel, then it's not a church; it's a community club. We don't need more community clubs; we need a church family that is covenanted and gathered together around Christ and sharing life together.

But once this criterion has been met, geography is next. You may have ten churches within your town that proclaim the gospel. I suggest you choose the one closest to the community where you most live, work, and shop. The more consolidated your life in these spheres, the more organic your church life will be. Why is this? It's quite simple. If you commute 30 minutes to a church on the other side of town, life becomes difficult to share with others there. You may run into someone at church who wants to get together for a meal. What do you do? You either arrange your calendar to combine as many things out as possible while you are in the area, or you commute thirty minutes again to meet with that person for a meal. And what if they live on the other side of the church in the opposite direction? Both of you will travel a combined two-hour round trip to have a meal. On the other hand, if your church body is ten minutes away, suddenly doing life with other people outside of Sundays is not just possible, it is nearly effortless and allows for life to spill over beautifully.

Don't Do Church by Demographics

In my own North American context, churches have been designed and planted around many niche demographics. Just in my town of 24,000 people we have a 'Biker Church,' a 'Cowboy Church,' a 'traditional church,' a 'satellite video feed church,' and so on. The traditional services appeal to an older demographic, so who attends? Older people. These other overly niche places are doing a disservice to forming a real community. It may be easier to interact with people who are the same, but we don't need more *same*, we need more *other*. If a church becomes the predominantly affluent 'rich-person' church, what will their outreach to the poor look like? It will naturally flow out of their pity to organizations, foodbanks, and charities that specialize in poverty alleviation. What will their relationships with poor people look like? They won't have any. Or rather, it will be formed into a tragic 'us and them' mindset, which ultimately undercuts the very goal of loving their neighbor.

If churches are selected primarily out of an ethnic comfort zone, what will be the result? You will see black, white, Hispanic, Korean, and every other ethnicity under the sun; not homogenized or blended, but naturally segregating themselves to what's familiar and safe (which is exactly what we often see). But the church isn't meant to be chiefly a safe place for our ethnic familiarity. If a church is selected primarily out of a predominant age-group, such as twenty-somethings or young professionals, that will create a demographically niched church which cares most uniquely for people of similar age and looks. The enrichment that comes from intergenerational relationships and bonds will be neglected, if not wholly absent. The elderly wisdom from experiencing a full life of successes and failures won't be gleaned. The elderly couple who wants to disciple a young couple won't have the opportunity and the young couple won't know what they're missing. More tragic will be what happens when the elderly have finally spun out their 'useful' years. When they are finally unable to care for themselves, the lack of relationships with younger folks at the church will result in institutional living accompanied with spotty care, loneliness, and a diminished dignity seen in short sympathy-visits from acquaintances.

Why should veterans avoid clustering *only* with other vets? If we learn anything from the examples above, it is because non-veterans need to hear veterans' experiences. Non-veterans need to learn and glean from veterans' courage, honor, and sacrifices. Similarly, veterans need the stability of relationships from non-veterans who are available and faithful to them. My best friend in the Marine Corps may be there for a 2am phone call, but he isn't present for a Monday, Tuesday or any other afternoon dinner with my family. But my neighbor is. The widow in my church is. A host of other people, many who only touch the veteran experience through a relative with military service, are more readily available to do life with me than all of my Marine buddies. Not only does their proximity help, but their collective wisdom, talents, abilities, and resources are much more complex, deeper, and advantageous than the pool of veteran relationships I maintain. Why is this? One reason is because serving in the infantry attracted a certain type of person, in personality, disposition, and so forth. I don't need more people like me; I need more people *not* like me.

APPRECIATE DIFFERENCES

Sharing life together in the local body of Christ is not about diversity for the sake of diversity. Rather, it is valuing diversity because of a unity found first in Christ. As dearly as I hold my Marine brothers, I hold my Christian brothers and sisters even

113

higher. Why? Because the comradery I have with those bought by Christ's blood is irrevocably tied to who He is. I share a warrior ethos with my Marine comrades. But I share the forgiveness that Christ gave me with all Christians everywhere. Because Christ's sheep are a great diversity of people, they have more relational resources than my tribe of the Marines. I have come to appreciate and be enriched by the beautiful variety of Christ's sheep. These include the shut-in widow who eloped during WW2, the couple whose children are missionaries in Turkey, the young students on the high school track, golf, and basketball teams, and the disabled woman who has trouble making friends outside of her caretaker. All these people have what we often need in our own lives. But if you never value diversity, if you never pursue others who share in the same unity in Christ, you will never know that the person who may be most loyal to you, to weep with you, to listen, care, and walk with you, may not know anything about military service. And that's more than just 'okay.'

RELATIONSHIPS OVER PROGRAMS

A program is like a helpful trellis that provides a framework for life. No one wants to go to a church that doesn't schedule a regular and predictable time to meet. Programs can be good. But if they are the heartbeat of a church, ministry, or non-profit, they are less than ideal. Why is this? It's simple. Anytime the recruitment of volunteers, scheduling, logistics, advertising, and so on takes precedence over relationships, relationships suffer. If the heart-beat of the local church is its events, being seen as active in the community, or appearing to look healthy at the expense of something as simple as eating together, then their priorities are inverted. Look for a church that desires to get to know you more than it desires to do stuff for stuff's sake. The way you spot this is by looking at their calendar of events and by making a couple of attempts to meet with people for meals or coffee. If the priority is on the events, they won't make time for people. If they are available and eager to get to know you, then it could be a good place to put down some roots.

STAYING FAITHFUL

Community doesn't just happen overnight. It takes the steady replacement of event orientation with relationship orientation. It takes the gradual consolidation of our geographically separated lives to come closer together. It takes more than just a single meal with another person to form community. It also takes more than the slow and steady digital detox from binge watching shows and endlessly scrolling through social media. The faithful ministry of presence and curiosity in the midst of diversity takes time. It also may start happening sooner than you expect.

Here's one way to know when true community is forming—someone takes a risk. Most conversations are but veneers of communication. The mere formalities of 'How are you?' 'I'm fine, thanks for asking,' are so thin they're anorexic. But you know people taking a risk when they say something to you that places you on the edge or outside of your comfort zone. A person puts forward the risk in a desire to be reciprocated. Do we dare do so? Do we dare risk in return? The vulnerability of community is indeed risky, but it's also redemptive when those who profess Christ bear each other's burdens and confess to one other, so that they may be healed. This is a huge risk for veterans. Will others understand us? Probably not at first. But they *never* will understand if we never take a risk. We must subordinate our pride of being a veteran to our warrior motif of faithfulness. Stay at it. Risk being burned. Risk sharing too much. Risk being misunderstood. Do this in order that you might confess the weight of depression, PTSD, the grief from a suicide, divorce, or any other loss or pain. The community in the family of Christ's body isn't just beautiful; it is a little picture of the eschaton (the end of time) when our faithfulness will be fully restored and we will be made whole.

10

VANITY OF VANITIES

Sergeant Seth M. Algrim:
March 20th, 1984–October 30th, 2006

I never would have imagined that the safest place in all of enemy territory would be the place of one of my most harrowing memories from the conflict.

'THE TRUST GAME'

My second deployment to Iraq placed us just north of Fallujah. Our COP (Combat Outpost), called COP Viking, was situated about 300 meters north of the busy interstate, that we referred to as MSR (main supply route) Milo. This COP was bigger than my first deployment and contained our entire company plus attachments and segments of other units. Our rectangular shaped COP was situated parallel to the MSR. A fortified post was in each of the four corners of the COP, with two Marines standing watch at all times. These posts were numbered 1-4, respectively, starting in the Northwest corner moving clockwise. In addition to these posts, there was a fifth more prominent post on the roof of the three-story building, around which the combat engineers had built the COP. The overwatch this post provided was armed with an m240 machine gun sighted down the primary southern entrance that zig zagged around serpentine wire and large cement jersey barriers.

If someone with ill-intent desired to fill a truck with explosives and turn their vehicle into a VBIED (vehicle borne improvised explosive device), they would fail. Besides the challenge of having to drive through the zig zag of jersey barriers that would slow down anyone, post five could light them up almost instantly. Even if they let them travel the 300-meter road all the way to the gates, the entire COP was surrounded by double stacked HESCO barriers. These barriers are essentially giant mesh containers filled with sand. One HESCO stands about seven feet tall and seven feet thick. No bullet could penetrate the sheer weight and density of the sand, and a VBIED wouldn't do more than create a giant spray of sand over the COP.

At any given time, two squads were on stand-by for QRF (quick reaction force). One squad would have their gear staged and by the CO's order would not be allowed to be less dressed than taking off their blouses. Like minute-men, they could be fully geared up and ready to engage the enemy in a minute. The second squad on QRF was on a five-minute trip warning, as they were allowed more freedom to move about the COP. If QRF had to be called upon, there would be two Marine Corps infantry squads standing ready to fight, within five minutes.

The distance around Viking, if one were to run from post to post at the longest extent (something we often did) was a little less than ¼ mile on each side. The two original buildings for Viking were Iraqi-built and consisted of retrofitted living spaces. The main building, upon which the overwatch rested, was a large three-storied house that housed the Company Commander, the COC (company operation command), the briefing room, another room for the CLIC (company level intel command), as well as small living spaces for sleeping. The other building was a long one-story structure for the various platoons and sections. To accommodate for attachments and other units, several 'hooches'—one room houses built by the engineers —were erected for the SCOUTs,

Marine attachments originally trained to scout before Tank units. COP Viking's organized layout, with the layers of security and fortification, made it a safe place.

The duty of the COG (corporal of the guard) was to walk the posts in full-gear and check on the Marines as well as overseeing the change of command in each post. The Marines coming off duty would brief their oncoming replacements of their sectors of fire and then would be supervised as they unloaded and showed clear their weapon from condition one (round in chamber) to condition four (no round in chamber and no magazine inserted). After making all the rounds and fulfilling the night duties, the COG would return to the CO to meet his replacement.

One evening, while I stood watch as the COG, I had just finished the change of command with every post following the 1800-00:00 (midnight) shift. In military time, the 2400 hour technically never arrives but flips from 23:59 to 0000. While I was walking from post three back to the COC, I heard what sounded like a muffled gun shot. I was unconcerned because we were surrounded by HESCO walls twelve feet high on all sides, and a shot at us would have sounded differently. Maybe it was the mechanics working on one of the trucks, I thought. As I continued walking, a flood of the SCOUTs came running out of their hooch. The light from the opened doorway streamed into the black night as several men ran out side by side. As my eyes adjusted to make sense of what I saw, it became clear that they were carrying someone.

There was a panic amongst the commotion. My mind raced, trying to make sense of things, as these men ran and shouted. One voice rang in my ears, 'He's been shot!' Fear and disbelief struck me as I tried to grasp how someone could have been shot by the enemy while inside the safety of the COP. The men carrying the wounded Marine bolted to BAS (Basic Aid Station—our medical room). I followed closely behind with my radio, ready to notify the COC of whatever crisis was unfolding. Waiting outside the BAS, I was met with my oncoming COG, who replaced me in the midst of the chaos. He seemed strangely eager to take my shift, perhaps excited to help coordinate emergency assistance. I immediately positioned myself outside the BAS, ready to assist carrying this Marine to LZ (a landing zone) for what would be a med-evac.

Other Marines and I peered through the open doorway as Doc Fox calmly treated the shot Marine. I could see his limbs twitching and Doc trying his best to clean and put pressure on the wound. Doc's face was serious, and, even though he was brightly lit, it looked as though a shadow had fallen over him. First Sergeant Griffith was there with a ground medevac on standby. Not yet processing what occurred, I and other Marines pressed against the outside of the BAS to carry him when the time came. And then Doc Bethesda, the senior enlisted corpsman in BAS, who was helping Doc Fox, walked toward the doorway where Griffith waited for a status update. He shook his head and crossed his hands in a wave, indicating that it was done. He didn't make it. We just watched that Marine die and didn't have a clue how it happened.

We were disbanded and sent to return to our tasks. An informal company formation was called to alert the rest of the COP, most of whom had not heard the shot, that something terrible had occurred. What we learned was both tragic and insanely vain. The SCOUTs had a game that had infiltrated their ranks called 'The Trust Game.' Someone would take an empty M9, our 9mm Beretta pistol, put it to the head of someone else, and say, 'Do you trust me?' In the course of this game a magazine had been ejected from the pistol, but a round remained in the chamber. A Marine had been shot in the face because of another's stupid and meaningless action. Our place of safety was undone. Not by an invading enemy. Not by a coordinated attack. But by a brother in arms. The question invariably asked was simply: 'Why?'

ANGER, PAIN, AND CONFUSION

There is no satisfactory answer for such a tragedy. I spoke with others who watched that man die that night, and we all felt the same thing. Anger. We're angry for a man we didn't know. He wasn't in our unit and was only about a month away from going home. Why did he have to die? Sure, we can state the obvious. One guy put a gun to his head. Or we can blame the squad and team leaders for allowing this kind of culture to persist. We can blame those not in leadership for not speaking up. Humorously, Marines will joke that when a Marine screws up they don't blame him, but his drill instructor. But there's no humor here. We can even blame Saddam for creating weapons of mass destruction that prompted the US invasion, setting this Marine down a road that inevitably led to that place on that night with that 'game' taking place.

Nothing is pure meaninglessness. Nothing. But some things lack answers. Most people have lost someone. Many people have lost more than one person. Most Marines have lost many 'someones.' Loss is never meaningless. But it doesn't always make sense. Anger wells in the souls of those who have lost someone. After hearing of another suicide, I feel a spark of bitter despair within. Death stings. Death takes. Death hurts. Death, we reason, is supposed to have a meaningful end, to be the last epic chapter of our lives. If we're not going out in the proverbial hail of gunfire, we're going out swinging after we've emptied our clips. 'We will not go silently into the night!' we cry out, and then we hear those fateful words. Whether by another Marine taking his life or dying by seemingly senseless means.

Another Marine shot today, another life taken. Vanity. Pain. A whirlwind of emotions and no answers. But it's not meaningless. It takes a dissonance of the mind to live with paradoxes, two truths that appear to contradict each other, and to say they are both true. One person looks at a suicide and says, 'That is meaningless.' Then the voice in our heads screams out, 'How does this fit with the preacher who said that our life is purposeful?' Death and suicide make us wonder: *'Perhaps there is no meaning to life after all.'* But the reality is this: it doesn't take *dissonance* to live with paradoxes. It takes faith. There is no balance to be struck between understanding suicide and trusting in a sovereign Lord. We are not always able to understand an unexpected and seemingly meaningless death. The truths of a sovereign God and the facts that surround a death pull on each other in a tug-o-war. While a contradiction does not exist between them, a tension does. No moral or logical contradiction exists between these two realities. It's the absence of an answer that makes it so difficult.

Not having an answer shouldn't influence our grieving process when people die, particularly by their own hand. But not having an answer influences it, nevertheless. When it's a death like the Marine getting shot at COP Viking, the brokenness of the situation rears its ugly head, and we can be driven to despair. That despair breeds in the darkness of our lacking an answer. There isn't always an answer. What do we do in such circumstances? What can someone look to for hope when a friend takes his or her life? Doesn't God care? Doesn't He see all and know all? Why didn't He stop it? What is He doing up there?

SETH ALGRIM

In high school I was on the wrestling team with Seth Algrim. Seth was a senior my freshman year, and we were both in the same weight class, forcing us to vie for the varsity spot. Seth was quite the athlete, and even though I could beat him wrestling, he was a much better runner, able to finish a 5K over hilly terrain in an impressive sixteen minutes. Although Seth was a white kid like me, he bore a tattoo from the Mexican gang he was a part of. Near the end of high school, he realized that things were not moving in a positive direction, and he needed a way out. Seth and I shared an apathy toward school, and this narrowed the field of possible futures after graduation. Seth improved his grades so he could graduate and joined the Marine Corps.

Being good at math and able to make calculations on the fly, he was initially trained as a mortarman in SOI (School of Infantry), but when he arrived at his unit, 1st Battalion 3rd Marines (1/3) in Hawaii, he jumped at the opportunity to be in the sniper platoon. The Sniper Platoon is very hard to get into, so Seth endured a grueling indoc (indoctrination, the initial period of testing to allow entrance into the Sniper Platoon), and from accounts of his former peers at 1/3, he crushed it.

His athleticism served him well and accelerated his standing, as he first deployed to Iraq in 2003 and was a part of the push on Fallujah in 2004, cementing his place in the long lineage of the United States Marine Corps. I can recall his reception at the small regional airport in Garden City, Kansas. He had just returned home from that first deployment, and when I saw him step off that plane, I saw a different person from the one I knew in high school. He was a man. He was a *Marine*, tried and tested. Although he was only a lance corporal at the time, he was already well-decorated. He later deployed a second time, this time to Afghanistan.

During my high school senior year, I was considering the Navy and Army, and then Seth returned from his second deployment. He was now a corporal and made no attempt to convince me to join the Marines. But I wanted to be like him. I remember snippets of his story in high school and saw the dramatic change to his life that I ascribed to the Marine Corps. I joined the Marines, opted for the infantry, and was soon underway to MCRD (Marine Corps Recruit Depot), San Diego, in July, 2006.

At the end of his first enlistment, Seth re-enlisted after a successful attempt to join Recon. The attempt is just a retainer; those who successfully make it through the 'try out' get a full shot while in RTP (Recon Training Platoon). Seth was a stud, though, and I had no doubt in my mind that his physical fitness, experience, and expertise would enable him to make the grade. He was the ideal candidate for Recon. He knew his call-for-fire (the lingo referring to calling for mortar fire), was in pristine physical fitness (with his amazing run time a full two-minutes beneath a 'perfect run-time'), and above all that, he was a professionally instructed sniper for two combats tours. Seth was not just a good candidate for Recon; he was a dream team pick.

I graduated from boot camp on October 20th, 2006 and was pleasantly surprised to be met not only by my family, whom I was expecting, but also Seth. I'll never forget the special memories from those days with him and my buddy Cody. We went down to Mission Beach, swam in the water, enjoyed our time in San Diego and ate at 'Fat Boys Pizza.' Seth was getting me excited about trying out for Recon, an opportunity that would come up in the next few months in SOI. He took me around Camp Pendleton which felt awesome to me as a new Marine, being shown all the training areas that, in a sense, now belonged to me.

We went for a run the next morning and had an encouraging talk that got me pumped for the next four years. I knew it would be tough. I knew I'd be repeatedly pushed to my limit, but I was excited to be going through this journey with such an incredible Marine and friend, despite the fact that I was a boot and he was by far my senior. I told Seth goodbye around October 22 or 23 and continued home for a short leave before I headed back to California for training at the School of Infantry (SOI). The days flew by. I spent time with friends, some who were college-bound and others who were beginning full-time jobs. In all, it was one of the most enjoyable times in my life. It was a new chapter with what seemed limitless and attainable opportunities.

On October 31, Halloween, my friends and I congregated in Cody's basement to watch a movie together. We were watching *Silent Hill*, a horror flick for the holiday. While we were watching the movie, Jacob and Lucas, Seth's younger brothers, came in. I was delighted to see them; they had come over to Cody's place many times and we were good friends. But their demeanor seemed different. Jake seemed stiffer and tense, with his head tilted back slightly, the way one does after being insulted or threatened. It was a posture of defense. His hands were in his pockets and his face did not reciprocate our delight. Tyler and I invited them to join us with our tone. 'Hey guys, what's up?' Jake's response shook me to the core, 'Seth is dead.'

I felt lightheaded, my stomach dropped, and I felt sick. My mouth became dry and pressure started to build in my entire body. Thoughts raced in my mind like a whirlwind, but the foremost was disbelief. Seth can't be dead; we just talked a few days ago. He was telling me about some insoles that were good for people who run a lot, *Superfeet*. That was the brand. I was lost, grasping for meaning in those words, 'Seth is dead.' It didn't make sense. What did he just say? Everything in the last week was about future plans; there was nothing on the radar about dying. My thinking wasn't even coherent. I turned my head forward with my back pressed against the couch and looked straight down. Waiting. I was bracing for impact. I knew it was a bombshell that just fell and I couldn't put words to it yet. I can't even tell you what happened next. The night was like video snip-its in vivid detail and blank blurs of action and discussion without knowing what was going on. It was like being drunk and watching an old movie with a choppy frame rate jumping from scene to scene. It was as though my brain was unable to process the new information and would skip from short bursts of lucid clarity mixed with gaps in memory. I was intoxicated with grief and pain.

Seth had checked into 1st Recon Battalion early. Like me, he was eager to get on with his next chapter of life. He began training with RTP while it was awaiting to fill class slots until they had enough Ropers to begin their training cycle. They had been doing some vigorous PT (physical fitness) and some basic preliminary training when they went out to a MOUT (military operations on urbanized terrain) town for a night-time training exercise on October 30th, the night before we found out. The new guys in RTP were assigned to be the OP-4 (opposing force—playing the 'bad guys'). Some were given rifles and blanks while others just had rubber rifles and would have to yell 'bang, bang' to 'shoot.' But on that night, one of those Recon Marines was armed with live ammunition.

Live Ammunition

The man who shot Seth had been at a live-fire range one week prior and gotten sick with pneumonia. The regulations at this point are clear. No one is allowed to leave the range with any ammunition, even empty casings. To observe this protocol, his gear and magazines filled with 5.56 ball rounds were left there while he was taken to BAS (Basic Aid Station). The SOP (standard operating procedure) at the end of a live fire range is for everyone to line up, remove all magazines, show clear their weapons, and have whoever is conducting range safety shake down Marines, check pockets, flaks, magazine pouches for rounds that were retained. Presumably, because his gear was left there, no one was assigned to remove the rounds. So, after this range was conducted, everyone cleared out, but his flak with magazines and live rounds was not. Someone else, later, returned his gear to him and he walked onto this new range, one week later, with ammunition when he should have had only blanks. When arriving at a new range, there was yet another failure in protocol. If you leave a range with no ammo, you will arrive at a range with no ammo, including blanks. The man would have been issued blank rounds, that are encased in a different kind of box and are lighter in the hand. He would have had to fill his magazines with his own blanks. Had there been a simple oversight, he should have caught it when he removed one of his magazines to load the blanks. According to one account, however, he had charged a private to load his magazines for him, though. When it came time to load, he grabbed the wrong magazine.

Even filling in the gaps of this story with presumed actions, all who loved Seth still lack a definitive 'why.' Did this man not load his magazines? Did he not check his gear before leaving for another range? I can understand an oversight, but I don't know how the man who shot Seth didn't realize his mistake sooner. I don't know how he didn't catch that he had live ammunition when he was given blanks. I don't know why he didn't (did he?) have a BFA attached to his rifle (blank firing apparatus, a screw that plugs into the end of the barrel and creates pressure when a blank is fired to send the bolt back, reset, and mimic firing a live weapon). Many safety precautions must be ignored to arrive on a non-fire range with live ammunition and not know it.

Seth had been role-playing when at a fatal moment in the training exercise, this particular Marine aimed his rifle at Seth and shot. Seth was lying on the ground, pretending to be dead, when the first bullet tore through his left cheek, likely killing him instantly. His body jumped where he had been hiding and the other Marine shot again, thinking he was simply being a good actor. Seth didn't move a second time. He was dead.

Within a couple weeks of having graduated boot camp and becoming a Marine, I attended my first military funeral. And it was for my friend, Seth. I watched him lowered into the ground, honored by many Marines, his family, his many friends, and even the Patriot Guard. The Patriot Guard was there to escort him and provide a buffer for the families so they could grieve while Westboro Baptist Church protested the funeral with their 'Fags Go to Hell' signs.

It hurt. It was heart-wrenching. Even as I write this, I feel the pain of his death well up afresh. I can't make sense of his death outside of the recklessness that led to it. It was a waste of potential. It is a tragedy for such a magnificent person who fought his way through two deployments to have such an anticlimactic ending. Seth Algrim was so godly, kind, and yet had a vigorous and roaring spirit within him. Seth is gone. To this day I still occasionally see him in someone's face at the store, to have my heart speed up, anticipating, hoping against vain hope it's him. VA psychologists told me that my reaction is a normal part of grieving. Years later I'm still searching for his face on a stranger, and he's still young, though it's been a decade since he died. Part of me wishes that Seth was selected for some top-secret kind of special forces that had to fake the death of its operatives in order to admit them into an elite team. But this is all just coping, grasping for a way to ascribe meaning to what was seemingly meaningless.

It was meaningless. It was vanity of vanities. And it hurts. Death hurts. Death stings. Though I can tell someone with confidence in many other instances how the narrative of Scripture makes sense of hard situations, I cannot make sense of this.

Horatio Spafford

In 1871 a fire swept through Chicago destroying hundreds of homes, killing over 300 people and leaving over 100,000 people homeless. One successful businessman, Horatio Spafford, lost nearly all of his investment in real estate along Lake Michigan's shoreline, consumed by the fire. Horatio decided to send his family back to Europe, where he would join them later after tying up unfinished business. Later that year his wife Anna and four daughters boarded a ship bound for Europe with 308 other passengers. Four days underway, the ship collided with an iron-clad, a Scottish ship. Horatio's wife brought their daughters to the deck where they prayed that God would spare them if it was His will or prepare them to endure whatever happened next. In a span of only twelve minutes, the ship sank claiming 226 lives, including all four of Horatio's daughters. Horatio's wife managed to cling to a piece of debris and was rescued by a sailor searching for survivors after the ship sank.

Shortly after being rescued, Anna said, 'God gave me four daughters. Now they have been taken from me. Someday I will understand why.' The survivors were taken to Wales, where upon arrival Anna telegraphed her husband the words, 'Saved alone.' Horatio immediately booked passage on another ship to join his wife. While on this voyage, the captain of the ship brought him onto the deck when their ship reached the approximate location that the other ship sank. Walking onto the deck, Horatio wrote the lyrics to the song, 'It is well with my soul.'

When peace, like a river, attendeth my way,
When sorrows like sea billows roll;
Whatever my lot, Thou hast taught me to say,
'It is well, it is well with my soul.'

Refrain
It is well with my soul,
It is well, it is well with my soul.

Though Satan should buffet, though trials should come,
Let this blest assurance control,
That Christ hath regarded my helpless estate,
And has shed His own blood for my soul.

My sin—oh, the bliss of this glorious thought!—
My sin, not in part but the whole,
Is nailed to the cross, and I bear it no more,
Praise the Lord, praise the Lord, O my soul!

O Lord, haste the day when the faith shall be sight,
The clouds be rolled back as a scroll;
The trump shall resound, and the Lord shall descend,
Even so, it is well with my soul
It is well with my soul,
It is well, it is well with my soul.[1]

---

1. https://hymnary.org/text/when_peace_like_a_river_attendeth_my_way

SEARING LOSS

We are never guaranteed an explanation when tragedy strikes. God created us to be interpreters. We find meaning as it is woven through all the cosmos by our Creator. We want to find the meaning behind a death, but sometimes there isn't one that satisfies. When meaning is elusive, sometimes healing can be as well. What we do in the midst of loss is important and can even be healing. Our society, churched or not, does not grieve loss well. We are awful at lamenting death, not just in a right or wrong way, but in just plain lamenting. We don't do it.

The closest thing we have when it comes to lamenting is funerals. But even then, our guard is often up so high that we don't let out the underlying anguish. If our guard isn't high, our affections are distracted by sanitizing the death with a 'celebration of life.' There are certain unspoken rules that many of us obey. If you're a guy, you don't show any sign of grief greater than a somber stare. You must never cry, unless the person was your relative. Even then, it's best not to be seen doing that any more than a week or so following the burial of that person. We're told that we'd better 'move on' once the formal process has ended.

But we don't move on. Many of us are still grieving, or rather, many of us have never grieved. This is especially common in the military when only a few close friends can be spared to be a part of a friend's funeral. It's just as difficult after leaving the military when unexpected death comes. Of all the men I knew who died, I have only been to one military funeral—Seth's. This wasn't by choice, but by circumstances. When I reflect upon the men who have taken their lives, in many ways I can't come close to 'letting go,' because, in my mind, I never buried them. I didn't hear the eulogy. I didn't hear the stories of their friends and family. I didn't mourn with them in community. One of the best Marines I ever knew, Nicholi Diamond, was not given a funeral after he took his life. His wife abandoned him. He had no direct, living family, and was buried in an unmarked grave for many years. But grief doesn't just 'go away.' It's still there, lurking deep inside many with whom I served. Many know this lurking feeling of undealt-with, suppressed guilt.

It's often easier to ignore than confront the pain of death. Though I too struggle to lament, I've learned some difficult lessons along the way. In the process of writing this book I was confronted with never having grieved Yund's death (see chapter two). My seminary held a memorial service, the first of its kind, for those who had lost children through miscarriage, stillbirth, or early in their youth. Our seminary community's married couples have had many such deaths, and, like suicide, they aren't spoken about. In that memorial service there was not a dry eye. And even though the deaths that were being lamented by parents were primarily children, my heart was with Yund. It ached as never before, and my tears flowed.

Scripture says, 'rejoice with those who rejoice and weep with those who weep' (Rom. 12:15). Both the culture at large and the military are good at rejoicing. We celebrate everything that can be celebrated: birthdays, anniversaries, new jobs, the Super Bowl, and the birth of a child. There is a huge bandwidth of celebrations that are culturally acceptable. Grieving, though, does not have that same luxury. To our hurt, grieving is limited to only a narrow set of circumstances in a thin window of time. But we need to grieve. We need to foster a culture that allows wailing and mourning at funerals. We need to be allowed that space to cry out from the deep, dark places of our soul and name the pain we experience. We need to lament.

As part of the process we need to open up to hear people's stories. We need to fill ourselves with the stories of life, of successes and failures, of the one we bury. Those closest to the dead need this the most. They need to be listened to. And if they don't want to talk about it, we must not assume that they want to be left alone. Sometimes the pain is so searing and numbing that we don't know what to say. Then say nothing. Just minister to that grieving person by your presence. In meeting people in the pain of loss, we feel *with* them, not just *for* them. Empathy is far more healing and comforting than sympathy. And we will still struggle to understand it. We won't always be able to make sense of death, but we should never be left alone to grieve.

HIS SON

At times I want to be angry at God. In the death of one of my Marines, I'm left with the emptiness of their former life. I don't get it. I hate it. I could kick, scream, with all of my might. But even if I were the strongest person who ever lived, I'd still find my strength to be in vain. I can't save them. They have faded into oblivion, washed into the blackness where the souls of those remaining are tormented by the thoughts of 'What if I had said this? What if I had done that?' There, we could be swallowed up and lose the battle with grief if not for God's Son.

The anger I have felt toward God is absorbed by the anger He once had toward me because of my sins. As much as I resist Him, His slow and unrelenting love draws my gaze back to His Son. And there He is, hanging on a cross. Really, God, your Son? The Scriptures say it was the will of the Father to crush Him (Isa. 53:10). The Son says, 'I lay down my life that I may take it up again' (John 10:17). Christ was obedient to this path, and He did not tread it lightly. Christ did not give up His life for any merit or goodness in me. The God of the universe, who mightily created all things, gave up His Son to pay the price for my transgressions. And in that weighty glory my mouth is silenced and my knee is bent to behold the God-man who took the sting of death and crushed it. He *did* that. He is taking His enemies now and putting them under His feet. He *is doing* that. My anger and grief have no meaning apart from the Son having died and risen again.

If you want to know what pain, suffering, and grief look like, look at Jesus Christ, the Son of God. If you want to know where those dreadful emotions lead, look at the pierced feet of the Son. Under His feet, He will lay all grief. Under His feet, He will place His enemies. Under His feet, no more sorrow will arise. I knew nine men who have been taken from this life by their own hand. Two killed in car accidents, two more in training accidents, and one that I watched die after being shot in a vain act of stupidity. I don't know why God allowed these things to happen—but one day I will. I may never get the comfort of an answer to all my 'whys,' but I do get the comfort of a 'who' in Jesus Christ. Even though pain persists, and grief still comes in waves, 'even so,' because of Jesus, 'it is well with my soul.'

11

GRIEVING DEATH

The sorrow that comes when death has claimed another victim seems insurmountable. It is a towering mountain of darkness, with lonely valleys and perilous ledges. Grief comes like an unwanted relative. It unpacks its things and indefinitely lays claim to your ongoing life. We are already reeling from the death of the loved one; the closer they were, the more we find ourselves in a cascade of disarray. This one we knew is now gone, and this new arrival of feelings and anguish lays down its demands and an ultimatum—*Deal with me now or deal with me later.*

Most have probably heard of the five stages of grieving—Denial, Anger, Bargaining, Depression, and Acceptance. They are common in media that touch on grief. They are more demanding than the four horsemen of the Apocalypse. After all, there are five of them. They also can be helpful for navigating a long, messy process. They have, however, often been misleading. They tend to suggest that everyone grieves similarly, or that these five stages are always encountered chronologically and one after the other. If you miss one stage, you might think, you're grieving incorrectly. This couldn't be further from the truth. Here I unpack my process through the death of a loved one and share ways we can grieve and help others who are grieving. Unlike some books on grieving that contain a certain logic and chronology, I wrote this in a bout of grief, and it bears less neat categories and more of the intertwined ideas associated with C. S. Lewis's *A Grief Observed*.

MY GRIEF OBSERVED

It felt like it was passively happening to me. After my friend Seth died, I felt like a child in a store, defiantly resisting my parents' demands. Though I dug my heels in, my strength eventually gave way to a power and circumstance more powerful than all the rebellion I could muster. What was I resisting? I'm not entirely sure. Perhaps it was the death, the planning of the funeral, or facing the emotions that came with it all. It could have been many conversations, clumsy condolences, and diverted eyes from acquaintances. Though I tried with all my strength to remain unmoved, this mighty torrent washed me away with waves of pain. I tried to press the brakes, but everything kept coming. The inevitable planning of a funeral descended upon us. It was every bit as unwelcome as the news of the death, and every bit as pointless to fight. Some might have called this stage of grief 'denial'; some labeled it 'shock.' To me, it was an oscillating clock of angst from one emotional state to another. *He's gone. I don't want him to be gone. I can't believe he's gone. This can't be happening. But it did.* I found myself constantly torn between a present reality and a completed action.

The weeks and months passed, and I found I quickly accepted the terms of the death. But as soon as I had accepted them, a wave of depression and shame hit me. Shame that I accepted that he died. If I accepted that he was gone, I felt as though I was also accepting the manner in which he died. I could neither accept it nor allow my mind to forget him, though I desperately wanted this cloud to lift. Then, another fresh tide of shame washed up, pressing me back into denial and bargaining. These progressive waves of emotion were more like standing in ocean waves than I cared to admit.

Of course, it wasn't bargaining the way some might think of it. It is not as though what I bargained for was desirable; rather, it was as though I was trying to fool myself into a lie I desperately wished were true. In reality, I wished he was recruited from some special ops that needed to sever family ties to maintain plausible deniability. In the recesses of this lie, he is alive somewhere, and in this false hope, he might return. The corpse that I saw at the visitation looked nothing like him, after all. It was just a shell of a person I once knew, but it wasn't him. It was merely an empty husk of the once great man who occupied that body.

My denial mixed with bargaining, as vehement and fanciful as it was, accomplished nothing. I moved between anger spliced with bouts of depression. Why didn't anyone warn me about this? I could have been ready to embrace death and move on. But, I suppose, we're terrible at talking about death as a whole in our society. Witnessing death is an experience many will have, but it is less a part of the collective experience today. Today, it's distant and sanitized. If you lived fifty or more years ago it's more possible you saw someone die in your home when a doctor's home visits were more common and terminal illnesses weren't outsourced to a wing in the hospital. The infant mortality rate in previous eras was also much higher. As a nation, we faced death more routinely, and as communities and families we knew how to grieve better than we do now. In the wake of greater hospital care, the nuclear family, and segmented communities, death is less visible because the structures of our society have pushed it out of sight. People die behind closed doors in hospital rooms. Even if they were to die in a tragic automobile accident, the scene is cleared and traffic carries on within hours, undisturbed by the previous collision. No one bats an eye, because no one saw anything. When death finally arrives, its presence is as unwelcome as before, but we are less prepared to deal with its visit.

Why didn't anyone ever tell me about death? I knew it was a certainty on some cognitive level, but why didn't anyone ever tell me about the waves of feelings and numbness that would accompany it? The grief with death feels like pent up anticipation, like I'm waiting to catch my breath, exhale, and be refreshed with my heart returning to a healthy rhythm. But the tightening around my chest, and the disruption of my bowels are unpleasant to speak of. About 95% of the body's serotonin is stored in our gut.[1] Not surprisingly, many of our bowel problems can be linked to depression and vice versa. I didn't know that before. A regular diet that includes probiotic yogurt can help offset this. Add some Vitamin D for the days I was cooped up inside, and you can take two legitimate steps toward dealing with grief. But this isn't information covered in a Death 101 class in high school, is it?

Days came when I felt I had 'arrived.' Is this what acceptance looks like? I slept well, awoke to a new day, praising and confident in the promises of God. Then, someone from work made a miscalculated, though well-meaning, comment, 'It's good to see you're doing better.' I *was* doing better, but little did they know that my respite would regress back to waves of depression. But it wasn't that I was wrongly grieving, necessarily. It was simply that I was grieving the way humans do—in waves. Complex waves enter the grieving process through interactions that we have with people, work, and society. As far as I knew, there was no way to calculate what feeling or memory would trigger more grief, or a greater respite. As I said, it just happens.

I could be doing 'fine' in other people's perception, even my own. And then, I would be triggered by something

---

1. Adam Hadhazy, 'Think Twice: How the Gut's "Second Brain" Influences Mood and Well-Being,' Scientific American (Scientific American, February 12, 2010), https://www.scientificamerican.com/article/gut-second-brain/.

unexpected and out of my control, emerging from the depths of my subconscious and hitting like a tsunami. On one occasion I was at Mission Beach, enjoying the sunset, the time with friends, the water, the smell of salt in the air. The sky was layered in deep broad strokes of blues that faded into lighter tones. As people walked hand-in-hand along the sidewalk, the birds followed, scavenging the fallen scraps of food. Then came the trigger. Two friends, running joyously stride for stride and laughing, making indiscernible conversation at a distance as they went on running barefoot in the wet sand. The light patter from their feet came and went quickly.

Suddenly, I'm in a memory, now. I'm on the beach with Seth running in the sand. We're barefoot, enjoying the wet surface beneath our feet as we talk and make plans for the future. It's a quick memory. It comes quickly; it seems to last no longer than the dash of the two friends going by. But then I looked down and the ice cream I held had melted over my hand and I feel a bit foolish as I sheepishly discard it into a nearby bin. How long had I been lost in this wave? Two minutes? Ten minutes? I thought only seconds had passed, but my mind had stopped—frozen trying to remember (or forget?) what it was like when Seth was still alive. In a brief lucid moment, I felt as though I could recall every detail. And then the memory faded.

Another time I was at the store. I caught a glimpse of someone who shared some facial features with Seth—that shorter upper lip which makes for a bigger smile. That's all it took, and my heart quickened in anticipation. *There he is!* Within milli-seconds I figured out it wasn't him and blood returned to my face as the memories of Seth flashed before me, again.

GRIEVING AND ANGER
After one of my Marine buddies died, I was angry when people would say something. Usually what they said was

miscalculated or superficial. Often, I was mad because people didn't know what to say or were overly interested to hear details in the wrong setting. When I'm passing you at the store, I don't really want to share my deepest thoughts. Paradoxically, I was also angry with people when they said nothing. *Don't you know what I'm going through?!* I'm not sure if there's a way to 'fix' that. Part of this was the way grief came and went without taking out the trash it piled in my mind. Part of this was being in areas where people could have just let me know they were thinking and praying for me and move on. I would have settled for that. I still needed people to minister to me through their presence.

For years, I never felt anger towards the man who shot Seth. Denial would come and go perhaps even still lingering or planning a future visit. Bargaining often laced itself with denial. Depression would ebb and flow. But anger? It was absent—*unusually* absent. I thought perhaps there was something broken in me that I didn't feel what was readily present in others when they grieved in similar circumstances. It was nearly twelve years after Seth died that I felt my first wave of anger. As I was reading articles on Seth's death in preparation for writing this book, I became curious to look up the man who shot him. I was curious as to why I was curious. Why now? Why over a decade later? Hadn't the thought occurred to me before? I suppose it must have. It seems natural enough. But I couldn't recall why it hadn't. Perhaps this was a coping mechanism—a way for my mind and heart to digest the grief in smaller portions by holding one blow of grief off, delaying it until the heart had mended and braced itself for the next.

A Google search revealed the man's name and another search on Facebook yielded a profile picture of the Marine. I was shocked. I had met the man about three months after Seth's funeral. I remembered him well. I was at the Recon pre-indoc, the "try out." This was where we conducted our PFT, did a 1500-meter swim with cammies on, treaded water and other tests. A portion of the exam required us to swim underwater 50 meters with our cammies on. This man was the cadre proctoring my lane. He gave me a thumbs up when it was my turn. I completed the swim and came up shouting the mandatory, 'I'm okay!' He began to yell something to the following effect, 'Hey! Did I give you permission to go?'

'Yes, sergeant.' I guessed his rank.

'NO, I did not. Watch this one,' motioning to a lance corporal holding a clipboard. 'Maybe we shouldn't let him pass because he can't follow instructions!'

I did the swim, again, and passed. I was angry and irritated that he had done what he did. No one was behind me in line and I couldn't understand how I could have misinterpreted his thumbs up. How could that have been 'Don't go, yet'?

I sat at the computer, shocked. I felt another wave of shame well up inside of me. Shame wasn't the first thing I felt. It was anger. But the anger I remembered was the anger I had toward this man for what he did during that examination. And then came the shame. It came because I had more anger against him for what he did to inconvenience me and postpone my passing this exam than what he did to my best friend. And then came anger. Maybe even rage. I didn't storm about knocking things off my counter or anything like that. But I allowed hatred to fill me as though my blood were turning septic. I couldn't believe someone would be telling another person they didn't follow instructions when, of all people, *he* didn't. *Are you kidding me?* The anger could have taken great root, then, if not for the grace of God.

A lot happened in the twelve years from Seth's death to finally googling the name of the culprit. God taught me much about my rebellion against Him. He showed me much about my sin, its consequence, and the impossibility of paying for my sin by anything I, or anyone else besides Christ, could ever do. The words of my Redeemer haunted me, 'For if you forgive others their trespasses, your heavenly Father will also forgive you, but if you do not forgive others their

trespasses, neither will your Father forgive your trespasses'
(Matt. 6:14-15). These words pierced me like a spear. And
then I wept, collapsing under the weight of melted anger,
disbelief, and wonder as to why a spotless Savior would die
for angry sinners like me.

Finally, after twelve years of waves of grief, sometimes
coming for long visits, sometimes shorter, I experienced
acceptance. The greatest feature of acceptance of death was a
gospel dimension I was not ready to experience at an earlier
time. Without the gospel, acceptance is only getting used to
the idea of grieving. It's similar to the distinction between
repentance and resigning yourself to the facts. Repentance is
accompanied by a change of heart. Resignation is giving up.
With the gospel, acceptance is trusting God to be merciful
with whom He is merciful. The first person who comes to
mind with that is the grief-stricken individual. Secondly,
acceptance has more forgiveness embedded in it than we
care to admit. After other suicides I have felt more anger
toward the deceased than I care to admit. It wasn't the first
feeling, but it did rear its ugly head. If a loved one has taken
his or her life, anger followed closely by shame may very
well make its rounds. It also could be years before it comes.
But without a doubt, there is an element of forgiveness
that must be granted when it comes to the person who has
opted to leave this world behind. Forgive them. Let go of the
resentment toward them. I'm not saying you should try to
talk to them after they're gone (you shouldn't), but that the
experience should affect your heart in a way that enables
you to see your own shortcomings as big, and Christ's
forgiveness as bigger.

GRIEVING AND COMMUNITY

Grief may or may not follow a pattern like the one I experienced. However, community definitely can help you grieve
better than you can on your own. There is much healing

to be gleaned from and experienced in a community that allows you to grieve openly and allows the waves to come when they will. Grief isn't rational in the same way eating food is. If I don't eat, I get hungry, and then I eat—regularly, predictably, day in and day out. But grief doesn't act like that. It can stay for intense periods of time, and then abruptly leave you periods of bright days and needed respite. In the midst of this cycle, we need community. Finding a place that allows you to emote, fail, mourn, and process; community is often the missing element in processing grief and moving toward a place of acceptance. Grief, whether we face it or not, will come to those who face loss. Whether it's an accidental death, an expected one, or a suicide, grief comes. The greatest guardrail we can put on our lives during an observed grief is a gospel-shaped community. All other alternatives outside of Christ are counterfeits promising relief but coming up short on those promises.

Deal with grief as it comes, even in its passing waves and your often numb reception. You are under no obligation to cycle in and out of grief according to a checklist. The death of someone you care about will cause you to limp, perhaps for the rest of your life. But you can ride the waves of grief buoyed by the gospel, waiting out the visits while filled with the promise of Christ: 'I will never leave you nor forsake you' (Hebrews 13:5). That you can stand on. Truthfully, grief takes time to process. You are never under compulsion to deal with grief and move on. Deal with it as it comes. And if you are unable to deal with it, even in the midst of community, remain anchored to Christ. He will never, ever leave you. And He will never, ever forsake you.

HELPFUL AND UNHELPFUL RHYTHMS

Not every action, rhythm or decision after the death of a loved one was helpful. Some things assisted in grieving; others deepened it in the wrong way. The instinct I discovered in myself, and I've since confirmed as similar in others, is that we will make a move toward finding comfort when washed under by grief. These may vary in intensity or type, but the usual suspects include binge drinking, painkillers, sexual exploits, media-numbing, and food. On a bio-chemical level, there is something good about endorphins being released in the brain. Food, for example, is a good and necessary thing, but this, like the others, can quickly form a vicious cycle of deepening depression. Here's how that works: The news of death zaps your energy, so with the desire to avoid doing dishes, and wanting comfort food, you order pizza. You don't get enough to *fill* you, but enough to *stuff* you. You overeat. This can often be followed by regret. *Why did I spend so much on that?* The diet you may have been on is subsequently abandoned and on its heels is shame, perhaps only mild, for giving up something as simple as watching your weight. Whatever sociological reason accounts for what happens next, it's all too easy to then turn to another vice to numb the guilt from overeating. You may turn to drinking. One beer seems fine, two aren't bad, but the increased consumption gives way to lowered inhibitions which in turn, eventually trade themselves for a night of getting sloshed. Perhaps you throw up everything you ate, reminding yourself of the wastefulness of spending money on something that satisfies for only a moment. The next day at work is terrible because of the hangover and loss of sleep. The previous sources of comfort didn't work, so why not try painkillers? Some won't try them, but they will try their 'go-to' comfort like it's a magic formula, adjusting the amounts and trying to get the balance right while chasing the elusive promise of satisfaction and comfort. A grief-stricken person's search for comfort in their idols comes up woefully short and, in fact, heaps guilt and shame upon an already emotionally taxed individual.

TALKING

Alternatively, instead of looking for comfort in a vice, I've found it helpful to be with others and talk about the good memories we've shared with the departed loved one. It's cathartic to laugh, cry, remember, and finally, after the conversations have spun out, to release. For myself, I tend to be more introverted and don't necessarily like to talk all night. But being near people who are ready to engage when I was ready to engage was extremely helpful. I've found it to be less than ideal to say, 'Just let me know if you need anything.' Perhaps some people take others up on that offer. It strikes me like an empty platitude of fulfilling a friendly obligation. Having friends and family that can be around for a committed week of grieving and lament in community can facilitate conversation that can be healing and soothing.

SHARING A MEAL

As an alternative to telling a grieving person, 'Just let me know if you need anything', it's good to simply say, 'I'm going to make you a meal to bring you this week. Just let me know what day works best.' By taking this extra step of initiative, there is less pressure in the grieving person's court. They don't have to take additional risks; they only have to give a date. When dropping the meal off, be ready to leave right away or stay around and have the meal with them. This takes an emotional intelligence of sensing where the person is and where they're not. I've been both on the receiving and giving ends of meals. People will send cues if they want you to stay and talk, so read their body language.

Interestingly, I've found that as the initial waves of grief subside, doing 'slow food' can be a great time of distraction from other numbing strategies and reflection. Slow food is cooking meals from scratch. Washing, peeling, boiling, mashing, and flavoring potatoes, for example, is a process. There is something cathartic about the process of using your hands to create something satisfying. Additionally, making a meal that others can eat with you creates a rhythm that opens the door for conversation and shared experience. It also has enough busy work that if the grieving person doesn't want to talk, no one has to. And because the mind and hands are busy, no one has to feel awkward and fumble through forced conversation. I know, not everyone can cook, but for those who can (or grill or smoke meats), it can be a great time-filler which involves our bodies. One alternative to making a person a meal is bringing them the ingredients to make a meal themselves. This also requires a higher emotional IQ by knowing the person well enough to know if they would enjoy this.

Praying

Pray for and with the grieving person. Pray the attributes of God and how they apply in this situation. No one needs to hear you teach in your prayer. You don't have to be flowery using a bunch of words. Just posture your heart before a God who listens and speak. Pray the Psalms of comfort. Allow for anger, doubt, and fear to well up before the merciful throne of the One who heals in His timing and according to His purposes. Pray silently and aloud. Pray as a group and when you're alone with the person. Whenever you have the slightest impulse that you should pray, pray. Don't just tell people you will pray for them. Pray for them. If the setting permits, stop, and pray for them on the spot. I have found it to be much more encouraging for a person to come up to me and say, 'I prayed for you this week,' as opposed to 'I'll pray or you.' We all know that the latter is often code for sympathy without action. So don't just tell someone you will, fulfill your duty to bear their burdens, and come to them to let them know you have, and will continue, to pray for them, and if they allow, pray for them on the spot.

WEEP

Don't forbid yourself from feeling emotions. Don't try to fake strength you lack. Let the waves flow out of you and weep as needed. 'Weep with those who weep' (Rom. 12:15). When there is nothing to say, be present and ready to mourn aloud and in silence. If you don't allow yourself to mourn, you may find emotions dammed up for years only to burst suddenly into a flood triggered around an entirely different life circumstance.

It was six years following the death of Yund until I finally grieved his suicide. And it was in an unexpected place. I was at a memorial service for the death of young children we hosted at our seminary, and I suddenly, in the middle of this service, found myself weeping over his death. I had never made room to grieve and had seen it as a weakness to do so. But finally, after years of suppressed emotion, it finally welled up and flowed out.

FOLLOW UP

Funerals can be a whirlwind. Often they are followed with a flood of cards, flowers, relatives, and emotions that make the ensuing weeks seem longer than the previous ones. Adjusting to a new rhythm absent of the loved one takes time. Mark your calendar for monthly check-ins with the person who lost a loved one. Do more than send a text. Show up. Call. Make them another meal. Invite them into your life. Take them out to do something sociable. But follow up. This is an often-neglected rhythm. If the one grieving has avoided you a couple of times, don't resign yourself to leave him or her alone. Be persistent and faithful, but sensitive to what's needed.

TAKE OVER FUNERAL ARRANGEMENTS

This isn't always possible. But where it is, it can be incredibly helpful. If you are in a position to take the logistics of planning, arranging, calling, organizing, and advertising off someone's plate, do it! The hundreds of small decisions and tasks that go into funeral arrangements are taxing and should not be callously heaped upon the grieving spouse or their loved ones. While family and friends are in town for the funeral, take the chance to give that person the room to grieve, lament, laugh, and cry with their family. I've seen family members harbor resentment for having to make funeral arrangements and thereby sacrificing the best opportunity to grieve with others. And then, when everyone left to go back to their lives, the grieving person found themselves more isolated and their grief accompanied by anger.

Everyone grieves differently, but everyone must grieve. These are some bits of advice that hopefully can give people room to work through their emotions. The end goal of grieving isn't to get a person back on their feet. It isn't to 'get over' the death. It's deepening our trust that God is gracious and that He comforts us even when He doesn't give us an answer. It's standing on the promises that God saved sinners from eternal death and that Christ rose again from His own death so that those who have put their trust in Him will rise again to new life.

12

ONCE A MARINE[1]

'Once a Marine, always a Marine.' This statement contains much truth. Becoming a Marine leaves an indelible impression upon people. It's not just the rite of passage of becoming a Marine, but the entire lifestyle of immersion into a unique culture. The impression is strong enough and lasting enough that whenever military service comes up in conversation, I do not say I am an 'ex-Marine' or 'former-Marine,' for if I do, civilians recite the adage. It would seem that others still want to view former Marines as Marines still, even when their service is over. I don't know if that's good or bad, but I do know that it complicates identity for Marines whose service has come and gone.

MARINE SUBCULTURE LOST
Service in the military, regardless of branch, is a life foreign to most people who don't have the opportunity to observe the regulations, specifications, culture, and language of the military. For the Corps, a bulkhead is a wall, a porthole is a window, even if one doesn't have an actual ship in view.

---

1. This chapter was published in part at Desiring God. https://www.desiringgod.org/articles/the-hardest-battle

The floor is the deck, the dorms are the barracks, shoes are go-fasters, toothpaste is fang paste that is squirted onto a fang brush. The issued glasses are called BCs, short for 'birth control' glasses, to correctly label their hideousness. Although much of the jargon Marines use is naval terminology, they adopt their own subculture of terms that is even more specific. Grunts are those who serve in the infantry and POGs (personnel other than grunts) is everyone else. A 'booteneiant' or 'butter-bar' is a boot Lieutenant, although 'butter-bars' can more specifically refer to a 2nd lieutenant's gold-colored signet.

We must not forget the plethora of acronyms, either. The military is bombarded with acronyms corresponding to its 'efficiency.' During my second deployment, we spent a few hours writing down every acronym we knew. I believe that day the list came in just north of 200! It's not just the language that makes military life distinctive, but everything about it. The uniforms are worn with much precision, the jokes, the lifestyle, the entire profession is unique—there is nothing like it. But, then, one day it ends. Although I went back into the reserves for a time after active duty, the end of active service closed a defining chapter in my life.

June 20, 2010. I finished checking out of service. With my wife of ten months and a vehicle filled with our belongings, I said goodbye to two Marines, Clark and Garner, and threw my worn-down boots over the telephone lines. I haven't been to every base in the Marine Corps, but I can imagine that this is a common sight in many places. Marines leaving active duty will often throw their boots over the telephone lines to symbolize their exit from service. They have proverbially 'hung up their boots,' which corresponds with the other way of referring to leaving the service, 'dropping your pack.' The joke in Twentynine Palms especially, is that Marines don't leave service because they want out, but because they want to see grass again. And that's how my active duty came to an end. I headed for our first stop in Phoenix on the way back to Kansas. When I looked back in the rear-view mirror and saw Twentynine Palms, I flipped the mirror up, not wanting to look at that same site ever again and I haven't.

It doesn't take long, and the distinct military look begins to fade. The daily shaves and weekly haircuts that make someone identifiable outwardly are the first thing to go. Many men leaving service as the very first thing grow a beard, something completely out of the question for their years in service. Veterans enter the workplace, some go to college, but all of them leave the service with a period of joy and many find that this period is met with a sense of loss that slowly grows and then wanes in the months that follow.

One day you're running live fire and maneuver ranges, the next it seems like you're in college with a bunch of snobby kids. One day you're leading men who are trusting you with their lives and millions of dollars in equipment, and the next you're filling out applications to work at Wal-Mart re-zoning shelves alongside an ungrateful and lazy high schooler. It's humbling sometimes, and it feels humiliating, but it's nearly always accompanied by the sense that something was taken away and is now missing.

Misunderstood as a Civilian

My freshman year of college I was partnered with two others for a project in my Spanish class. In getting together and drilling conjunctions, translations and so on, a conversation emerged about traveling to other countries. It didn't take long for the other two very vocally to share their opinion with me that they did not like the United States. Lest I be misunderstood, they were not disagreeing with what is common sentiment among many that the United States is not number one, or the greatest nation, or something like that, they were voicing a *detestation* for the country. I was taken aback, and asked them what countries they had been to, traveled and experienced in contrast. *None.* I can remember very much being grateful for the United States returning home after months of being deployed. I have no illusions in thinking the U.S. is the best nation in all categories of evaluation, but it is still a wonderful place to live, and I will probably always call it home. This kind of experience happened again and again in similar sentiments in similar conversations causing me to dislike many non-veterans. At the very least, it revealed how much of an imprint the military had left on me.

Another time at school, I attempted to explain some of the nuances of the culture in the military as a discussion about race emerged. I shared with fellow-students a fascinating anomaly on how racial differences all but disappeared while in the service, but at the same time, racial slurs that would make most ashamed were still used. Truly, this was one of the many sociological fascinations of the Marines and how a brotherhood could be formed despite the differences with which the rest of the politically correct world are enamored. How do you think they responded when I shared this insight? I was called a racist. The people, who were trumpeting the value of hearing everyone's story and valuing experience, categorically dismissed my own. Near the time I left active duty, I was getting my hair cut when the lady learned I was a Marine. Although I was already accepted into college, she informed me that I 'needed to get a real job and go to school.' When I returned home from my first deployment I was approached by a man in the mall, though I was dressed in my civilian clothes, who asked, 'Excuse me, are you a Marine?' 'Yes,' I replied shortly after I looked at him cautiously, not knowing what to expect. With contempt he said, 'Baby-killer,' and then walked away.

None of these experiences helped me transition from being a Marine to a civilian. Let me be clear, I still had a largely positive time in my undergraduate program, but these points of friction are a common feature of those leaving the service. If anything, these experiences have cemented my desire to be identified as a Marine no longer in service. Unfortunately,

I could tell you dozens of similar stories where perceptions were projected onto us without basis or even thought. These experiences still continue, but especially in those first four years, they were constant reminders that something had been taken away. No longer do we fit in with active service members, yet we don't fit in entirely with those with whom we work or go to school. The civilian life marches on with its mundane tasks and lack of excitement, and we veterans have our minds someplace else entirely. This constant reminder of not being fully compatible in one place or another is an additional way that veterans feel the loss of identity.

More and more, movies and television shows relate to the war in Iraq or Afghanistan to some degree, and I almost always do not want to see them. After *American Sniper* came out, many people who knew I had served eagerly asked my opinion. I was largely apathetic to their questions despite their innocence and sincerity, because it was yet another re-confirmation that others want to view veterans as war-torn heroes suffering from PTSD. That is true of some veterans, but to flatly assume that of all and then only be interested in a person's story if it is heart-wrenching has been hard for me to handle. Why on earth would I want to watch a movie full of strategic *faux pas* that will make me miss my friends and remind me that I am no longer in the service? Once again, veterans are faced with a sense of loss.

Much of the identity a veteran forms is due to unique features of the military's culture, as said above. But an overlooked aspect of that identity formation is that the profession comes with great pressure in its responsibilities as well as a fresh start from those you used to know. When we've grown up with people who know everything about us, our family, friends, successes, and failures, they often project an identity onto us with expectations. Many people leaving high school, whether entering the military or not, experience the elation of a fresh start to shed past failures and start anew with people who don't know them. They get to know us without biases or false assumptions. The military does this, allowing servicemen and women to form their new selves, put their best foot forward and show people the best things about their character. But the military also brings pressure. Particularly in the infantry, the pressure is immense. I came to know the men I served with through the experiences that we shared, good, bad, and ugly.

A Sense of Loss

Many of us leaving the service feel a sense of loss because we come to realize that some of the best aspects of our character won't be revealed to new people in slow-going civilian jobs. Many veterans don't look back on their service because there they see the worst version of themselves, that they want to leave behind in service. In other cases, leaving service comes with an inevitable sense of loss, sometimes searing. In fact, some days I almost miss it so badly I wish we would go to war with anyone—just or unjust—so I could become the same person I once was, that person I loved *and* hated.

To compensate for this loss, many plan battalion reunions with their old buddies who have been scattered across the country. Some get tattoos of their unit emblem, others try to find work as a security guard or in law-enforcement, knowing the likelihood of finding veterans in those career clusters. Interestingly, leaving the service often removes the barrier of inter-service rivalry between branches. I think that this is due in part because, once out of service, veterans realize they are a large minority, and have a desperate urge to have shared experiences with others who understand. I felt robbed of my identity as a Marine. I certainly strike a common chord with many, knowing there can be a minor identity crisis in transitioning out of service, just as there was coming into service, after Ramirez killed himself.

One of the most frustrating aspects about that change is that veterans want to talk to someone about their experience.

They want to process the highs, the lows, the honorable, the shameful; they long to pour out their souls to someone. The problem is civilians largely don't want to talk to veterans about their story; they want to talk to them about what *they want* veterans' stories to be. This complicates matters. When others approached me after learning I was in the service, often the first words were, 'Did you see any action? Did you kill anyone? Did you see anyone die?' I found such questions extremely difficult to deal with. The first time someone said those words, I wanted to punch him in the throat. What if I had killed someone and enjoyed it? Would they want to know? Do they know what the mindset of a constant readiness to kill is like? My response is largely silence or to turn the question back on them so they feel awkward. This hasn't always been helpful though. If I say nothing, people asking the question assume they confirmed their suspicion. 'Oh yeah, don't want to talk about it, that's cool. That means you probably were deep into some combat or saw a lot of crazy things, huh? That's cool man.'

UNHEALTHY IDENTITY MARKERS

Many of the identity markers in the military aren't healthy. High schools adopt mascots, but high schoolers don't identify with the substance of their mascot. If the mascot is a buffalo, as my high school's was, the characteristic of a strong creature wasn't what we students walked around thinking about. Maybe a sports team will take the mascot more to heart, but it's still superficial compared to the way military subcultures adopt identity markers. My company in the 7th Marine Regiment was Alpha Company, but we all referred to it as Animal. Being a part of Animal left a deeper impression than solely being in the Marines' uniform. The idea was to embody the most primal instincts when it came to warfighting, to show no mercy, take no prisoners, and animalistically wreak havoc. Even the poetry of Shakespeare is invoked selectively to underscore this darker side of the infantry, 'Cry havoc! And let slip the dogs of war!' Part of me likes this. It's bold and embodies strength; yet another deeper part questions it. I question it, for I knew that it led to other identity markers. One such dark marker was accepting the name 'baby killer' as if it were a good thing. I hated it. I hated it in the Marine Corps even at my most callous point. Baby killer? This was the insult that civilians had used to point at some tragic events, such as the Haditha Dam incident. *Baby killer? Really?* It also makes me question the name of our sister company in 1/7: Charlie Company, better known as Suicide Charlie.

I wonder what the cumulative effect is of identifying yourself with the persona of a 'baby killer' or even the subtle influence of Animal. I don't know. But I do know parting with it is hard. Hard and confusing. It's confusing when you carry this mentality that is hardened and ready to fight, into a culture of civilians whose greatest fear is to be late to work. It's confusing because in the Marines we were understood. There was pride in appealing to our carnal nature. But on the outside? It wasn't appreciated. We feel misunderstood, and worse, no one seems to try to understand. How ironic that the place we were most understood was on foreign soil! Leaving the military isn't like leaving a job. It's extremely difficult for many to go back into service, and it is best to do so right away. Thus, leaving feels like banishment, exile of warriors to the land of misunderstanding and apathy, filled with the weak and valorless.

Veterans inevitably replace their missing identity with a new one, sometimes two. There is the new identity they try to create for themselves in their work, and then there is the identity that is forced upon them by others' prejudices. Though some mean well when they project a wounded PTSD-ridden persona on me, I do not need sympathy. Veterans need empathy. Sympathy is feelings of sorrow *for* someone. Empathy is feelings of sorrow *with* someone. Sympathy pushes away. Empathy draws near. Sympathy treats veterans like wounded ducks, while empathy yearns to enter into their feelings from their point of view.

To be honest, it has taken years for me to talk about my service and deployments. It's nearly impossible to find someone willing to listen to my story without looking for embellished stories of war glory or fighting off one-thousand insurgents with a knife and hand-grenade. This also makes it difficult for veterans who served with each other to get to know each other outside of the military. When my first battalion reunion came around, we all hungered to talk about things we understood. We spent our energy re-living, in a healthy way, those stories with people who understood them. But as we packed our bags to return home, we realized we didn't even meet the new persons they had become, which is tragic. It's tragic because one's story doesn't just stop, it continues as it is shaped by a new context, new job, new family, and so on. Without a steady trickle of processing your story with someone, that old military-self remains untouched and hinders digging deeper with military friends.

My dearest friend in seminary served in the Navy as an officer, and he was the first in seven years I told stories to that I hadn't told anyone before. They weren't stories of war and killing, but simply of service, some funny, some hard, some even a little embarrassing. I was willing to do this because he was willing to listen. Being ignored and forgotten strains veterans and continues to strain them exiting the service, groping for a new identity amidst the loss of the old.

As you can imagine, the loss of identity can be incredibly difficult. Much of our self-worth is tied up in how people perceive us. Those veterans who face a difficult transition and are unable to connect and share their story are isolated—a fate that haunts many. From the outside, they are perceived as pathetic, like the thirty-year-old man still talking about his glory days as the high school quarterback. But the mark of service is deeper and even harder to relate to most people.

The loss of identity cuts deep. It doesn't feel like losing a small part of yourself; it feels like your entire person has been ripped away and replaced by everyone else's perceptions.

It's in that loss that the pain of a previous death or traumatic experience is enhanced. With no one to trust, no one to listen to their story, veterans are in a dangerous place. Their family may have already parted ways with them, they may already have a skepticism or hatred of the church, and then this is coupled by habits they carry with them from before. When drinking without the constraint of beloved brothers, sorrows are drowned out in bottle after bottle. The VA may already be prescribing pain medication for service related injuries, so this gets thrown into the gaping void of losing the identity they loved. With no family, no friends nearby, no support from a church, and left to the devices of self-medication, that loss of identity is truly tragic. That veteran is as exposed as crossing an open-field and being fired upon with no support and no weapon to shoot back. It is in this empty darkness that suicide becomes a viable option that can offer a seductive release which nothing else can bring.

Seeking a New Identity

Only humans face identity loss. No other creature wrestles with thoughts of suicide after a loss of self; no other animal in all the glory of creation faces this challenge. It is wholly unique to humans. And even when a hint of this is seen in the animal kingdom, such as a whale beaching itself, it is measured *according to* the experience of humans. In other words, we try to describe it by the unique features of human suicide. Loss of identity is not unique to veterans exiting the service, though it is greater than many other comparable losses. People deal with loss of identity all the time. Those having lost a limb have incredible battles in this arena. Those who have lost sight, their business, a loved one, often believe a piece of them is lost too. We are, in many ways, what we love and what we do. An extension of ourselves feeds our own self-image, our self-worth, our persona as we project it on our actions and our identities.

I cannot begin to fully understand what it is like to lose a limb, but I do know what it's like to lose hearing. I'm nearly deaf in my right ear and have tinnitus, a perpetual ringing, in both ears. It is frustrating and embarrassing asking people to repeat themselves, only to have them condescendingly shout as if my loss of hearing was a loss in IQ. After leaving the service I wore my new hearing aids for a time only to abandon them largely to avoid the stigma of wearing them. They are a visual reminder to me of something I no longer have or will ever regain, and I just want to forget about it and move on. But I can't. That experience, that loss left an imprint that can't be un-rung. And what are some of the options? In my own opinion, it seems that society at large wants veterans to identify with their disability, not just their service. They want them to *become* what they have lost. But how does that help? After years of being called a wounded warrior or a disabled veteran, it will begin to seep in, and sooner than most think—we become that thing we don't want to be, while longing for wholeness.

Being a Marine is great, but it isn't lasting. Deploying to Iraq with some of the finest men in the United States leaves a lasting impression, but it isn't everlasting. Professions come to an end, even for career military service members, and, sooner or later, we are faced with loss. The problem is we put stock in something that fades, something that is temporal, something that does not last. The identity we need, and must seek, is not one found in ourselves. It is not one we make for ourselves by pulling ourselves up by our bootstraps—it is one we are given.

IDENTITY IN CHRIST
Identity in Christ is more than identifying with our Warrior Redeemer, it's more than identifying yourself as a Christian.

159

Its deep contours trace out a stupendous doctrine of the faith called 'union with Christ.' We can begin to grasp this new identity when, at the time of being reconciled to Christ, we are clothed in His righteousness. It is 'in Christ' that, before the foundations of the world were even laid, before we were ever born, we were given grace in Christ. In Christ's death our redemption was purchased and secured. In Christ the promise is given that we are made alive. In Christ is the peace of God that surpasses all understanding. All of these promises and blessings are in Him because they couldn't be found anywhere else.

We often fool ourselves into thinking we have strength but are suddenly paralyzed when a searing loss grips us. We can fight hard to make our own way in this world and make our own name, but nothing we can secure for ourselves will measure up to the riches that Christ has secured in His redemptive act. We can put a lot of stock in being a veteran, and for time, for a season, it may be satisfying. But I know, without a doubt, nothing about being a veteran will last. People will forget, others will move on, and an honorable war will become misunderstood, a misunderstood war will be forgotten, and we will be left remembering 'the good old days.' If we find our identity here, we will always be disappointed and feeling loss. But if we find our identity in Christ, in His death, resurrection, and the promises of union with him, we will never, *never,* be disappointed. We all desperately need the identity that is found in Christ.

When we were yet sinners, enemies of God, Christ died for us (Rom. 5:8). As we bent the knee of surrender to Him, He not only forgave the transgressions of the former rebels as if we had never disobeyed, but He lavished on us His riches, placing His righteousness on us as if we had always obeyed (2 Cor. 5:21). In Christ, we are given a new identity and can satisfy our deep hunger in Him (John 6:35). There is a pride of being a Marine that is real, but it isn't lasting. And then there's the identity of being in Christ—and that is for eternity.

Being eternally satisfied in Christ's redemption produces many responses, but primarily it corrects our longings to be satisfied elsewhere and directs our affections toward God. That response is correctly called worship. No longer is the fleeting desire to be recognized as someone *we were* primary, but it now rests in who *we are*. In Christ we can be truly satisfied. Only in Christ will your identity never fade, lose meaning, or get old. We can rightly say that our identity does not rest in *who* we are but *whose* we are. We are Christ's.

Even with your identity in Christ, challenging circumstances remain. Despite the legitimate and difficult seasons that await veterans (or anyone) grasping for a lost identity, they can rest assured that an identity in Christ means that He will never leave us nor forsake us (Deut. 31:6). Hope rests in Christ (1 Pet. 1:3), not in who I am, but in Christ and who He is. In Christ, God will mercifully prune the worst aspects of our own character. In Christ, God blesses us and nurtures the best aspects of our character. In Christ, we get a fresh start each day, where He renews His blessings every morning because of His great faithfulness. In Christ, we gain an identity that appreciates our time in the service, but also finds ultimate satisfaction in Him and in an enduring identity.

13

THE HAUNT OF HONOR

Every action in the military, from the smallest detail of wearing one's uniform, to the way one walks, to the performance of one's job, is filtered through an interpretive grid of honor and shame. It is in this honor and shame dynamic every action is weighed, evaluated and assigned their respective honor or shame. You could think of it as though honor and shame are the currency by which the Marine Corps functions. The premium status is to be without shame, or when shame comes, for it to be balanced by honor.

Even before recruits leave for boot camp, they learn there are three core values of the Marine Corps: honor, courage, and commitment. These become more than words; they become part of a Marine's identity, imprinted deep within. Henceforth, whenever they hear these words, they invoke the memories of these attributes that are impressed upon young Marines. Sadly, as they are repeatedly espoused, they lose their meaning within months, or even weeks, of arriving at the final duty station, where one spends the bulk of the first enlistment. These words are on tattoos, t-shirts, barber shop signs, bumper-stickers, and, sadly, become satirical. I suppose this is how it is with many careers. During the orientation and initial training at a new job, videos are played to paint an ideal picture of the company. And when that occupation doesn't match your high expectations, excitement turns to disappointment and disillusionment. Despite this pattern, Marines are quickly confronted with the truth. There is a deep sense of duty in which those core values reveal themselves as central doctrines for Marines.

HONOR/SHAME CULTURE

Military funerals, for example, bring that sense of honor to the fore, and Marines are reminded *why* they are Marines. Suddenly, the calling into the Marines is tangibly felt again. A sense of calling is woven into the fabric of each Marine, and it isn't as mundane as the daily tasks that can slowly erode a young recruit's passion. Honor is a reverence given to people, a high respect or esteem, usually in light of what someone does. The military at large, and the Marine Infantry especially, is an honor/shame culture. Some actions are esteemed, others are shamed. The boundaries of what makes an action honorable or shameworthy are not always consistent, but they normally follow how well one performs given duties. For example, those who underperform on their PFT (physical fitness test) are shamed. In my company, our command collected a special contingent of about ten Marines to remediate PFT for those out of shape. We called them 'fat-bodies.' Likewise, a Marine who *looked* overweight but easily passed the PFT, would still probably be considered a fat-body due to appearance. Hence, the inconsistent application of the honor/shame culture. At other times, the shame is appropriately placed.

We had one man fall asleep on post. He fell asleep! His action was deeply shamed, and he paid the price for it. For Marines to undo the sense of shame is difficult, and some can never erase the stain of their failure, deserved or not. The fat-bodies will always be referred to as such, until their body composition and run times change. It is possible to try to undo this sense of shame. But it's also possible, and common, for someone to gain a reputation for screwing up. If a soldier performs exceptionally with one, *maybe* two screw-ups, it may avoid labelling. But others label someone who makes multiple mistakes negligent. In order for the honor/shame culture to maintain boundaries, the negligent are pushed to the fringes until they redeem themselves or are pushed out of the Corps. If they show up to formation late in a dirty uniform when everyone else is clean, they will be shamed. Conversely, if they do not join the rest of the company in the field and embrace the dirt and grit, their crisp uniform will be shamed. This is because their appearance stinks of complacency. Other shameful behavior includes not having a fresh shave, being unable to recall basic Marine Corps knowledge, general orders, etc. Honor helps conform and re-conform Marines into the image of the ideal Marine. At its best, this type of honoring is good and should remain. However, this honor/shame culture can be toxic.

A Darker Side

A darker side to honor reigns in the service, and its damaging effects are long-lasting, even after transitioning out of service. One quickly realized consequence is the stark contrast between hopeful expectation and the disappointing reality. A famous recruiting commercial depicted a recruit rock-climbing his way up a perilous mountain to meet his final challenge, a fire rock monster dragon. The recruit takes up the NCO sword and slays the beast, thereby showing his bona fides to be a Marine. *'Earned. Never Given.'* The commercial makes it seem like Marines slay fire-breathing rock monsters daily! But most quickly meet the reality that not everything feels honorable, in fact, some tasks are dull and even humiliating. One joke was that if that commercial reflected reality, the guy would climb, not meet a monster, but to get to the top and start picking up trash. Another joke was that many would file for a service-connected disability of finger-cancer for all the cigarette butts picked up. I picked up thousands, and hated them all. I smoked five times during my service, breaking the stereotype that all Marines smoke. Nevertheless, this 'honorable duty' was always assigned to the boot (new recruit). As boots, we would wake up and police the thousands of cigarette butts around the barracks grounds.

This disenchantment period makes many new boots resolve never to re-enlist. The task doesn't seem so honorable, and when boots asks, 'Why?' the answer is the demeaning, 'Because I said so.' Nevertheless many good life lessons can be gleaned from this. Most of life is mundane and involves tasks that we regard as below our rank. But we need to get up and do them anyway. That's called being grown up. Nevertheless, the Corps quickly rips away the grandiose expectation of honor and courage.

Ingrained in the culture is the often reiterated belief that each new Marine troop is inferior to their immediate predecessors. We are told, those who deployed one cycle before us *really* saw action. Many of my seniors were decorated with combat action ribbons and purple hearts and sometimes shared stories validating those medals. Generations of veterans who either joined during peacetime or never fought a battle find this particularly hard to measure up to. I never fired a shot at an enemy, and I feel a great sense of shame in that. I feel ashamed and cheated, that the honor I worked and trained for all that time was robbed from me.

The honor-shame contours of our armed services need to be realigned to reality. Unless we reform the way we think about honor and shame, we will continue to foster a culture in which servicemembers feel shame for the wrong reasons, and no shame when they should. One particular story that pains me to this day is a cache sweep during my second deployment. We discovered hundreds of unexploded ordnance. EOD and our sister company, Charlie, arrived to help us dispose of it. I worked with and spoke to these men, only to learn a few hours later that four of them died in an explosion. I replay those times in my head and ask, 'Why wasn't it me?'

Our convoys were occasionally hit by IEDs, but, thankfully, during my first deployment, we managed to spot many IEDs before we were hit. Marines, however, might have preferred to be hit, so we could bear the combat action ribbon to reflect the danger we faced, despite not fighting with insurgents. Although we discovered hidden IEDs and narrowly escaped death many times, I and many with whom I served feel strange but deep-rooted shame for our lack of fighting action. We could not have changed the circumstances, unless we negligently allowed ourselves to be shot. On raids, we saved many Marine lives by capturing HVTs (High Value Targets) who had killed many Marines before us. And yet as twisted as it is to feel shame for not killing enemy insurgents, we feel an odd sense of shame. And I suppose all those I served with would compare themselves to their predecessors. Each subsequent generation would measure themselves according to those that were in OIF-1 and on the push through Fallujah, and so on.

Although during my first deployment we went on multiple raids where we used intelligence to pre-emptively locate enemy insurgents, there was no firefight. I remember a particular disdain I felt for one lieutenant (the same one who got us lost), who, fresh out of school, met his new team-leaders and excitedly asked, 'Did you get in a lot of firefights?' Hundreds of patrols, multiple raids, tens of thousands of hours being tensed up waiting to make contact all reduced in his mind to, 'Did you see action?' Honestly, it felt shameful saying, 'No.' It is sickening to have four years of active duty reduced to a single question. It's equally sickening that many I speak for allow it to define our identity, self-worth, and honor. During our last night in Iraq during my second deployment, rocket fire hit our base, but that didn't count. *Shame* was what we felt in light of a sense of honor none of us had named, but all of us desired.

NEVER QUIT!

The single, most shameful thing to do in the Marine Corps is to quit. I'll never forget labelling myself a quitter, for the shame follows me to this day. I was scared trying out for Recon, primarily because of swimming. I grew up in southwest Kansas, where there is no body of water for over an hour in any direction. Even the Arkansas River is dried up near my home town. I lived in the country, and if I wanted to swim, I would have to bike 5.5 miles to a tiny swimming pool in Ingalls, Kansas. I knew how to swim, but not well. I knew no strokes, or at least by their formal names. After Seth died, I wasn't sure I wanted to try for Recon, anymore. The pattern emerging was that this was going to be a transient chapter of my life. And who would be a trusted friend?

I passed the pre-Recon indoc (short for indoctrination), which was simple enough. It was merely a screening to see if we should have a chance. It consisted of a 1500-meter swim, thirty minutes treading water in our cammies followed by some techniques for blowing up your cammies (putting air in them), diving for a rifle, and a 50-meter underwater swim. Following the pool function on a cold morning in Camp Pendleton, we ran a PFT as the second half of the indoc. I passed, running a 19:30 3-mile (my personal record, to date), and was starting to get excited for Recon, again, even though Seth was no longer going to be there.

Following our completion of SOI we were sent to Camp Margarita to train in the RTP until the indoc class's slots were filled. We arrived on a Wednesday, which was to our advantage since we didn't have a full week of training before us. The first day we ran another PFT and had our first pool function. I greatly respect those who make it through Recon training because the swimming and pool function was pure madness. About thirty of us were on one end of a tiny pool crammed so tight we could only tread water with our legs. If we used our arms, we would drag someone under, which is what happened—a lot! Two guys who made it as Recon Marines, one still in, almost quit that first day. I was amazed I made it through a single pool session.

I made it to the weekend and was relieved for the opportunity to recover. Even though SOI finishes off in a 12-mile hump (hike) in full gear up and down the foothills of Camp Pendleton, I was super sore from those first few days. The next week we began with more pool sessions, aggressively escalating in difficulty. Monday's pool session opened with a 2000-meter swim. I finished last while everyone else treaded water in the deep end of the Olympic sized pool. The deep-end was an immense forty feet deep.

After that opening swim, the rest of the platoon was waiting in the deep end treading water in formation. All had their space, and we did this for about thirty minutes. The cadres added rubber rifles to the exercise, stepping up this session to a new level. Each rifle is a replica of the size, shape, and weight of an M16A-2 service rifle, weighing eight lbs. We would count off holding the rifle above our heads while treading water. Counting off consists of the first person of the first row shouting '1!' Then the next person '2!' and so on until a full count was made. The drill was to tread water with your elbows above the water, forcing us to practice a corkscrew leg kick pattern to keep our bodies buoyant and upright.

I was already struggling and barely 'making it.' Then we started inverting our rifles. That means turning the rifle vertical and letting it sink to the bottom of the forty-foot pool. When all the rifles were at the bottom of the pool, we were then instructed to swim down and grab one. I managed to do this about ten times. The immensity of the water pressure beyond twelve feet was unlike anything I had experienced. Each time we would swim down my lungs would feel like they wanted to explode as I was desperate to fill them with air. It felt like getting a head-rush. My vision focused only on what was in front of me, and my peripheral seemed to disappear. It was like the frame rate of my eyes was being reduced, not unlike the effects of intoxication. Even in the bright of day, the bottom of the pool was noticeably darker and colder. I gasped for air each time I came up out of the water, and I felt as though I was more out of breath each time. And then they started playing a game of taking one rifle away, like musical chairs, forcing someone to come to the surface empty handed. 'Play' is not a good word for it. I didn't come close to being fast enough to grab a rifle at the bottom of the pool. As I turned to swim downward, I would see others several feet past me grabbing rifles. I was only making it about thirty feet, and I would turn up fast, in panic fearing that I was not going to get enough air.

I came to the surface more gassed than the time before, and I was downcast. And after the fifth attempt at this, I came to the top while we were treading and made a swim for the edge to get out of the pool. I grabbed the side of the pool and was met by several of the Recon Marines standing over me. 'What are you doing, Holler?' they said flatly. 'I don't want to do this anymore,' is what I replied, gasping for air. This went back and forth a few times, and they let me out of the pool. I had quit. I was instructed to sit in a corner along the chain-linked fence that surrounded the pool facing away from the pool. I had quit.

I was disheartened. Everyone whom I had gotten close to had rapidly left my life, and I did not know if I still wanted to try for Recon. That morning in our PT session, one of my friends had quit. He had grown up surfing, had been a lifeguard, and was a strong swimmer. The psychological toll had taken its effect, for I reasoned, 'if he can't make it, then surely I can't.'

LASTING SHAME

I sat along that fence feeling both ashamed and relieved. And then one of those men said to me while my back was turned, 'Holler, Algrim would be ashamed; get back in the pool.' I didn't move. I felt a numb shock like I had felt when I first learned Seth had been killed. There followed a mix of anger and disbelief that he would invoke my friend's name to shame me. Deep shame. For years following that failed attempt, I always lied to people and told them I passed out in the pool, which wasn't uncommon. One of the men, who is a Recon Marine to this day, was bleeding from his ears from the pool session. For years, I've modified the staff-sergeant's words, 'Algrim would be ashamed,' to 'Come give it another try.' This was more honorable in my mind. There was less of the sting of failure in it, even though it wasn't true.

I've carried that shame for years. It's the pain of failure and self-loathing. That night after the pool session, I moved my things to the barracks where the other drops were living until we were sent to a different infantry unit. RTP has a log that weighs a few hundred pounds, is twenty feet long and painted black. When a class starts, the names of the people beginning it are written on it in red paint. As the people drop from RTP, they are crossed out, leaving those who make it to the end. Seth's name was carved permanently into the log. 'Algrim' and one other Marine who had died in training were etched as if always in the class, but never finishing. I sat alone on that log in the dimly lit barracks and cried. I wasn't sad about quitting. I wasn't feeling sorry for myself and didn't want anyone to feel sorry for me. *I* quit, and no one made me do it. I wept over my friend who was taken from me. I moved my finger over that etching and said goodbye, though I had done so at his funeral three months prior. It hit me hard that we would not be in the same unit as we had desired. I would walk a different path. He would in a sense remain there.

That painfully deep, but false, sense of shame and dishonor followed me to the fleet. Though, to my surprise, and to my benefit, the grunts didn't care if I was a Recon drop. Life in the fleet was difficult enough, so I suppressed that failure and sense of shame, shoving it down deep. I never brought the subject up except for those who had dropped with me. Sadly, the idea behind this sense of honor and shame bleeds over into many facets of service. We all, in one way or another, measure ourselves up to this perfect ideal of honor. But sometimes it isn't even ideal. We imagine that it would have been more honorable to have killed many enemy insurgents, lost friends, and seen endless combat. But not all of us had. And then, we face the reality of suicide, the ultimate act of shaming oneself, which carries deep cultural shame.

Shame begets shame. When we fail to reach the honor we sought, a sense of dishonor replaces it. And how can we undo what has been done? What could anyone in my platoon have done to change the circumstances of our deployment? We showed up to the fight, but didn't. Yet we went home with wounded hearts as if we had been cheated. Why do we burden ourselves with such a twisted sense of honor? The men I knew who fought in Korea and Vietnam, who lost friends are forever scarred by their deaths. They have never once said it was more honorable to face combat in the hell-like conditions they did than it was to show up prepared to fight and not done so. Those men would trade the world to have their friends back. Yet, many I served with who committed suicide were plagued by this very sense of shame. It haunted them. Years of preparation under grueling conditions, and constant mental awareness to be met by the letdown of a relatively quiet deployment comes packaged looking and feeling like shame. But why?

PTSD?

Many find this unbelievable. Nearly *everyone* to whom I speak about veteran suicide assumes that it was because of PTSD. The reality isn't uniform for every deployed veteran.

172

Some of the men I knew who have killed themselves saw combat. But several of them did not. At least three approached combat situations, such as going on raids and having an IED hit a convoy. We *must* rethink our assumptions about suicide in this regard. Many men take their lives who did not see combat as it is traditionally associated with PTSD. My 'answer' is only an anecdotal observation. Some of these men had accepted a false sense of what is honorable and were made to feel cheated by a culture filled with blood lust, enamored with stories of combat.

Most of the armed forces do not involve combat roles. Many conventional combat jobs, like tanks or artillery, saw most of their action at the beginning of the Iraq War, but as the fight became less and less conventional, they were less and less needed. When grueling training is rehearsed over and over, leading to an anti-climactic deployment, many feel cheated. And this is not only due to inaction. It is also because they sacrificed much of their health and relationships to get there. The infantry is tough on the body and tougher on marriage. Many men I served with have onset osteoarthritis from the wear and tear of the many hikes, patrols, ranges, and constant state of fitness required. We are not disgruntled. We do not point a finger at the Corps and say, 'You broke me, you did this to me!' Rather, this is a humble observation and a sad irony.

My hearing is diminished largely due to the many ranges we conducted. I can hear some out of my right ear, but have perpetual tinnitus in both ears. Twentynine Palms has more live fire time than any other Marine Corps base. It is a double-edged sword, of course. While the thousands upon thousands of rounds fired down range were only ever at a simulated enemy, some men even have overuse syndrome, commonly called tennis elbow, from so much trigger time. This is the same feature some men have who return from months of endless firefights. In this irony, the shame runs deep, so we don't talk about it, but pretend it doesn't exist. We keep it bottled up and allow others to think we experience the horrors of war, because we think it's more honorable than the truth. But this distorted sense of honor shackles more than it liberates.

Being haunted by this false sense of honor makes suicide difficult to process. We hold the most noble death to be that of dying for your friends. A half-step down from that tier is dying in combat. A gap then separates this ideal from everything else. Accidents are seen as honorable in a sense, but suicide? We pass judgement and think less of that person. That judgment is rarely voiced, and is not meant to be disrespectful. I have no disrespect for men I knew who took their lives. But we can't help making a value judgment of suicide compared to those the Marine Corps regards as the highest honor, like Corporal Dunham jumping on a grenade. Two of my uncles committed suicide, though they were not Marines serving in recent years. Immediate family attaches the same sense of shame to their deaths, as do family and friends of those in the service who take their lives. This unspoken shame leaves suicide deaths largely undiscussed, and thus never processed, rarely grieved, and, if lamented, done in silence and isolation. Suicide and this misshapen sense of honor have transferred the awful practice of suffering in silence to those they leave behind. Men who suffered in silence for too long now pass on their suffering to loved ones.

Breaking the Cycle

We need to reform our sense of honor. Not so that suicide is revered, but so it can be talked about, grieved, and prevented. We need to reject the false idea that faithful service is not as honorable as combat. We must wrestle with the false notion of inferiority attached to service outside of infantry, or of not being deployed, or of anything else not meeting the expectations of our culture. Honor should be measured in terms of faithfulness, not experience. This kind of honor can gently speak into the brokenness and allow suicides not to be grieved on the basis of the type of death, but on the basis of people being image bearers of God.

The Marine Corps Hymn contains the line:

First to fight for right and freedom
And to keep our honor clean,
We are proud to claim the title
United States Marine.[1]

Whatever to 'keep our honor clean' means, it must at least mean to speak the truth. This includes two things. First, it means we must speak about what happened, and even more importantly, what didn't happen. We will have an entire generation of veterans plagued by increasing rates of suicide, and it will be partially our fault, if we do not speak about our experiences. This means all of it, warts and all. It also means that, as a culture, we must work to undo the blood lust and false honoring of combat. Secondly, it means that we tell the truth. We must not embellish the truth, allowing others to falsely believe a false narrative, nor believing we are less honorable because we lack a certain experience. A clean honor is not something the United States currently possesses, and the Armed Forces are constantly under pressure from outside influence that wants to define what is honorable and what is not. Redeeming a clean sense of honor is a culture battle worth fighting for. The stakes are literally life and death.

A New Sense of Honor

In Scripture, *to honor* is to esteem, to give great respect toward someone or something. If we want to reform our understanding of what it is to honor someone in light of Scripture, then we can shed honoring in light of what a person has done, or failed to do. Peter writes, 'Honor everyone. Love

---

1. https://www.marineband.marines.mil/about/library-and-archives/the-marines-hymn/

the brotherhood. Fear God. Honor the emperor' (1 Pet. 2:17). Our honor is rooted in each person made in God's image. If we want our honor to be clean, then we must honor each person in life and in death, even if the death is complex and tragic—like suicide. If we want to keep our honor clean, it will also mean that we will abandon false notions of honor to cast out the darkness that has encroached upon the hearts of men struggling with thoughts of suicide. It will mean that what isn't spoken about will be spoken about, what isn't lamented, will be lamented, what is made to feel inferior, will be reformed in light of faithful duty.

Our honor can be made clean where we no longer have to be haunted by its false seduction and lies. We must honor what God honors, and in doing so honor Him. Our honor of Him, in all things, will be counted according to its faithfulness. Let us then be faithful. Let us keep our honor clean.

14

WEARY WITHOUT REST

'You can sleep when you're dead,' or 'sleep is a crutch,' are humorous, dark quips often cited during my time in service. When I recall the circumstances when they were said, I breathe a sigh of relief and thank God that I am no longer under the pressure of that profession. When overwork was commonplace and sleep was in short supply, these phrases accompanied our misery and numbed our objections to the endless labor. Many can relate to being overworked, and when someone has crammed eighty hours of work into one week, you can sometimes only summarize the entire deal and say, 'This sucks.' Work is a good thing; overwork is not.

A GRUELING PACE
A unique feature of the Marine infantry is its grueling pace. The work is more than just difficult or long; it is the definition of demanding. It steadily demands unrelenting loyalty with no end or rest in sight. I know of no non-military profession that consistently operates under the unique conditions of this kind of environment. The infantry would have E-3s (Lance Corporals) operating in E-5 and E-6 billets (those of Sergeants and Staff-Sergeants) all the time. The impossible is consistently required of the lower echelon of grunts. Imagine

having to be responsible not only for millions of dollars in gear, but also for the lives of the men in the team, squad, platoon, and so on. Add to this a few other facts. First, I dreamed of working *only* eighty hours in a week. My unit would regularly get four hours of sleep a night. That amounts to about a 140-hour work week. We didn't get evenings off or have time to watch the nightly news. We were mission-focused from wake to sleep. Add this to the pressure to perform with professionalism, being ready to fight at any moment, for weeks and months on end. There were breaks from the most grueling routines. Occasionally, there was downtime. But workups and deployments meant constantly operating at an *intense* level and at a demanding pace. The accumulative effects of this high stress environment in a demanding vocation leads to *operation fatigue*, and for those veterans who saw combat, it is more accurately labeled *combat stress*. Sometimes combat stress is the term applied to those with operation fatigue, which is largely the same concept.

My first deployment reached its peak of stress during the first few months in Iraq. The enemy's preferred method of engagement with American troops was laying in IEDs. Any piece of trash, rock, any natural or manmade terrain feature could conceal an explosive. Iraq is not a clean place. No sanitation departments clean trash from the street. Cans, wrappers, and trash were as commonplace in the city streets as rocks. This made the first dozen patrols mentally exhausting. We all tried to memorize our battle space down to the last detail. And when I say last detail, that's what I mean. This included every house, dirt pile, pile of trash, rock, and their location. This was always a difficult and taxing task.

After we basically knew our AO (area of operations), the routines solidified until the end of the deployment. We rotated back and forth between three days of post and three days of patrol. Posts were six hours long, followed by twelve hours 'off' that involved about six hours of duties. After completing duties, you had a six-hour window that you could spend on yourself.

Most wanted to decompress and lift weights, read, watch a movie, or sleep before their next post. We would try to squeeze in some free time at the risk of losing the opportunity to sleep, but 'sleep is a crutch,' so we often neglected it. It's sad that given the choice between some sleep or spending time on ourselves, sleep lost out. This reminds me of a famous experiment where a monkey was forced to choose between two fake mother monkeys. One, made of cold, hard wire, offered nutrition from a bottle, but no comfort. The other monkey offered no food, but was made of soft material, and gave comfort. After minimal attention was given to the basic requirements to live, comfort won out over sleep. The implications apply to humans. We would rather experience the fleeting joys of listening to music, working out, or snacking on potato chips, than sleep. But either decision came at a price. If we chose comfort, we lost a basic human need; if we chose sleep, we lost a taste of human flourishing.

Losing Control

Patrols were at least better in getting to leave the BP (battle position) for a little while. We conducted hundreds of patrols during my first deployment. We would vary our route, time of day, but would run anywhere between six to fifteen patrols during those cycles, not counting 'movements' to a smaller BP about a half a mile away.

I recall being about three months into my first pump (deployment) and being unbelievably irritable. Most people were like this; just beneath the surface was a war-ready Marine, ready to unleash violence at a moment's notice. Part of this was because of the difficult nature of the job; part because we were constantly in a state of preparedness. One of the core tenets of operating in that volatile and tense theater was memorizing the 5-3-5's, which had been drafted and instituted by our beloved General 'Mad Dog' Mattis (The 5-3-5's were a short list of habits of actions and habits of thoughts Marines were to memorize as guidelines for operating in theater). A portion of those 5-3-5's states, 'Be polite, be professional, but have a plan to kill everybody you meet,' so we did. All of us had a plan. From shooting to grappling to using our knives, if we were close enough. One Marine even carried a screwdriver which fitted neatly in the flak jacket's gear straps.

On one such day I had to stand post from 1200-1800. I was preparing by eating some chow first. I walked into our library/commons area, a wooden building about 20x20 feet, stacked with sandbags all-round the outside. The inside walls were lined with books people had read and then donated to the growing library that had a small area carved out for the commons' television. One Marine from 2nd Platoon, whom I will not name to save him from embarrassment, was sitting in front of the TV playing a game. He had discovered some sort of Frogger or Pong game that was built in with the TV remote. He and another Marine, Aguirre, were inside when I came in with a cup of Ramen Noodles wanting to watch some UFC before going on post. I voiced my disgust for wasting the TV and told the guy to change it to a show or movie we could all enjoy. He lashed out revealing the same level of fatigue and stress in him. I didn't like this, and so I resolved to punch him in the face. I slowly and calmly set my noodles down and, while he was kneeling in front of the TV glaring back at me to see what I would say, I threw a low right hook striking him along the right side of the face. I wasn't satisfied with this, and so I unleashed my rage in a flurry of angry punches. He mostly tried to defend himself by covering his face, and I continued to bombard my right against him while I used my left hand to hold him down.

The moment I landed that first punch I saw Aguirre out of the corner of my eye walk over to the door and peer out with it cracked to see if any of our seniors were around. Then while

I was continuing to punch this other guy, Aguirre came over and said, 'OK, Holler, that's enough.' And then just as quickly as I had snapped, I realized what I was doing and stopped. I walked over and picked up my noodles, sat down, and continued to eat. This other guy stood up, his face bruised and slightly bloodied, and said. 'Why the h&%$ did you do that, Holler?' I as calmly as I had been before, sheepishly apologized. I didn't know why I had done it. It just came over me, and I wanted to hurt him before I realized what I was doing. 'Okay, this wasn't a fight … no one won; let's tell no one,' he replied. When he said this, the anger in me welled again. I wanted to make him acknowledge his defeat—but I let it slide while I pondered what had just happened. I didn't have any ill-will toward him. My anger simply spilled over from the ocean of fatigue, stress, and anger that I was constantly trying to keep at bay. I didn't even realize what I was doing. It was like I was watching myself do it, distant and detached and, yet, simultaneously swimming in the rage like it was pleasurable. It *was* pleasurable.

And the deployment went on like this. This wasn't unique to my experience; everyone shared it, and no one spoke of it. Everyone stood in a perpetual state of readiness, ready to snap and unleash hell. I remember one night we were conducting a raid on an HVT (high valued target), and when the 'breacher tool' failed to break open the door, I watched my team leader smash open that door in the most violent kick to a door I had ever seen. He had tapped into that same anger, that same stress, and broke the bolt on a door considered impenetrable. Everyone was like that—always stressed, angry, and wanting to kill something, usually *someone*.

Toward the end of the deployment, I snapped at a Marine who had given me lip after we had been ordered to police call outside. 'Police calling' is the routine chore of picking up every bit of trash on the ground. It can also be used for specific material. For example, after a live-fire range we 'police our brass,' that is, we pick up the expended casings from the rounds we fired. I don't even know what I told him to do or even what he said. All I remember is overwhelming anger that caused me to run after him with violent intent. He tried to run along the small corridor, but I caught up quickly, grabbed the back of his neck and slammed his face against the wall bloodying his nose. I released him as I then threw him to the ground and unleashed another flurry of punches. I don't know how long I would have continued had I not been interrupted by a fellow Marine. I felt like I had temporarily lost volition, and I could only watch as a third party as punches flew. I was ashamed at what I did, and, yet, oddly at peace with it. No one reprimanded me. No one shamed me. In fact my platoon sergeant watched this second fight and praised it.

DECOMPRESSION?

Again, and again, we would press into our duties, operating sleep-deprived under immense pressure with stress increasing with compound interest over seven months. It's almost humorous that the two weeks in Kuwait after a deployment were called 'decompression.' This so-called decompression is akin to taking a violently boiling pot of water and turning the burner down. The water doesn't stop boiling instantly. And when it's no longer boiling, it remains hot for a long time. Everyone knew that after their month of post-deployment leave, they would be back at the beginning of another long training cycle, pushing through weekends, nights, holidays and more, to come back to Iraq or Afghanistan to face the same circumstances.

The first weekend back in the states after my first deployment I went with Jones and his father to Palm Springs. We went to a steakhouse where I ordered my first legal alcoholic beverage in the States. I had turned 21 in February of the deployment, a day I humorously remember my squad leader saying, 'Happy birthday, Holler. Now, get to post.'

Nearly two months later, I was finally enjoying this overdue privilege. After eating, we went to a bookstore and picked up some new reads, and I remember a man eating outside the Subway next to the bookstore. Bluetooth headsets weren't new, but I had not seen someone use one for seven months. I noticed the man eating his sandwich and speaking, to seemingly no one. And then I snapped, screaming at him, demanding information as I sometimes did of Iraqi civilians: 'Who the h*&% are you talking to?!' His shock was met with my own, not realizing what I had done, and in hindsight it seems funny, because all he said was, 'I'll call you back, dear.' I don't know if he was expecting me to attack him or what, but as my buddy exited the store, I simply turned and walked away, embarrassed at my behavior and not realizing the guy had been on the phone.

This is what operation fatigue does. It combines stress and fatigue into a new lifeforce that slowly eats away at the simple native boy I was before enlistment. Eventually, it devolves into a kind of beast of unending work in a terribly demanding profession. The cruelty of this profession is that many men go home to their wives and families with this stress. A Marine, named Smith, shared with the RBE platoon I was in near the end of active duty, that even with this last deployment behind him, he still had been snapping at his wife over small things, such as not being able to find the milk in the fridge. Everyone deals with it differently. Some internalize the boiling anger, embarrassed and, eventually, in several months up to a year later, the boil fades to a simmer, and fades away. Others internalize it as their identity. They reason, 'If you have a problem with me, it's your problem,' and, to some degree, all adopt that attitude for a time.

It's difficult, though, because one day you are operating in a high stress environment thousands of miles from home, and another you are supposed to blend in and behave like other civilians. But when civilians complain about working overtime, losing sleep or their job, or whatever, we veterans quickly remember how hard we had it, and how they don't have a clue how easy they have it. I worked security in Chicago for a brief period and listened to an overweight guard who was 'training me' complain about the AC being too weak in his gate post. Like other vets in that situation, my mind was back in Iraq, conducting 8-hour cache sweeps in full gear in excess of 140 degrees. Dwelling on those thoughts raises that same swell of anger, again. Years out of service, that stress can still be there, coursing through our veins, ready to find an outlet on someone through a fist to his face.

Longing for Rest

As you can imagine, prolonged periods of operating like this aren't healthy. They take their toll on many vets who can't hold down a job and are overlooked in favor of inexperienced, complaining civilians who wield supervisory authority over them. Every marriage takes the strain. It takes a special woman to put up with the BS we give our wives when we come home. Those who faithfully wait, endure long months only to trade them for longer months with us when we vent in fury—often show much grace. But the months are long and hard after getting home out of service. Some vets unintentionally isolate themselves, trusting nobody, still ramped up, still ready to snap at any moment, still feeling utterly alone.

The inability to release the burden of operation stress drains the veteran's already fragile psyche. This added burden shatters marriages, splits families, and further isolates those who yearn for a freedom from this vicious cycle. Some look for freedom in the wrong places, resorting to anything to help them cope—video games, alcohol, violence—yet nothing completely removes the pain. A single sip won't help. There is no relief unless we are blackout drunk, so that the burden of that never-ending fatigue can be forgotten for a night. This cycle isn't satisfying, nor does it provide rest. Soon, reprieve is sought elsewhere, and for far too many, the only lasting freedom is suicide.

When one is worn down day after day and month after month, strength is slowly sapped. We veterans are told that we are strong and that we shouldn't tap out. We should dig deeper, and use the reservoirs of unending strength. But it isn't unending, and many feel simply depleted. Similar to the ALS ice bucket challenge, when the videos of the 22-push up challenge were circulating on social media to raise awareness of veteran suicide, one veteran vehemently disapproved. His reasoning was first rooted in contesting that 22 veterans actually take their lives, though we don't know for sure whether the number is lower or higher. His second critique was that in openly discussing suicide among veterans, it was flying in the face of the strength we have. He urged others to stop talking about suicide as if it makes veterans weak. I agree with at least part of his sentiment. We shouldn't talk about suicide in terms of 'feeling sorry for poor weak veterans.' The projection is condescending. But I also disagree in terms of creating a facade of strength where it has been depleted.

As veterans we *hate* to admit weakness. Nothing is more humiliating than displaying a gap in our internal defenses. So we stay tight-lipped and gruff about it. A well-known USMC shirt declares on the back, 'Pain is weakness leaving the body.' There is something good, true, and right about sometimes having to suck it up. Sometimes we must stay quiet and not bicker, becoming a burden to your unit and lowering morale. But as manly as that statement is, it is also largely a farce. I wonder about the pain in many of the men I knew who took their lives: were they casting their weakness away because they were feeling it? It is easy to show the untenability of that statement even though some pain is indeed good. Pain is not always to be dismissed as bad, but neither is it always to be accepted as good.

Admittance of weakness, weariness, and the need to be replenished is not an identity marker. Veterans aren't 'weak' because they struggle. Rather, it is a display of strength to reach out and confess the burdens that we bear. Many of us ask, where can rest be found? Where can weariness be relieved? Whose strength can we tap into and be replenished?

CHRIST PROMISES REST

We must never lose sight of the fact that Christ bore a burden that no one else could bear. Yet, He was able to say: 'Come to me, all who labor and are heavy laden, and I will give you rest. Take my yoke upon you, and learn from me, for I am gentle and lowly in heart, and you will find rest for your souls. For my yoke is easy, and my burden is light' (Matt. 11:28-30).

Even though His yoke is easy, many find it difficult to come to Him. Why? The reason, in the context of this passage, is unbelief. Despite the miracles that authenticated Christ, many of those who saw Him perform them did not believe His identity and promises. We do the same thing. But if Christ is who He says He is, then His promises are what He says they are.

Make no mistake—the call to bend the knee to Christ and cast our cares on Him is not easy. But Christ, the Warrior Redeemer, is faithful. Christianity isn't a cakewalk of blessings and riches. Hardships remain for everyone to varying degrees. But Christ is faithful. His promises are forever, including this one: 'Be strong and courageous. Do not be frightened, and do not be dismayed, for the LORD your God is with you wherever you go' (Josh. 1:9).

Scripture's call to be strong is more holistic than many realize. It is to have both a strong arm (physical strength), and a strong heart (spiritual strength). When we cast our cares on Christ, our bank account isn't suddenly enriched. Our struggles with painkiller addictions do not usually go away instantly. When we cast our cares on Him, we are required to confess our weakness and seek God's strength. To confess means admitting our sins and asking God to forgive us. This results in aligning our internal reality to the way things really are.

Our strength is not sufficient, but Christ's is. Though we may have physical strength, our hearts are not always strong. We confess that Christ can bear the pain, brokenness, and shame we have, and everything that separates us from Him. God in Scripture says, 'I will never leave you nor forsake you' (Hebrews 13:5). The transient nature of the military brings people in and out of our lives like a revolving door. After the first enlistment, it is sometimes difficult to bond with anyone as deeply as you did previously. But God's promise does not change because He does not change. He says He will never leave us, and He won't. So where does that place us?

This promise is most expressed when we are in great need of Christ's strength to be poured into us while we—especially when we are—weak, weary, and heavy-laden. Christ not only enriches the soul and pours Himself into us, but He also uses others for this mission too. This is one aspect of the mission of the church. As image-bearers of God needing life together in community, we can strengthen one another. We can't do it alone. We never could. And the great humility of confessing our weakness is that we must shed a false identity *and* deal with the disenchantment we may have experienced because of the church previously. I truly know the rejection some of my buddies have against all forms of organized religion. And therein lies the challenge to find rest. The challenge is primarily to overcome the skepticism and reticence to believe who Jesus says He is and to believe what He has done. But if we confess who He is, the promises are there. In Christ we can be filled with a strength that enriches our soul and replenishes our vitality.

15

VOLUNTARY EXTRACT

This has been a difficult chapter to write. First, because it's depressing to jump right into. How do you find meaning in the suicide of a veteran? I struggle with this question, and it's even harder for those without service experience to understand the cultural contours of the military. Only with a larger context (hopefully given in the previous chapters) can we begin to understand veteran suicide. A myriad of factors can lead someone to contemplate taking his or her life. A holistic worldview can help us find meaning in the tragedy of a veteran. Some who read these words might reject Christianity, but it has been my greatest source of comfort in tragedy. This is why it is so important that we recognize the uniqueness of everyone's story.

Second, it's equally important to know about certain disciplines to which we commonly look for answers to these questions—psychology and mental health. Doubtless these have a place, but not psychology, psychiatry, medicine, individual experiences, or any other sub-discipline has all the answers. These disciplines help us ask important questions behind the questions. The big picture conversation when it comes to veteran suicide looks like this:

Experts: Studies suggest that the main reason veterans commit suicide is related to depression.

Average person: Okay. Why are they depressed?
Experts: Studies suggest that depression is caused by these ten contributing factors.
Average person: Okay. Which factors are present for veterans?
Experts: It depends.
Average person: What does it depend on?
Experts: Their individual experiences.

Although these are generalizations, they are not inaccurate. All suicide is a multi-disciplinary issue. We must interact with people as individuals. Veterans are individual people with individual circumstances and stories. Generalizations are unhelpful if we neglect the person struggling with suicidal thoughts. While the broad strokes of the stats and articles give us good ideas about what contributes to veteran suicide, we must subordinate them to the grand narrative of the inspired Word of God. Without God's Word, our lives lack meaning. We need to hear other voices on this issue, but ultimately any voice lacking the gospel lacks what is needed to address the greatest need of every human heart.

Veterans share overlapping circumstances that may have brought them to a similar end, but they have unique stories of their triumphs and failures. Some might challenge that the previous chapters don't apply to their loved one who committed suicide. First of all, thank you for reading this far if that is your view. By reading this much you have demonstrated your desire to know my story and those of these other men. Secondly, I hope you will reread the previous chapters before you conclude definitively that they don't apply to the loved one you knew. Though every story is unique, most veterans will, in fact, face many of the following aspects.

Stereotypes
'Well you know, suicide is just a selfish action.' 'Someone saying they're going to commit suicide is just looking for

attention. If they were going to kill themselves, they would've done it.' Tragically, these sentiments are commonplace and, on the surface, aren't questioned, until you've known someone who struggled with suicidal thoughts or has taken his or her life. Many times I've heard people recite these oft-used and misguided ideas about suicide. These observations are unhelpful to say the least. My response to hearing them has been to shut myself off from others to simmer in dismay or disgust. Is suicide a selfish act? Well, it *could* be. But this view holds little value. It doesn't explain suicide. Different people take their lives for different reasons, even if the result is the same.

It's a common occurrence that when veterans, or at least Marines, have died, they are commemorated on social media by a set of words to replace their birth and death. It looks something like, 'John Smith- *insert* 2–10–87, *extract* 3–23–17.' The *insert* is to invoke the military 'speak' or vernacular, for a helicopter drop off and pick up. By doing this, we are interpreting their lives totally through the grid of their military experience. In their death such language remembers their whole life as one long battle, even if the last casualty in that war was their own. It is a way for veterans to humanize and honor their fallen comrade. If the person's 'extract,' then, was a suicide, it is a voluntary extract from this life.

The death of loved ones by their own hands raises many questions for both Christians and non-Christians. The question of the after-life comes into full view as do its accompanying questions. Where do people go when they die? Do warriors go to Valhalla to live as Vikings do in their afterlife? What about the nature of suicide itself? Is it an unforgivable sin? Is the Roman Catholic Church right in holding that it is a mortal sin?

I wanted to include many stories of great men in this chapter. These stories are all heart-wrenching and depressing. Many stories of suicide are controversial. Rather than tell all the stories I knew of those who killed themselves and offer no answers, I will tell the stories of a few that were illustrative to help us understand the others. We don't always have all the details or reasons for a suicide; nevertheless the question remains: Why do some take their lives? Why do some veterans kill themselves and others who experience the same circumstances do not?

IS SUICIDE AN UNFORGIVABLE SIN?

Many people believe that suicide is an unforgiveable sin. Many, religious or not, believe this. Though this belief has seeped into the popular culture of religious beliefs, it is not found in the Bible. So why do some people believe it? The Roman Catholic Church has long taught that suicide is a mortal sin, a category of sins that includes willful rejection of the faith. It states that those who have taken their life forfeit salvation. Specifically, the Catholic Church defines a mortal sin as: '*Mortal sin* destroys charity in the heart of man by a grave violation of God's law; it turns man away from God, who is his ultimate end and his beatitude, by preferring an inferior good to him' (*Catechism of the Catholic Church*, paragraph 1855).[1]

That doesn't clarify what kinds of sins are mortal or what the consequences of such sins are. The reason most suicides are considered mortal sins is because of what the *Catechism* says in paragraph 1857: 'Mortal sin is sin whose object is a grave matter and which is also committed with full knowledge and deliberate consent.' Most suicides are deliberate. It is difficult to imagine a suicide that is accidental. If someone is killed by accident, it is because there was no forethought or deliberateness to the action. It seems that suicide meets the definition of a mortal sin. If that is the case, what are the consequences? The Catechism continues in paragraph 1861:

---

1. *Catechism of the Catholic Church*, 2nd edition (New York: Continuum International, 2000).

Mortal sin is a radical possibility of human freedom, as is love itself. It results in the loss of charity and the privation of sanctifying grace, that is, of the state of grace. If it is not redeemed by repentance and God's forgiveness, it causes exclusion from Christ's kingdom and the eternal death of hell, for our freedom has the power to make choices for ever, with no turning back. However, although we can judge that an act is in itself a grave offense, we must entrust judgment of persons to the justice and mercy of God.

The key aspect is stated here. It results in the loss of a state of grace which cannot be atoned for without repentance. Since persons who kill themselves cannot repent, the Catechism demonstrates that Roman Catholic doctrine teaches that suicide is a mortal sin that sends those who commit it to 'the eternal death of hell.'

I say 'most suicides' above because of this qualification in paragraph 1860:

Unintentional ignorance can diminish or even remove the imputability of a grave offense. But no one is deemed to be ignorant of the principles of the moral law, which are written in the conscience of every man. The promptings of feelings and passions can also diminish the voluntary and free character of the offense, as can external pressures or pathological disorders. Sin committed through malice, by deliberate choice of evil, is the gravest.

The Roman Catholic Church is correct to assert that suicide is a sin. It is. The unjust taking of life is always sin. But they are wrong to assert that it occupies a category of mortal sin, which is not biblical. Of course, this is not a green light to commit suicide. Who would want to face their Creator on the terms set by their last action?

A SCRIPTURAL VIEW OF SUICIDE

Suicide is self-murder. Self-murder is wrong just as much as any murder is wrong. It would be unwise to try to help anyone grieving a suicide by hitting them over the head with this truth. The Bible makes it clear that murder is wrong through the sixth commandment: 'You shall not murder' (Exod. 20:13). It's not simply wrong because God declares it wrong, for when God reveals His law, He reveals His character. When God reveals His law, He teaches His creation how we should be like Him. The reason suicide is wrong is because it falsely confesses that God is 'like this.' Suicide follows this line of reason. Our faithful Redeemer does not self-malign, hurt, or murder Himself. He could not. As we reflect the image of God, we are to reflect His character and be like Him, so we ought not to falsely confess the character of God, but rightly confess His character by upholding the dignity of human life.

Those who have known someone who committed suicide are often quick to skip over the details when sharing the news of that death with others. That absence of information, I believe, is because we associate shame with the death. Military or not, trained for combat or not, people know that the wrongful taking of a human life is wrong. We must distinguish between murder and killing. All murder is killing, but not all killing is murder. All cars are vehicles, but not all vehicles are cars. There are also trucks, motorcycles and so forth. Servicemembers would not voluntarily enlist into the military if they thought all forms of killing are always and everywhere wrong. It would be a mistake to conflate killing and murder. Sometimes killing is permitted because the causes of war are just. But murder is always wrong. Because people naturally know that murder is wrong, there is a shame attached to it. How far did a person have to sink in the view of their self-worth to think that taking their life was permissible or even necessary? So, we neglect the details when informing others because we do not want to continue to project the shame that person felt in his or her final moments upon their memory.

Suicide is not an unforgiveable sin. To think otherwise is to misunderstand the heart of the gospel. The death of Christ redeems rebels who put their faith in Him, who died for them and rose from the dead. His death and resurrection purchase forgiveness for all sins, even suicide. Because salvation is not something that can be gained by works, we cannot lose it by works, either. It is true, suicide is a sin. But the blood of Christ paid for the sins of those who believe in Him. When Christ said, 'it is finished' on His cross (John 19:28-30), He meant that His work of salvation was completely finished. Christ accomplished salvation forever for all who trust Him to save them. That's why Jesus said: 'I give them eternal life, and they will never perish, and no one will snatch them out of my hand' (John 10:28). We can never thwart God's will. Some protest, 'but we can remove ourselves from His hand.' But this misses the point of Christ's atoning work. It says that God has the power to keep His sheep completely, but not those who reject Him. If someone rejects Christ, they never knew Him. Suicide, though heinous, never undoes people's worth. It never erases the fact that God made us in His image. No sin is unforgivable for those who love Christ and are called according to His purpose (Rom. 8:28).

Those in Christ cannot be separated from God's immeasurable love, as Paul says:

> What then shall we say to these things? If God is for us, who can be against us? He who did not spare his own Son but gave him up for us all, how will he not also with him graciously give us all things? Who shall bring any charge against God's elect? It is God who justifies. Who is to condemn? Christ Jesus is the one who died—more than that, who was raised— who is at the right hand of God, who indeed is interceding for us. Who shall separate us from the love of Christ? Shall tribulation, or distress, or persecution, or famine, or

nakedness, or danger, or sword? As it is written, 'For your sake we are being killed all the day long; we are regarded as sheep to be slaughtered.' No, in all these things we are more than conquerors through him who loved us. For I am sure that neither death nor life, nor angels nor rulers, nor things present nor things to come, nor powers, nor height nor depth, nor anything else in all creation, will be able to separate us from the love of God in Christ Jesus our Lord (Rom. 8:31-39).

Paul's quotation of a Psalm in the Romans 8 passage is overlooked. Paul cites a Psalm in which the writer doesn't feel God's presence. The next verse says: 'Awake! Why are you sleeping, O Lord? Rouse yourself! Do not reject us forever! Why do you hide your face? Why do you forget our affliction and oppression?' (Ps. 44:23-24). Paul's point in using this Psalm is that nothing can separate us from God's love, even when we can't feel His presence. When we fail to see God's hand in our circumstances, God still loves us. When we feel abandoned, He is there. Especially when hardships, suffering, grief, and death come, God's love remains upon us.

WHAT ABOUT SUICIDE IN COMBAT?

There is a key distinction between a suicide in view here, and suicide in combat, which I will refer to as 'sacrifice.' Those who sacrifice themselves by jumping on a grenade are taking their lives into their hands too. But it's entirely different. The reason they are taking their lives is to preserve other lives. A suicide by any sort of self-inflicted means is wholly different. Suicide goes against the heart of God's law and character, which we reflect in a love for God manifesting itself also in a love for neighbor. Sacrificial death should never be called suicide, in terms of self-murder, because sacrifice is the essence of love for neighbor, while suicide is the inverse of that love. Thus, it is not proper to call a sacrifice of one's life in combat a suicide.

SUICIDE IN GENERAL

Suicide in the U.S. is on a steep and steady incline. According to a study recently released by the Center for Disease Control, the rate of suicide in the U.S. is the highest since WW2 and is up 33% since 1999.[2] It is not just veterans and servicemembers who are experiencing the ravages of suicide. These staggering numbers have many people alarmed. The armed forces, veterans and servicemembers are still disproportionally affected but the parallel between the two populations could suggest that the reason why a veteran commits suicide may share common ground with a non-veteran. Do veterans experience unique circumstances and experiences? Yes, indeed. Most of this book has told stories unique to veterans.

THE STATS

The oft-cited statistic which says twenty-two veterans take their life each day is terrible. Writing for *The Washington Post*, Michelle Ye Lee Hee reports:

> This statistic comes from the VA's 2012 Suicide Data Report, which analyzed death certificates from 21 states, from 1999 to 2011. The report calculated a percentage of suicides identified with veterans out of all suicides in death certificates from the 21 states during the project period, which turned out to be 22 percent. (By point of reference, about 13 percent of U.S. adults are veterans, according to a 2012 Gallup poll.) Then the report applied that percentage against the number of suicides in the U.S. in a given year (approximately 38,000). Divided by number of days in a year, the report came up with 22 veteran suicides a day.

Some have criticized this study for excluding California and Texas, high volume veteran states, and thereby inflating

---

2. 'Suicide Rising across the US,' Centers for Disease Control and Prevention (Centers for Disease Control and Prevention, June 7, 2018), https://www.cdc.gov/vitalsigns/suicide/.

the stats. But the truth could cut the other way. It's possible that the stat would be higher if the states were included. But there's more data to examine. She goes on:

A new study[3] funded by the Army shows the suicide rate for veterans who served in recent wars is much lower than 22 a day. The study, published in the February 2015 Annals of Epidemiology, is the first large population-based study of post-service suicide risk among this population. Researchers used veteran records from two Defense Department databases, verified Social Security information and used the CDC's National Death Index Plus. They studied 1.3 million veterans who were discharged between 2001 and 2007. Among deployed veterans in this report, 32.6 percent were born in 1978-1981 and 30 percent were born in 1982-1990. Between 2001 and 2009, there were 1650 deployed veteran and 7703 non-deployed veteran deaths. Of those, 351 were suicides among deployed veterans and 1517 were suicides among non-deployed veterans. That means over nine years, there was not quite one veteran suicide a day.

Obviously, there is quite a disparity between veteran suicide of one per day versus twenty-two per day. So, which is it? Both studies approach the questions from different angles. On one hand, quibbling over which number is right is beside the point. Veterans still possess a suicide rate 50% higher than their civilian counterparts.[4] With recent attention on veteran suicide, hopefully there will be a more definitive study in the future. For now, we should hold loosely to

---

3. Han K. Kang et al., 'Suicide Risk Among 1.3 Million Veterans Who Were on Active Duty During the Iraq and Afghanistan Wars,' *Annals of Epidemiology* 25, no. 2 (February 2015): pp. 96-100, https://doi.org/10.1016/j.annepidem.2014.11.020.

4. Alan Zarembo, 'Detailed Study Confirms High Suicide Rate Among Recent Veterans,' Los Angeles Times (Los Angeles Times, January 14, 2015), https://www.latimes.com/nation/la-na-veteran-suicide-20150115-story.html.

the figure and simply recognize that whatever number we choose, it's too high.

Several studies in the last decade have researched the cause behind this. PTSD is the usual suspect at a popular level, but may not be to blame as much as we might think. In fact, as hard as it may be to hear, PTSD and combat experience appear to be poor predictors if someone will take his or her life.[5] Writing for the LA Times, Alan Zarembo notes, 'The rate was slightly higher among veterans who never deployed to Afghanistan or Iraq, suggesting that the causes extend beyond the trauma of war.' While his tone is guarded in the interpretation of the statistics, he's probably correct about where the causes behind suicide are *not*.

When we look at all the evidence, we see that the popular belief on veteran suicide is wrong. This is puzzling because the popular belief is essentially that after people see something horrific in combat, they get PTSD. PTSD leads to isolation and depression and, over time, might lead to suicide. Looking at the suicide rates of servicemembers more closely quickly shatters this popular belief, that combat is a primary cause of PTSD, which increases the risk of suicide.

For example, examining suicide rates in the Air Force raises more questions. To begin, we note that the Air Force is not a combat branch of the military like the Marines or Army. Their primary mission does not include ground fighting. There are exceptions, such as the Air Force's elite Special Forces, the Pararescue. But, by and large, most occupational roles and specialties are in supportive functions, not tanks,

---

5. At least two studies highlight this loose connection with PTSD and suicide as not being definitive. Jaimie L. Gradus, 'PTSD and Death from Suicide,' PTSD Research Quarterly 28, no. 4 (2017), www.ptsd.va.gov/publications/rq_docs/V28N4.pdf.
Holly C Wilcox, Carla L Storr, and Naomi Breslau, 'Posttraumatic Stress Disorder and Suicide Attempts in a Community Sample of Urban American Young Adults,' *Archives of General Psychiatry* 66, no. 3 (March 2009): pp. 305-311, https://doi.org/doi:10.1001/archgenpsychiatry.2008.557.

artillery, or infantry. Nevertheless, 78 active-duty airmen took their lives in 2019.[6] This statistic excludes reserves and veterans transitioned out of service. Before we seek further to unearth the causes, we must understand this: combat and PTSD are not the primary causes of suicide among veterans. Several studies indicate that PTSD is connected to combat and this, in turn, is connected to suicide.[7] But this does not account for most veteran suicides even though it is the widely accepted view that veteran suicide is a result of PTSD as it is derived from combat. So why are so many veterans taking their lives?

The Biggest Link Is Depression

The most common link to suicide, including that of veterans, is depression. *The National Institute for Mental Health* lists five reasons people are suicidal. They are: 1) depression, 2) substance abuse, 3) anxiety, 4) borderline personality disorder, and 5) psychosis.[8] The first three are common among veterans. Of course, this is just kicking the can down the road. The natural follow up question is, 'If they didn't see combat or have PTSD, why are they depressed?'

Depression is person variable. It pivots around each person's story and can be enhanced or diminished by things as little as lack of sunlight and an imbalanced diet.[9] But

6. Stephen Losey, 'With Deaths By Suicide Rising, Air Force Orders Resiliency Stand-Down,' Air Force Times (Air Force Times, August 2, 2019), https://www.airforcetimes.com/news/your-air-force/2019/08/01/with-deaths-by-suicide-rising-air-force-orders-resiliency-stand-down/?utm_expid=.jFR93cgdTFyMrWXdYEtvgA.0&utm_referrer=.

7. This single volume of thirty-eight articles on the topic of Veteran Suicide is the best single resource to follow this thread of evidence. Robert M. Bossarte, ed., Veteran Suicide: A Public Health Imperative (Washington,, DC: American Public Health Association, 2013).

8. 'Suicide in America: Frequently Asked Questions,' National Institute of Mental Health (U.S. Department of Health and Human Services), accessed March 2, 2020, https://www.nimh.nih.gov/health/publications/suicide-faq/index.shtml.

9. Writing for Christianity Today, points out the increasingly common link

the question posed here is this, 'What is common among veterans that leads to depression?' The answer to that, I hope you will see, is given in the other chapters' stories. Common to veterans are lack of community, loss of identity, loss of a friend, divorcing a spouse, losing rights to children, disconnect with peers upon exiting service, cultural barriers that prohibit veterans from connecting with others, substance abuse, etc. All these contribute to depression. All of them take different redirection and gospel application to each person's story. When answering the question, 'What causes veteran suicide?' depression is a helpful answer, but when we dig deeper, since the causes of depression vary innumerably, it doesn't move us closer to a satisfying answer.

At day's end, statistics are cold, disconnected, and at best raise good questions. The questions I hope you will ask veterans are best done in community, relationship, with empathy and patience, while ministering to them with your love, presence, and curiosity. It is *good* to see a doctor about depression. Medical assistance *can* help for items such as chemical imbalance. But where it falls short is with relationships. It may be that the reason we throw prescriptions at veterans is not so *they* can walk away, but so that *we* can. Don't do that. Press in. Use the previous chapters' stories as a foothold to understand veterans' stories, to provide categories to talk with them, and pursue relationships rooted in community and nourished by God.

Recognizing the Signs
Much has been made accessible on knowing and recognizing the warning signs for suicide. They include:[10]

---

between nutrition and depression for veterans: Paul Pastor, 'One Hamburger, Hold the Depression, Please,' CT Pastors (Leadership Journal, September 4, 2014), https://www.christianitytoday.com/pastors/2014/fall/one-hamburger-hold-depression-please.html.

10. 'Suicide Prevention - Mental Health,' Veterans Affairs (VA, September 3, 2008), https://www.mentalhealth.va.gov/suicide_prevention/.

201

- Hopelessness; feeling that there's no way out
- Anxiety, agitation, sleeplessness, or mood swings
- Feeling like there is no reason to live
- Rage or anger
- Engaging in risky activities without thinking
- Increasing alcohol or drug misuse
- Withdrawing from family and friends

These Signs Requires Immediate Attention:

- Thinking about hurting or killing yourself
- Looking for ways to kill yourself
- Talking about death, dying, or suicide
- Self-destructive behavior such as drug misuse, carelessly handling weapons, etc.

As a community, we can do better than simply be reactive to these signs. I have had a handful of veteran friends on Facebook who suddenly and unexpectedly, out the blue, posted on Facebook something like this, 'I'm so sick of this blankety-blank, I just want to end it all.' This, dear friends, is a cry for help indicating contemplation of suicide. The replies I've seen, though well-meant, fall woefully short of what we must do as a community. 'Hey, man, how are you doing? Give me a call.' 'Hey, knock that off. You're better than that.' 'Give me a call, brother.' More often than not, a call is made, a short catch-up conversation is had, and the count-down continues the moment the person hangs up until the next flirtation with suicide. Why? Because Facebook, for all its bells, whistles and blessings, has allowed us to erase the meaning of true community from our lives. While we distance ourselves from others and peer into each other's lives with overly sanitized versions of ourselves in a clean timeline, someone is in desperate need to be in a relationship, to have their story heard, to unpack what they are feeling, and to keep their life from spinning out of control. All that is to say, these warning signs above are helpful. But they reveal themselves only when a person has traveled the long distance of many months, perhaps years, toward the threshold of suicide. We can do better. We must do better. Instead of putting a band aid on someone's chest when heart surgery is needed, we must press into the long, taxing and uncomfortable process of loving that person.

Using the Recognition Signs

Many of us don't know what to do following a phone call with a person you just talked down from suicide. In our heads, we're calculating the cost of our time and relational capital it will take to help this person. What can we do when a person we love dearly reaches out for help or shows one or more of these signs? Below are several starting points.

HOW TO BEGIN TO HELP
Showing up

Never underestimate the power of being present. Some call this the 'ministry of presence.' Your presence and curiosity, driven by a love for people, can do an immeasurable amount of good, and it might even save a life. If you live near a struggling veteran, get together for a meal. Do something that gives you face and talk time. Going to a movie can be okay, but the lack of communication isn't as well spent as sharing a meal, where you can converse together in real time. If he or she works at a place you can pop in unannounced, do it. If such a person invites you to an important event in his or her life, go. How do you know if it's important to them? Here's an easy barometer: 1) Do they talk about it often? 2) Do they post it on social media? 3) Is it a major event like a birthday or wedding? The more you attend to that relationship, the more you will be given a window into their life through which you can minister to them. Of the nine men I knew who took their lives, only one was not alone. Suicide is typically a solitary act that is the epitaph of all areas of their lives. They were left alone. And we should never leave our friends behind or alone. We must tend to their wounds and include them in our lives.

Preprograming Phone Numbers
Having the suicide-prevention phone number in your phone and your friend's phone can be tremendously helpful. Take this a step further and make it personal, make a pact with your friend to be their '2am buddy.' Fully commit to giving them complete access to you by putting his number on the list of approved numbers that the 'Do Not Disturb' function will filter out. It also means that you give assurance to your friend that if he ever needs to talk, even if it's 2am, he can call. Take it yet one step further and make your friend promise you that if it's 2am, he isn't allowed to make any decisions that would drastically affect himself or others. Though our honor is sometimes misplaced and in need of being reshaped, we can invoke our honor behind this promise. Don't violate it. If that person does call, be patient with him. Always thank him for having the courage to call. Avoid the impression that you wanted to look like you cared but when it counted, you really didn't.

Listening Long
Remember Job? After he lost everything, his friends ministered to him. If you read his story in the Bible, you'll quickly learn that every time one of his friends tried to help, they ended up sticking their proverbial foot in their mouth. We are often at our best when we say nothing and listen to everything. The more we allow people to talk, the more we learn about them, grow in empathy for them, and learn the reasons behind a desire to commit suicide. Suicide is not a contracted disease. It is the misplaced solution to a long

series of defeats that we need to unpack. Listen. Close your mouth, and open your ears.

Asking Good Questions

Ask questions often and in varying ways. The reason Joe Rogan and Oprah Winfrey get paid the big bucks is because they can ask good questions! Here's a sample:

- What's going on? (This is always a great place to start)
- Why are you thinking about doing this?
- What needs to change?
- How can I help you?
- How have you been dealing with (sample problem) on your own?
- Is it working?
- Who in your life have you looked up to? Why?

If you don't know what to say, reassure them of your love for them. Asking good questions is like peeling back an onion. There will be layers of past-hurts, contributing circumstances, truths, self-told lies the person believes, and more. And you will need to be selective of what stories to follow. Your goal is to disrupt this self-destructive thinking and redirect that person to Christ. This may happen in a single, fifteen-minute conversation, or it may happen after fifteen fifty-minute conversations. Keep showing up, keep asking good questions. The more you do that, the more authentic your relationship with them will become and the more ready you will be to help them and point them to Christ.

If you are a friend or family member who does not share their military experiences, it is better to start before they joined the military. Their story is no doubt complex and, for those contemplating suicide, there is no way to understand their life story by merely asking, 'Why do you want to do this?' While that question can be helpful in a moment of crisis, for the on-going relationship with someone it is better to start at the beginning. These questions may help.

Getting to Know Veterans

- Why did you join the military?
- Did you have a friend or family member who joined?
- With whom did you serve?
- What was your job?
- Where were you stationed?
- Where were you deployed?
- What did you like about it?
- What did you not like about it?

These questions are a good starting place. They are the typical questions people ask that want to know more over a car-ride or sitting on an airplane, but they also just scratch the surface. They are like walking the perimeter around a grand cathedral. You may see the extent and bounds of a person's life, but until you've explored the archways, nooks, ruins, and monuments, you can't deeply know that person.

Going Deeper

- What was it like the first time you came home after boot camp?
- What did it feel like to see your old friends?
- What did your family say/do?
- What did daily life look like when you weren't deployed?
- What did it look like when you were deployed?
- What are some of the most memorable things about being in the military?

The brain is a funny thing, sometimes. While we have millions of memories stored, catalogued, and cross-referenced, sometimes an initial question, like 'What is your favorite memory?' comes up blank. It's like our mind is a ship that has built momentum and takes great force to slow it down and turn it toward a new heading. But once the memories are flowing, the details will spill over in abundance. If you ever have the privilege to be a fly on a wall while two military buddies share and swap stories, take it! You could learn more in an hour of listening *to* a person than you could in a week of reading *about* that person. No amount of posts on Facebook, no amount of threads on Twitter, can compete with the non-verbal cues and dialogue that happen in relationships. We are emotional, embodied beings who miss out on the richness of people's character and stories when we keep each other at arms-length.

What Not to Say or Assume

Don't assume that because people are veterans their difficulties in life or contemplation of suicide is a direct result of PTSD or combat experience. It may or may not be. But asking, 'Is this because of all the things you saw?' may inadvertently cause a veteran to invoke that haunt of honor and feel shame. The reality could be that they never had PTSD, but it's easier to say 'Yes,' because they feel more honor associated with it than admitting their marriage is a mess because of the 100-hour work weeks the military demands. Don't assume that because a person has PTSD it is because of combat. Though PTSD is over-diagnosed and over-filed for fraudulent disability requests, PTSD can happen for other reasons. For example, women in the military who have been raped have been traumatized and may suffer from PTSD.

Partnering with Outside Help

Sometimes, helping someone struggling with PTSD or suicidal thoughts will quickly move beyond our expertise.

I've included an appendix with some helpful ministries, non-profits, and resources to help guide the process of assisting someone. The mistake we can make, though, is to think that the experts will take care of the person and provide for them better than we ever could. That isn't entirely true. A counselor or psychologist does not have the relational capital, history, or time to be a friend to that person in the ways you can. Friendships and community can do wonders to heal the hearts of the wounded. Though most can appreciate the value of a good friendship, this is a distinctly Christian notion. Christ, who became a neighbor to us, who structures what community is to look like, and upholds friendships, is the reason these things are so notable and worthy. The gospel cannot be supplanted by counselor care. But we would be fools to think we can do nothing or that the counselor can do everything.

A RESPONSE

Suicide is permanent. It cannot be undone. Death cannot be rolled back. We cannot count on the person on the verge of suicide giving a second thought. There are no double takes, no do-overs. Prevention is the only way. We can help prevent suicide by casting down the unfulfilling idols of worship. We can press into the lack of community. We can grow superficial friendships deeper. We can help fill nights of depression with comfort and can minister to others through our presence, empathy, and listening. People ministering to someone contemplating suicide must bring the whole story of redemption, the full story of the gospel, and the fullness of Christ.

When responding to suicide, we impulsively look toward the creation of non-profits, ministries, and programs that specialize in dealing with PTSD, suicide, veterans, or all of the above. This is a double-edged sword. While it is often necessary to be equipped to deal with recognizing suicidal thoughts, and while it is good to have specialists who are competent in mental health, there are some complicating consequences. When a program is created for a particular niche group, for example, homeless people, there is a natural affinity among homeless people to open up only to fellow homeless people. When the goal is to help someone build up to integrate back into the rhythms of normal life and community, the artificial community of homeless people is more appealing. This says a lot about the human desire for community. The same is true of veterans. Veterans are often naturally more comfortable around other veterans. The shared experiences, language, and culture make for a good fit. This is great for a support group, but also creates the difficulty of assisting veterans back in their lives and community.

The previous chapters have attempted to help others grow in empathy for veterans, to expose veterans to the truth of Scripture, and to subvert the cultural idols we turn to for comfort. Thus, it is incumbent not only upon the specialists, government programs, the VA, or the individual to reach out to veterans. It is for every Christian believer on mission for God. In other words, it is the church's duty to care for those hurting, and the church is not composed of only one kind of person or specialty, but all kinds of people with varying experiences and specialties. The best response to suicide will be by the church, through a relationally driven model that listens long, ministers patiently, and pursues others lovingly and tenaciously. Our best responses will not be those that re-route veterans to programs or prescriptions while ignoring the relationships that should be built through the local body. Can programs, ministries and non-profits help? Yes. Do they help? Yes. Should that be the replacement for our primary outlet of community? No. The relational cost may be high to press into a relationship with a struggling veteran. But the cost for neglecting those relationships is greater.

16

POST-TRAUMATIC STRESS DISORDER

Post-Traumatic Stress Disorder (PTSD for short) has become a common buzz word in the last decade thanks to the greater awareness of its symptoms due to new research. It is also partly due to an increased number of movies and television shows highlighting characters who have been negatively affected by war and afflicted with PTSD. In any case, almost everyone has an idea, accurate or not, about PTSD. A simplified definition offered by the Mayo Clinic is:

> Post-traumatic stress disorder (PTSD) is a mental health condition that's triggered by a terrifying event—either from experiencing it or witnessing it. Symptoms may include flashbacks, nightmares and severe anxiety, as well as uncontrollable thoughts about the event.

A HISTORY OF TERMS

Though the definition of PTSD has been expanded and clarified in recent versions of the Diagnostics and Statistics Manual (DSM), the phenomenon is not new. The concept of PTSD is rooted in the related state of 'melancholia' used to describe soldiers in and around the time of the Civil War in the United States. This term probably better describes depression, but its association with a soldier's traumatic

211

experience of war links it with modern PTSD. Similarly, the term 'shell-shock' was coined to describe troops from World War I, easily disturbed by loud noises. Those noises were triggers associated with the shelling of indirect fire weapons in trench warfare. In World War II, the term used (incorrectly?) by troops in the south Pacific was 'Asiatic.' E. B. Sledge's memoir, *With the Old Breed*, paints a picture that the term 'Asiatic' was like 'shell-shocked,' mixed with an aloofness, or what we might call a numbness or a blunted affect-disconnected emotions.[1] It was also termed 'Combat Fatigue' or 'Combat Stress Reaction' during that war era.

The variety of these terms contains a common thread. All of these terms are tied to stressful and traumatic events in wartime. Because of the variety of historic terms and the close association of PTSD with the military, a variety of misconceptions have arisen. Here we aim to dispel misconceptions about PTSD and then answer the following questions:

- How do you get it?
- What does it do?
- How many veterans have it?
- How can we care for someone with PTSD?

MISCONCEPTIONS OF PTSD

We've all seen PTSD portrayed in movies. It's a normal day, and a man is seated on a park-bench in the middle of the city, while life moves around him. He's lost in his own thoughts,

---

1. 'Asiatic,' as Sledge describes in his memoir, did not denote things Asian (as you might find in a dictionary definition) but was used as a Marine Corps term to denote 'a singular type of eccentric behavior characteristic of men who had served too long in the Far East' (*E. B. Sledge, With the Old Breed: At Peleliu and Okinawa (New York, NY: Presidio Press, 2010), 34.*). Sledge uses the term to refer to unexpected, odd behavior, and under this umbrella he included items consistent with PTSD as we define it today.

pulling a sandwich from a lunch box for his meal. Suddenly, a nearby car backfires. The noise is startling, but not overly frightening. As people resume life after the brief scare, they see the man has taken cover under the park bench. Embarrassed, he discards his sandwich and leaves the area to avoid the lingering eyes. What just happened?

This kind of story has been told many times. It's what is most closely aligned with the idea of 'shell-shock.' Individuals facing indirect fire develop a survival routine that trains their fight-or-flight response. Taking cover was the routine for many in WW1 and for my peers mortared on their first deployment. Hearing a loud noise triggers that reflex. They hear the noise, and the bodily action they rehearsed hundreds of times, under fear, stress, and adrenaline pumping, instinctually takes charge. Thus, even when removed from the dangerous environment, they retain the protective behavior. Does that constitute PTSD? The answer is not that simple.

As PTSD has been studied, the criteria for diagnosis have expanded and become better articulated. When I returned home from my first deployment, for a couple of weeks I woke up delirious and confused about where I was. I found myself in a panic looking for my rifle—and looking in odd places. The first night away from base I stayed in a hotel in Palm Springs. When I woke up in this half-awake state, I groggily searched for my rifle under the bed and in the shower. I opened the door to the hallway and glanced around there as well. It was only after I went back to the bathroom, splashed water on my face, and began to wake up completely that I realized I was in some sort of half-sleep operating on muscle memory from my previous environment. For seven months, my M249 SAW (Squad Automatic Weapon) never once had been more than 20 feet from me, and most of that time, my hands were firmly clasped on it. In my first week in Iraq, my squad leader yelled at me while on patrol because I rested my SAW on one of the 500 round drums attached to my flak jacket causing me to take my right hand off the pistol grip of my weapon. His fierce reprimand fixed that mistake, and I never took my hand off it again during patrols for the rest of the time in Iraq.

Though many can identify with such an experience, this is not an example of PTSD. It is common among deployed veterans, is often mistaken for PTSD, but it is not PTSD. It is related to operation fatigue, and though akin to PTSD, it lacks a traumatic experience. Below is a summary of the criteria for PTSD:

Criterion A: Stressor (at least one of the following)
The person was exposed to: death, threatened death, actual or threatened serious injury, or actual or threatened sexual violence, in the following way(s):

- Direct exposure
- Witnessing a trauma
- Learning that a relative or close friend was exposed to a trauma
- Indirect exposure to aversive details of a trauma, usually in the course of professional duties (e.g., first responders, medics)

Criterion B: Intrusion Symptoms
The traumatic event is persistently re-experienced in the following way(s):

- Unwanted upsetting memories
- Nightmares
- Flashbacks
- Emotional distress after exposure to traumatic reminders
- Physical reactivity after exposure to traumatic reminders

Criterion C: Avoidance
Avoidance of trauma-related stimuli after the trauma, including:

- Trauma-related thoughts or feelings
- Trauma-related external reminders

Criterion D: Negative Alterations in Cognitions and Mood (two required)
Negative thoughts or feelings that began or worsened after the trauma, in the following way(s):

- Inability to recall key features of the trauma
- Overly negative thoughts and assumptions about oneself or the world
- Exaggerated blame of self or others for causing the trauma
- Decreased interest in activities
- Feeling isolated

Criterion E: Alterations in Arousal and Reactivity
Trauma-related arousal and reactivity that began or worsened after the trauma, in the following way(s):

- Irritability or aggression
- Risky or destructive behavior
- Hyper-vigilance
- Heightened startled reaction
- Difficulty concentrating
- Difficulty sleeping

Criterion F: Duration
Symptoms last for more than 1 month.

Criterion G: Functional Significance
Symptoms create distress or functional impairment (e.g., social, occupational).

Criterion H: Exclusion [2]
Symptoms are not due to medication, substance use, or other illness.

Many, if not most, of my peers have met several of the criteria, but do not have PTSD. My sleep was very chaotic the first year back from deployment. When I slept, besides the nights of confusion of looking for my weapon, I had frequent bouts of a stress-induced sleep apnea, where my wife would wake me up because she noticed I would stop breathing. Since leaving service, I have not had this. I have seen a traumatic event—the Marine at COP Viking which triggered many emotions due to its similarities with Seth's death by friendly fire. Though these were obviously negative experiences, and though one event triggered a lot of emotion about the other, it still doesn't quite qualify as PTSD. When I was evaluated, I was diagnosed as 'sub-threshold;' an evaluation I feel is accurate. What I have found to be the key factor that tends to push someone to true PTSD is flashbacks. If it were not for flashbacks, I and thousands of other veterans could say they have PTSD.

- A traumatic event? Check.
- Irritability or trouble sleeping? Check.
- Negative thoughts and feelings of isolation? Check.
- But flashbacks? Not so much.

---

2. Diagnostic and Statistical Manual of Mental Disorders: DSM-5 (Arlington, VA: American Psychiatric Association, 2017).

Flashbacks are not merely remembering something about a traumatic event. They are not simply seeing something that reminds you of that traumatic event. Flashbacks are more intense and more upsetting than simply recalling something to mind. The best way I could describe it would be like having the inability to push the pause button on it, the inability to stop thinking about the memory conjured. Many can relate to buying a new gaming system and putting in that new video game. You spend hours playing the same racing game. Those hours seem to make an etch in your mind so that when you close your eyes after all that playing, you see the same car being raced. Without being able to help it, it's like your mind defaults to a screensaver of the image or images that replay again and again. With video games it isn't that bad. It could be interesting, or it could be annoying. But with a traumatic experience, replaying unwanted images again and again is torture.

One fellow Marine experienced PTSD most sharply in his sleep or when near sleep. Like me, he would awake delirious about his environment. But I did not share what he would do. The images of his dying friend flashed before his eyes uncontrollably. While awake, he could suppress these images. But every night, when he entered that half-asleep, half-awake state, images of his traumatic event would play, and his muscle memory kicked in. He described to me the vicious cycle this created. The more he would have a flashback, the more it became a habit for his body, and it became ingrained into his routine. His nightly hauntings began to haunt his day. He began spending more of his days thinking about the night before and dreading the night ahead. The more he thought about it, the more it happened. The very thing he needed a respite from had accelerated itself.

I've heard of this sort of occurrence happening with people who experience irregular heart palpitations for the first time. They had never felt their heart skip a beat that causes shortness of breath. Such a thing doesn't necessarily mean bad news or the onset of heart problems. It could simply happen because they are dehydrated. But, having the irregular heart palpitation can lead to an ill-advised Google search which will yield a variety of deadly diseases. If people are convinced that they have a bad heart, the stress of this news (even if untrue) causes more palpitations. Although a skipped heartbeat is different than PTSD, this analogy demonstrates how PTSD can regress into a kind of trigger cycle that's difficult to disrupt.

The one time I stood duty with this marine in the Barracks, he warned me before taking a nap on the couch in the duty hut, 'If I wake up screaming and walking around, just sit me down and wake me up completely—and don't freak out.' For him the nightly triggers reinforced a cycle of creating a new habit of deepening his PTSD. For him, it helped to count ceiling tiles. Doing this thing would help 'ground' him, allowing him to use the opposite side of the brain to shatter the feeling that his half-dream was real. After a few moments of being oriented to his surroundings the feeling of being in the environment of the original traumatic event would melt.

By no means is this story the norm. But hopefully it is illustrative in contrast to my own of why I do not have PTSD, and he did. But what is the norm? What are those misconceptions that complicate our understanding about this?

Ten Myths about PTSD
1. *Only People in the Military Can Have PTSD.*
This myth is born out of the close association the military has with PTSD. In a similar vein, sometimes it's believed that only the traumatic experience of seeing someone shot warrants the diagnosis of PTSD. This is not true. Some of the most often overlooked and underreported victims of PTSD are rape victims. Because of the difficulties in the tedious process of reporting a rape, including the shame that stigmatizes victims, it is highly underreported. Yet the trauma of being sexually

exploited by someone overpowering you is extreme. The triggers may be different than someone who has PTSD from being blown up by an IED, but it's still PTSD nevertheless. The triggers may not be loud noises, but instead realized through the sense of touch of their attacker's gender.

During a PTSD awareness training hosted by the Veteran's Administration, our instructor told stories of two female veteran victims of rape. For one victim, the trigger was the smell of the after-shave of her assaulter. The other one was raped in a laundromat. The sounds of the machines, the smell of laundry detergent and fabric softener, were all equal triggers to relive the event. One complication of these triggers was that she, perhaps as a defense mechanism, remained extremely unkempt. Her clothes were almost always bought new, then worn until filthy, and then discarded. She gained a great deal of weight in order to mar her own appearance. She didn't want to be an attractive woman victimized again, but someone no man would want. As you can imagine, this can bring a host of peripheral complications. What we might see as the problem (obesity, for example) is the defense the person mounts to prevent experiencing trauma.

Those two triggers are different than those from seeing someone die. And yet the trauma these victims experienced is similar to the veteran plagued by nightmares of a different sort. It is important for pastors, chaplains, counselors, friends and the family of the veteran not to project a false shame on the victim. A faux shame would be to think of their PTSD as second-tier because they didn't see combat. Such shame invokes a haunt of honor that can take years to dismantle.

2. PTSD Only Affects Those Who Have Seen Combat.

This myth is related to the first. Since PTSD is tied to any type of trauma, not just combat, many with PTSD have never seen combat. Dispelling this myth raises some questions and concerns. If veterans have PTSD, but didn't see combat, why do they have PTSD? And flowing from this, what counts as a traumatic experience? These questions are difficult to answer, and need complicated answers. Part of the complexity is due to a shameful segment of military culture that has bought into a kind of entitlement.

Falsifying PTSD
While I was in my transitioning and assistance class coming off active duty, the retired Navy Officer encouraged veterans to continually apply for disability until they were at 100%. He described this as something that was 'earned' by the veterans. Without directly saying this, he also encouraged us to file for PTSD disability so we could receive a 50% rating and get free money from the government for the rest of our lives. This experience is not an isolated event, but a shameful trend that has unfortunately penetrated our military culture. Veterans, or anyone, should feel shame for falsifying claims for disability to receive free monetary assistance. The defense mechanism that is used to justify this is located in a distorted view of sacrificial service. The complication of PTSD for those who haven't seen combat is often found here, in veterans taking advantage of the fact that PTSD isn't necessarily tied to combat. They create a fictional story or exaggerate difficult parts of military life so they can capitalize on their experience for monetary gain. To further complicate the situation, rape in the U.S. military is a problem. The rape victims, usually women, don't report the rape. And because they don't report, they don't get the help they need. Meanwhile many who claim PTSD do not actually have it and then absorb the time and resources needed for others who do. Sebastian Junger observes this phenomenon in his book, *Tribe,* writing:

> [D]ecade after decade and war after war, American combat deaths have generally dropped while disability claims have risen. Most disability claims are for medical issues and should decline with casualty rates and combat intensity,

but they don't. They are in an almost inverse relationship with one another. Soldiers in Vietnam suffered one-quarter the mortality rate of troops in World War II, for example, but filed for both physical and psychological disability compensation at a rate that was 50 percent higher. It's tempting to attribute that to the toxic reception they had at home, but that doesn't seem to be the case. Today's vets claim three times the number of disabilities that Vietnam vets did, despite a generally warm reception back home and casualty rate that, thank God, is roughly one-third what it was in Vietnam. Today, most disability claims are for hearing loss, tinnitus and PTSD—the latter two of which can be imagined, exaggerated, or even faked. … Self-reporting of PTSD by veterans has been found to lead to a misdiagnosis rate as high as 50 percent. A recent investigation by the VA Office of the Inspector General found that the higher a veteran's PTSD disability rating, the more treatment he or she tends to seek until achieving a rate of 100 percent, at which point treatment visits plummet and many quit completely. (A 100 percent disability rating entitles a veteran to a tax-free income of around $3,000 a month.)[3]

Upon return from my first deployment I remember my company commander very clearly stating, 'No one owes you a damn thing.' He's right. If what was accomplished in carrying out faithful service was part of our duty, then there is no entitlement to money from a falsified report of PTSD. It will take time to redeem this portion of military culture, but it can be done if veterans hold each other accountable to the truth.

All this should not be understood, however, to think that PTSD has no bearing on veteran suicide, either. While the causes of veteran suicide most assuredly are not because of combat and PTSD, PTSD is still commonly linked to a high contributed factor of veteran suicides who have seen combat.

---

3. Sebastian Junger, *Tribe: On Homecoming and Belonging* (New York, NY: Hatchet Book Group, 2017), 87-89.

3. *PTSD Is a Result of a Lack of Resilience*

The Army and Marine Corps, in particular, have made 'resiliency' the focus for avoiding suicide. The title of the Army's training is dubbed 'Master of Resilience Training.' Though training tends to change in light of new data, the big idea continually pushed is that the training helps soldiers grow in resilience and strength to avoid succumbing to the unseen wounds of war.

An Army chaplain I knew informed me they were taught the reason young men take their lives is because their lower emotional intelligence doesn't allow them to have a high resiliency against the plight of PTSD, depression and so forth. The impulse behind desiring troops to be tough and hard isn't a bad one. But it is misplaced to say that if someone struggles coping with a traumatic experience, they lack resiliency. Perhaps inadvertently the military has associated its desire for resilience with something honorable, and lack of it as something dishonorable and shameful. Sometimes this desire is expressed among our own rather cruelly. A television show about the veteran experience called VET TV, known for its tagline, 'Raw, Dark, Military Humor' has highlighted the reality that often while persons are on suicide watch, they've been encouraged to take their own life. Because this veteran experience is the reality for many, it's painted in a positive and humorous light for insiders of this culture. The truth, however, is that at best this faux humor is a distortion of everything military culture stands for. Calling someone a 'weak b#$*h' because they are struggling with depression, symptoms of PTSD or otherwise is an overreaction to a culture at large that desires to create safe places for everything under the sun. At worst, it creates shame barriers for anyone truly struggling with PTSD to seek help. Who wants to be labeled as weak?

4. PTSD Is Only a Risk Immediately after the Traumatic Event

It is true that symptoms of PTSD may be the strongest near the time of the event, but this does not eliminate the risk of PTSD later in life. I can recall our Battalion Commander speaking with our company about a reunion event of Vietnam vets he had just attended. Some of the men broke down into tears and shudders recalling details of watching a friend die. The intensity of the recall was not merely a bad memory, but more like re-living the trauma. The risk of PTSD can follow people the rest of their lives. Indeed, it is an injury (see number 8), but it's not one that is worn in the same fashion. While some experience great healing after a trauma, there can still be a limp for many years similar to a flare up of an old injury. I've heard it described that PTSD never goes away, but it can go to sleep. Some triggers or memories wake it up. Everyone handles trauma differently. When someone says, 'No, I don't struggle with that,' it doesn't mean they are lying or putting on a tough guy façade. Relationships and listening to someone's story go further and deeper than allowing ourselves to be misled by wrong assumptions about PTSD.

5. If You Experience a Trauma, You Will Get PTSD

In the God-given capacity and complexity of our being, some were made with a greater ability to process, handle, and work through trauma. Some people could see hundreds die, and never experience PTSD, and someone else sees a single person die, and he's haunted for the rest of his life. It's similar to how some people see blood, and it doesn't faze them, while others see their own blood and faint. You might as well ask the question, 'Why are people different?' Without a doubt, some things can be more traumatizing to a child who hasn't developed the categories to think about death and dying than to an adult. By why is it two adults, with similar personalities, backgrounds, and upbringings can have the same occupation and experience the same traumatic event, and one walks away unfazed and the other scarred? Psychologists and sociologists have pursued that answer for years. I don't think an answer to that will be as helpful as simply arming oneself with the information: 1) being exposed to trauma won't necessarily traumatize you and 2) different people experience and process things differently. You don't have to understand why or why not, but rather, you need to empathize with someone who is struggling and not force guilt on someone who isn't.

6. *Those with PTSD Are Prone to Violent Behavior*

I wonder if this myth is due to the movie depictions of troops with PTSD. The muscle memory engrained through combat training fosters the belief that if people were soldiers and have PTSD, they will act out in violence, perhaps unknowingly, while in the midst of an episode. There's no way to predict how everyone will react to PTSD. It may seem too individualized, but PTSD is expressed in individuals. There's a scene in the movie *Saving Private Ryan* where Private Ryan, played by Matt Damon, has lost all his composure during the final battle. In the midst of the fight, he is curled up and screaming in fear like a child. The battle, at that point, was overwhelming. Death, destruction, dismay, sensory overload, it was all more than anyone was ever intended to handle. That might be the very way someone reacts to PTSD, curling up and weeping. It isn't necessarily going to manifest itself as violent behavior. The fight or flight response often results in flight. Because many withdraw and retreat after an episode of PTSD; and because there is often a shame associated with this, many never get the help they need. To assume someone may be given to violence, though, is a sweeping and false generalization.

7. *If You Have PTSD, You Can No Longer Be Productive*

I don't know why this belief circulates around PTSD, but it does. In some instances, it seems to be a myth born out of number 6. Unfortunately, this myth can also be traced to falsified disability claims that PTSD makes people unemployable. If people exaggerated their reported symptoms to be able to claim they have PTSD, they can ensure they receive disability payments by never being employed again. In order to defend their supposed unemployability, they point to PTSD as the culprit. There are many problems with this situation. It burdens our system and crowds-out others from employment who legitimately suffer from PTSD. It also creates an entitlement community of veterans who are insulated from critique about their welfare status. Unfortunately, the veteran card can be played to shield them from others who see a grown man playing video games all day claiming PTSD. 'You wouldn't understand; you're not a veteran.' This abuse of veteran status doesn't help veterans; it hurts them. There are many ways veterans with PTSD can remain productive people and contribute to society.

One such way is in the local body of a church. The church has a unique mission that uses all people of all backgrounds, gifting, and abilities under one calling to know Christ. Thus, Christians must reach those veterans who are isolated in their PTSD and those hiding under a false disability claim.

8. *PTSD Is Not a Wound*

PTSD is not like a gunshot wound. Such a wound has a clear path to healing. Apply pressure, stop the bleeding, extract the bullet and fragments, disinfect, close the wound, and allow the body to heal. PTSD is a wound of a person's mind that experiences a wide array of different emotions and responses. It can be compared to people who have issues in their marriage and seek counseling. Getting at the core of why someone is passive aggressive when they encounter conflict is not easy. To pinpoint this reflex, the counselor may use a family mapping tool called a genogram. The genogram can help locate trends and patterns of behavior that were modeled for this individual. Once located, which could take many hours of counseling, there are still many emotions and behaviors to investigate in order to arrive at a solution. The reason why someone may be passive aggressive and avoid direct conflict could be related to the way their father modeled conflict. Perhaps they experienced a divorce, and in this second marriage, they found themselves content to avoid conflict in order to maintain peace in the relationship. But, because humans are humans, emotions like dissatisfaction and resentment manifest themselves, and come out passive aggressively. The cycle continues as their behavior models for their children how to deal with conflict.

Counseling like this is not an easy process. A surgeon can take his skilled hand to a scalpel and make a significant difference in a person's life in a matter of hours. Counseling, something we should de-stigmatize and from which we could all benefit, is a process that is more akin to watching grass grow. PTSD is a complex wound of the mind, emotions, and the heart which requires greater time and patience to treat than a physical injury, because it's not immediately seen.

9. *Everyone with PTSD Experiences the Same Thing*
At this point you may observe a trend in these myths that already dispels this one. Because PTSD is caused by different experiences, it manifests itself differently for each patient. The trigger for a rape victim might be the touch of a male stranger. The trigger for a war-veteran might be fireworks on the fourth of July. These triggers are drastically different and may only be observed in a handful of contexts, or many contexts. It all depends. The thread of continuity to keep in mind when caring for those with PTSD is that we must enter into a person's story and get to know them without falsely assuming and projecting a preconception of PTSD onto them.

10. *Nothing Can Be Done for PTSD*
This myth is an easy cop-out, perhaps from complacency or a lack of compassion. It may be true that most people are unequipped or lack the knowledge of how to treat PTSD. It may also be true patients are unwilling to process or work through their issues at a given time. But to say 'Nothing can be done' is patently false. What can be done for veterans is listed in more detail below.

SYMPTOMS OF PTSD
The symptoms of PTSD vary in degree, number, and intensity, but some of the commonly observed symptoms are as follows:[4]

Re-experiencing Symptoms:

- Flashbacks—reliving the trauma over and over, including physical symptoms like a racing heart or sweating
- Bad dreams
- Frightening thoughts

Re-experiencing symptoms may cause problems in a person's everyday routine. They can start from their own thoughts and feelings. Words, objects, or situations that are reminders of the event can also trigger re-experiencing symptoms.

Avoidance Symptoms:

- Staying away from places, events, or objects that are reminders of the experience
- Avoiding thoughts or feelings related to the traumatic event

---

4. 'Posttraumatic Stress Disorder (PTSD),' Anxiety and Depression Association of America, ADAA, accessed March 2, 2020, https://adaa.org/understanding-anxiety/posttraumatic-stress-disorder-ptsd.

Things or situations that remind a person of the traumatic event can trigger avoidance symptoms. These symptoms may cause a person to change his or her personal routine. For example, after a bad car accident, a person who usually drives may avoid driving or riding in a car.

Arousal and Reactivity Symptoms:

- Being easily startled
- Feeling tense or 'on edge'
- Having difficulty sleeping, and/or having angry outbursts

Arousal symptoms are usually constant, instead of being triggered by something that brings back memories of the traumatic event. They can make the person feel stressed and angry. These symptoms may make it hard to do daily tasks, such as sleeping, eating, or concentrating.

Cognition and Mood Symptoms:

- Trouble remembering key features of the traumatic event
- Negative thoughts about oneself or the world
- Distorted feelings like guilt or blame
- Loss of interest in enjoyable activities

Cognition and mood symptoms can begin or worsen after the traumatic event. These symptoms can make the person feel alienated or detached from friends or family members.

How Many Veterans Have It?
Determining how many veterans have PTSD is very difficult. One way that this is determined is by the number

of veterans who received healthcare through the Veterans Administration clinics and hospitals. One set of statistics breaks down the numbers according to conflicts the U.S. has been involved in:[5]

- About 11 to 20 out of every 100 veterans (or between 11 and 20%) who served in operations Iraqi Freedom and Enduring Freedom have PTSD in a given year.
- About 12 out of every 100 Gulf War Veterans (or 12%) have PTSD in a given year.
- About 15 out of every 100 Vietnam veterans (15%) were currently diagnosed with PTSD when the most recent study of them (the National Vietnam Veteran Readjustment Study) was conducted in the late 1980s. It's believed that 30% of Vietnam veterans have had PTSD in their lifetime.

Interpretation of these stats presents challenges. Anecdotally, when I've spoken with veterans from the Korean War and Vietnam, they have voiced their exasperation and perhaps even disdain for the number of recent suicides. Part of this was rooted in generational shaming, that is, assuming their own generation was more resilient than its successors. When they are confronted with the fact that suicide rates seem to show more veterans are committing suicide that are not from recent conflicts, the statistics are suddenly reinterpreted. 'Well, WW2 was a much more difficult conflict that saw more death and dying than these recent ones in Iraq and Afghanistan.' This kind of bias should give us pause before we assume too much about one generation of war-fighters to the next.

---

5. Elaine K Howley, 'Statistics on PTSD in Veterans,' U.S. News & World Report (U.S. News & World Report, June 28, 2019), https://health.usnews.com/conditions/mental-health/ptsd/articles/ptsd-veterans-statistics.

My own position is to stick with what is safe: 12-20% of American veterans have PTSD. It's not helpful to infer why one is higher than the other. What is important to bear in mind is that everyone has a story, and someone may still need help in unpacking their story behind PTSD.

How Can We Care for Someone with PTSD?

How does anyone begin to get to know anyone? By starting at the very beginning. This is, after all, a very good place to start. Let's assume, for a moment, that you are not a mental health professional but that you care about the issues facing veterans today. There are two extremes which must be avoided when it comes to caring for those with PTSD. The first is outsourcing it completely to mental health professionals. The second is to think mental health professionals have nothing to offer. The answer is not a balance between these two, but rather, a tension. It requires discernment to decide within your context of ministering to veterans what is best for each person. Should you refer her to counseling? Are his issues at a level that is too much for you to handle? You must go before the Lord and others to make a final decision.

Identify Triggers

A trigger is something that activates the symptoms of and expression of PTSD. Our memories are complex, and often associate events with our senses. We are familiar with how this works. When adults smell a crayon, it can usher them back to kindergarten or primary school. I had a seminary professor who was reminded of his home in Australia by the scent of eucalyptus. Memories and our senses act like searching tags on a document. Without us actively attempting to search the recesses of our mind, the complexity of the brain begins an instantaneous search of our memories, cross-referencing, cross-checking, and making new search tags and memories for future reference. We've all experienced it with the mundane, the desirable, and for those suffering with PTSD, the undesirable.

I'm not suggesting something as clunky as asking a veteran, 'Hey, what triggers you?' A counselor, in a more tactful tone, may ask that, but I wouldn't suggest leading with that. I would suggest laying the foundation of a trusting relationship by, at least, learning each other's back-story and then taking the plunge into sharing something more specific. For example: we might ask, 'Could you tell me about when you experience PTSD?' This list may be helpful in looking for a trigger. The trigger could be:

- A scent
- A sight
- A loud noise
- A situation

What Do You Do with the Trigger?
In part, it may be easy to avoid triggers of PTSD. For some veterans, they never attend events where fireworks are shot off, like the 4th of July. Some things may not be so easy, like large crowds. Crowds are found in most routine places, such as the post office, the DMV, and grocery stores. Perhaps it is advisable to avoid the trigger, but where it is unavoidable, it is wise to seek professional counsel. They will help devise a plan to work through the triggers. The degree in intensity varies from person to person. This reinforces the need to enter into the person's story.

When I returned home from Iraq, I remember the feeling of panic when I saw trash on the side of the road. This had nothing to do with cleanliness, and everything to do with camouflaging IEDs. For seven months, every other three days I would patrol the streets and villages of Iraq. My training taught me to look for anything alongside the road that could be used to disguise IEDs with simple trash. The dreadful part is that Iraq is a very littered country. We take trash disposal for granted in the West. The first few weeks on patrol in Iraq were mentally exhausting. All of us were trying to memorize every nook, crevice, and detail of the town we occupied. And the trash? The trash was everywhere. So, when I returned home to America, I was relieved by the lack of trash on the side of the road. And then suddenly, I would be driving, and I would see a bag or something lying in the ditch, and I would inadvertently by muscle memory swerve and brake. Trash became a trigger. Technically, this lasted longer than thirty days, but by no means would I apply for disability for an issue I worked through and no longer experienced as I did in those first few months home.

If you're a friend of a veteran, learning their triggers can help you care for them. You wouldn't invite them to an event that would make them uncomfortable. At the same time, you wouldn't abandon them to live a life of solitude. Learning the triggers of your friend is an act of love. And for veterans, it takes risk and a redemptive vulnerability, both to let someone in so they can become known, and to allow others to shield you from what might cause you to be withdrawn.

Identify Coping Mechanisms

Equally important is being able to know what sources of comfort veterans turn to when they've been triggered and when, in general, they are seeking satisfaction. A coping mechanism is simply what someone does to deal with their issues. As humans, we often seek comfort, even at great cost. In the moment of pain, we want it to be gone. When it's not the kind of pain you experience from burning your hand, for example, but a pain from the weight of emotions, failure and so forth, we tend to go to one or more of the following: sexual gratification, alcohol, painkillers, food, or the affirmation of others. Have you ever sent, or been sent a text you normally would not, to a person while under the influence of alcohol?

I suspect this has less to do with the substance of alcohol, and more to do with our wounded hearts that seek the comfort of others' words and recognition.

In any case, being able to put a plan into place is critical. Removing substances that you have abused from your residence is a good first step. There is no reason to keep the thirty extra pain pills from having a tooth pulled. Simply remove those items that might be abused. If the person is known for abusing alcohol, remove it, lock it up, or do something that will keep that person from seeking out the false comfort it brings. The ease and access of pornography on our computers and mobile devices is not just something that should be avoided in its excess, like food, but something that should be purged from our midst entirely. I use a software called Covenant Eyes which sends reports to an accountability partner about my internet usage and browsing history. Studies show that people who use pornography have decreased satisfaction. And when it is introduced into marriages, it leads to increased problems and dissatisfaction there, too.[6] Flee from it. Avoid it. Have an honest self-assessment, or, if you're the friend of the veteran, an honest conversation about the places they turn when they are feeling low, beaten, and defeated. Formulate the plan so that it is actionable and not merely abstract.[7]

Friends and Family

'A true friend sticks closer than a brother.' A good friend is one who is there for you, even when it's inconvenient and difficult for him or her. That's the kind of friend you want—the available at 2 am buddy. A true friend will be able to look you in the eye, let you know you messed up, and confront you

---

6. D. Zillmann, 'Pornografie,' in R. Mangold, P. Vordere, and G. Bente, eds., *Lehrbuch der Medienpsychologie* (Gottingen, Germany: Hogrefe Verlag, 2004), 565-585.

7. See the Appendix for a sample support plan.

to change something. You know they won't love you any less even if you continually fail them. Friends and family are the first line of defense not only to help veterans struggling with PTSD, but also those facing bouts of depression and suicidal thoughts.

Professional Help

Seeking professional help through counseling should not be considered only as a last resort. Because of the stigma around the idea of someone laying on a couch being asked by an overpaid psychiatrist, 'How does that make you feel?,' we have a cultural doubt of a semi-pretentious occupation that only caters to the weak while lining practitioners' pockets with money. Perhaps there is some truth to this stereotype, but my own experience, and for friends who sought counseling, this is not the case. My wife and I received counseling during seminary and benefited greatly from it. It helped strengthen our marriage, identify places of weakness, patterns of unhelpful behavior, and more. We should never prioritize our pride ahead of our desire to see someone struggling with PTSD (including ourselves!) to get help. There are a variety of ministries, non-profits and networks of counselors that can help. On the extreme end, we should not depend upon the professionals at the neglect of our everyday relationships. The two aren't antithetical to each other, but partners.

De-deifying Troops with PTSD

This could be stated in a variety of ways, but putting troops up on a pedestal for the injury of PTSD isn't helpful. Don't read what I'm not saying. I'm not advocating disrespect or apathy toward veterans. Rather, I'm suggesting that we don't fawn over them if they have PTSD, assuming this will help them. It won't. It won't help their symptoms of PTSD, nor processing the complex emotions, memories, and triggers that come with the territory. Occasionally I'll be asked, 'Did you see a lot of action over there?' What they're looking for is a violent, shoot 'em up, story. Not everyone has a Black Hawk Down story, and that's okay. Veterans should dare to be boring and keep their honor clean. There is more honor in showing up faithfully for duty, standing at the ready, guarding that plot of ground and never being attacked than there is in letting someone believe a lie about you. Typically, my response to someone hankering for a combat story is, 'I don't want to talk about it.' I have no desire to talk to a person who wants something I'm unwilling to give them. I'm disgusted by the thought that a stranger could have a distorted appetite to potentially hear about a friend dying. Why would anyone want to open up like that? One of my former squad leaders would shamelessly turn the question back on them, 'Hey, how about you telling me about the most difficult time of your life?' When I have declined to indulge this, it has surprisingly, though not often, been met with, 'That means you saw something terrible.' And then I see the wheels spinning in their head as they try to envision what that might be.

CONCLUSION

It is unhelpful to assume that if someone has PTSD, it's because they 'saw something.' You don't know that. You couldn't know that. It's better for the information to come out in a relationship rather than a request as if we have entitlement to that story. We don't deserve to hear everyone's story. We aren't privy to it unless they let us in. It's equally unhelpful to assume that if someone has PTSD that this is something 'awesome' because they "saw some action.' Why would this ever be desirable? I submit that it's because some want the status of being a veteran without paying the price. Don't treat veterans as though they are gods. Treat them as humans. Truth be told, I don't particularly like the attention given to me on Veteran's Day. This isn't some kind of selflessness of pride paradoxically born out of humility. It's the fact that

I don't need a free meal at a restaurant to experience veteran status. I would rather have the stories and friendships with my brothers as my keep.

I don't need PTSD to feel better about my experience. I don't need others to think that I have PTSD or some riveting story behind it to validate anything. The same should be said for more of us. Any fawning over a hypothetical PTSD story keeps the veteran at a distance and deifies them as an object to be examined rather than a relationship which requires giving and receiving. You want to know how to approach a veteran? Do it as a human. Do it as a person. It is commonplace to thank someone for their service. Many mean well by this, but it's often superficial. Don't settle for thanking someone. Press beyond this, go deeper and use it as the onramp to get to know someone beyond their veteran status. Being known is a yearning of every human heart in the grand narrative that holds all stories together. We want to locate our meaning, know others, and become known. And ultimately, that deep yearning is to know God in this life and come to the privilege to be known by Christ, our Warrior-Redeemer.

17

NAVIGATING THE FIGHT

Land Navigation (Land Nav) requires a certain set of skills. In SOI (the School of Infantry), basic training with Land Nav begins with a compass and a map. Although we might think this would be enough to find most places, it is not. Navigating the variably elevated terrain, obstacles blocking the most direct path, straining weather conditions, and even the mundane details of our pace count and stride length affect the ability for people to find their way.

NAVIGATING THE LAND

Above all other challenges, there is one which renders the compass useless. Metal. Every good compass points North, well, magnetic North. But aren't they the same? What must be quickly mastered is the difference between magnetic north and true north. True north points toward the star, Polaris, which centers itself directly on the axis on which the earth spins. As it appears, it does not move and is consistent and objective in its location. A compass, though, cannot point toward a star. Thus, magnetic north provides a good estimate in which direction is north, but the problem is magnetic north *can change*. Depending on where one is on the globe, true north and magnetic north may not meet up at all. In fact, there are only a few places that they do, and even this isn't consistent.

Magnetic north, north of Greenland but south of the North Pole, actually moves around. Not only has it moved around, but sometimes its movement is sudden and unexpected. In order to compensate for this discrepancy, a simple mathematical calculation can be made by determining what is called a 'declination.' A declination refers to the difference between magnetic and true north. Any map worth its salt will have a correction near the compass rose that enables those navigating to know how many degrees to offset their reading of the compass, whether to add or subtract degrees from each reading.

Finding the declination is a big deal, but it's not the whole scope of Land Nav. Even with an objective, fixed polarity, the circumstances on the ground are greatly shaped by what the individual is experiencing. As much as one would like to simply draw a line between points *a* and *b* as the shortest and quickest possible route, it doesn't always work that way. Actually, it *never* works that way. The best route will have to account for the terrain, unforeseen obstacles, if there is a river that needs to be crossed, and so forth. So, when people plot their course, they may have an objective destination in mind, but the course they take may be very difficult and off-track.

NAVIGATING THE CHRISTIAN LIFE

Land Nav is not really very different from the Christian life. There is an objective goal for which we aim. God is unchanging and unmoving in character, but life isn't as simple as saying, 'I'm a Christian; don't I get a free pass to the destination?' No, sorry, it doesn't work that way. What is true for Land Nav is also true for the fight of faith—sin gets in the way. The magnetic correction for true north helps make a correct plot of the course, but without accounting for the metal in one's rifle, if the plotter is standing near a vehicle, telephone lines, and so on, the destination can stay 100% correct but the intermittent checks to see if the person is on course can be thrown off again and again.

In the Christian life, God is the objective, unchanging true north. We might describe the general awareness of God's presence as the magnetic north. That is to say, we agree with what Paul writes: All know God, 'but by their unrighteousness suppress the truth' (Rom. 1:18). All people know God in a general sense, though they may not know of Christ. Christians are made aware of Christ when they hear the gospel message. When disciples are equipped, they are given a map, which we might call Scripture. The Bible is sufficient since it is authoritative for all matters in faith and practice. The Bible objectively reflects the terrain of life, obstacles and common pitfalls, and shows us 'the way we should go.' The compass, then, is the right interpretation of Scripture by the people of God. The compass isn't the standard; it's an interpretation of the standard—a reflection of right teaching.

BAD COMPASS READINGS

The fallibility of humanity has led some to believe they are rightfully interpreting the map of Scripture when they were not. They thought they were following the compass as it reflected the map, but they weren't. The great departures from the faith that misuse Scripture do not reflect Scripture or the character of God. A common objection to Christianity is that it has caused religious wars, condoned slavery, segregation, suppression of women's rights, etc. I would simply point out that the common factor between those atrocious things isn't Christianity, but a departure from it. More specifically, it's a good example to show that we shouldn't always trust the reading of a single person's compass. We must always ask the question: Does the compass they follow point toward Christ? Or does it point to their own ends?

Scripture clearly teaches the fallibility of humanity everywhere in every age. When honest people vehemently reject Christianity, they are most often unintentionally rejecting a misapplication of Christianity. Rather than following their logic to its ultimate conclusion, they simply trade one wrong map for another. They may reject Christianity, but always replace it with a different philosophy. They may cast aside Christianity, but Buddhism, Hinduism, or even a religiously zealous atheism springs up in its place. The reason for this is underscored in the chapter on worship—we are hardwired to worship *something*. Humans will always give glory to something, whether it's themselves or something else.

What, then, do people reject when they reject Christianity? Some have a problem with the idea of objective truth. But I wonder, does objective truth exist? Perhaps it's the variation of this that is often uttered today, 'Your truth is for you, but my truth is for me.' This sometimes is stated more subtly, 'Listen man, you can be a Christian and all that, but don't force others to believe it.' The problem is, though, that Christianity is either true, or it's not. Certainly, we experience truth *subjectively* (hence the analogy of magnetic debris screwing up the compass), but that doesn't change the essence of truth being *objective*. Some reject the notion that there is a meta-narrative that ties all stories together. But, of course, they must privilege *that* narrative over others. So, what is the reason people reject Christianity? It's a simple answer, but it's not simplistic. The reason is autonomy. To be autonomous means 'self-ruling' or 'self-governing.' It means we like to be the ones in charge, the ones who call the shots. To put it in the words our culture values, it means we're free.

FREEDOM?

We like freedom. Many of us have fought for freedom. But freedom doesn't always mean what we think it does. As

Americans, we love those famous words of the poem *Invictus*. The last line is practically a prayer and hymn for many:

> It matters not how strait the gate,
> How charged with punishments the scroll,
> I am the master of my fate,
> I am the captain of my soul.[1]

Freedom does not mean the ability to do what we want, when we want, how we want. We may phrase it like that sometimes, but no one has that kind of freedom. If you think you can go running down the street naked, shooting bullets in the air, you're wrong. You wouldn't try this because you know that even in a free nation like the United States, freedom isn't permission to do such crazy things. Freedom is largely meaningless unless we can answer two questions: freedom from what? and freedom for what?

FREEDOM FROM WHAT?

Our will is not free by nature—it is rebellious. We don't want to hear that God has a law that we have violated. We don't want to know that our sin is a burden that binds and restrains us. But it is and it does. Freedom, true freedom, is that which makes us free from sin. When we are made alive in Christ, it's like getting that declination correction. It is more dramatic than having piles of metal debris removed from on top of us. The only freedom that matters is freedom from sin.

FREEDOM FOR WHAT?

The second question pairs with the first. When the shackles of sin are lifted, freedom only matters if it is placed in something fixed, permanent, and true. Freedom to do whatever we want isn't freedom —it's anarchy. Freedom to fulfill our own desires and follow our own will isn't freedom either; it's merely

---

1. https://www.poetryfoundation.org/poems/51642/invictus

our burden. Freedom matters only when it is for God. This brings together our need to worship and finds satisfaction in a freedom lived for Christ. This satisfies our hunger and need to give glory to something when freedom is lived for God. Freedom from sin and for God—the two greatest aspects of declination correction and plot designation. Where we go in life matters as much as how we travel the course.

Like every analogy, the illustration of navigating life by means of Scripture breaks down if we think that any path is equally valid to reach God. The fact is that Scripture shows an exclusivity in the person of Christ. This is why He says, 'I am the way, and the truth, and the life. No one comes to the Father, except through me' (John 14:6). Jesus is saying, 'I am truth. I am the gateway to truth, I am the path to truth, and I am the destination of truth.' This is a bold claim. It's not as though all religious lives are equally valid pathways to God. Jesus says that He is *the* way. The pathway to God and reconciliation with Him is through, and only through, Jesus Christ. That's a capstone sum of what our map, Scripture, says definitively. Will we still struggle with sin? Sure. Will it impede our course and get us off track? Of course. But God's character hasn't changed because of our fallibility or inability to keep the metal debris away. So, what happens when we do get off track?

COMMUNICATION WITH GOD
Fortunately, we can communicate with God. We aren't left alone to figure it out, but we have a direct connection to Him. How does this work? How exactly can we speak with God? This way of communication is something veterans are particularly familiar with already.

In boot camp, the muscle memory I gained through seemingly endless repetition of drills underlined the foundation of the training I received. Particularly, the adage of relying on an unrealistic ability and ethos of 'one shot, one kill.' But as morbid as that phrase may sound, and despite the emphasis this mindset demanded, it was to my own dismay to discard it.

When I arrived at my new unit after SOI and was in that RBE platoon described in the first chapter, the Marines I arrived with came under the guidance of a couple of salty Marines tasked with passing on knowledge and training while they waited to finish out their contract time.

At least four of us boots were brought into a barracks room where a corporal, who had deployed twice to Iraq and was soon to leave active duty, gave us a period of instruction that I will never forget. 'What is the most important item to have on a combat load?' he asked, looking each of us directly in the eye. Confidently and without hesitation we three replied at once: 'Your rifle, corporal.' I felt almost insulted being asked such a question. After all, I had just completed six months of training and was sure of the answer. There was a short but effective pause, followed by a flat, 'No' from the corporal. As we pulled out our note-taking gear to learn more about this new piece of information, I silently challenged what was being said. I knew I was right. How could all those times screaming 'one shot, one kill' be wrong?

What this corporal was teaching us challenged my belief that the rifle was the most important piece of gear. At least that is what I believed at the time. 'The most important thing to have on a combat load, is comm,' he began ('comm' was shorthand for 'communication,' i.e., our radio). At that moment my understanding of both infantry tactics and prayer were completely transformed. 'Take for one moment,' the corporal went on to explain, 'that I have a thirty-round magazine, and I have even pre-loaded one round in the chamber, giving me thirty-one rounds at my disposal. Now, suppose you boots are really amazing shots, that you in fact could hit every target and down it with one shot. Take this a step further, and let's say you could kill two birds with one stone, doubling your ratio. That kind of uncanny effectiveness with a rifle will still not, nor ever could, equal the importance and effectiveness comm has in combat.'

Any kind of coordinated efforts or fighting, from the lowest level of small unit leadership to the largest commands with dozens of overlays and moving parts, must have effective communication. Even without your rifle, your assets are vastly more substantial than only the weapon on your person. If I have no rifle, but I have effective comm, I can call for QRF (Quick Reaction Force—usually composed of a Marine rifle squad). I have 'call for fire' (a process of requesting mortar fire in support to execute a variety of missions on behalf of the forward observer or the Marine calling for fire). I may have artillery, which is more capable and deadly than mortar fire. I may have CAS (Close Air Support—comprised of F-18s, gunships, and/or helicopters that have their own onboard weapon systems and support they can provide). I even have the necessary access to emergency casualty evacuation which in numerous circumstances is the only way to save the life of a fellow Marine. All these assets are in direct support of the individual Marine looking to close with and destroy his enemy. This support, however, can only be available or directed into the fight when comm is utilized correctly, acting as a gateway to overwhelm the enemy. The importance of the rifle pales in comparison to comm, which drastically increases the confidence and deadliness of a Marine in combat. All of this is to say that comm is a whole lot more powerful than a few bullets.

PRAYER AS ARMOR
The apostle Paul writes to the Ephesians:

> Finally, be strong in the Lord and in the strength of his might. Put on the whole armor of God, that you may be able to stand against the schemes of the devil. For we do not wrestle against flesh and blood, but against the rulers,

against the authorities, against the cosmic powers over this present darkness, against the spiritual forces of evil in the heavenly places (Eph. 6:10-12).

Paul draws an analogy between physical and spiritual warfare. He mentions parts of a first-century Roman soldier's gear: 'the belt of truth,' 'the breastplate of righteousness, as shoes . . . the readiness given by the gospel of peace,' 'the shield of faith,' 'the helmet of salvation, and the sword of the Spirit, which is the word of God' (verses 14, 17).

Even as soldiers would be incomplete without rifles, people are incomplete when they remove any piece of their spiritual armor. But had there been such a thing as a two-way radio when Paul wrote to the church in Ephesus, the Romans would have undoubtedly used it in combat as part of their advanced war machine. And if the Romans had them in use, Paul could have symbolically attached this piece of equipment used in battle.

Last Paul mentions a part of armor too easily overlooked, when he speaks of 'praying at all times in the Spirit' (verse 18). Many Christians today, and even books about the spiritual armor of God, do not place enough emphasis on prayer. Prayer should have equal emphasis with every other piece of armor and weapon. John Piper gets it right when he says, 'Prayer is a wartime walkie-talkie.'[2] Prayer should never be excluded from the armor of God, just as we should never exclude the armor of God from prayer.

In Scripture we find numerous examples of prayer in spiritual warfare and as part of a Christian's life. Our greatest biblical heroes regarded prayer as integral and essential to living for God. The epic story of Daniel and the lions' den centers on the act of prayer. Daniel refused to lay down this

2. John Piper, 'Prayer: The Work of Missions,' Desiring God (Desiring God, March 2, 2020), https://www.desiringgod.org/messages/prayer-the-work-of-missions.

piece of armor, and was victorious only because he continued to do what was outlawed—pray (Dan. 6:10-23). Elijah's life also demonstrates the power of God answering prayer: 'Elijah was a man with a nature like ours, and he prayed fervently that it might not rain, and for three years and six months it did not rain on the earth. Then he prayed again, and heaven gave rain, and the earth bore its fruit' (James 5:17-18).

Before the Battle of Jericho took place in Joshua 6, the Israelites marched around the city with the trumpets leading the way, silent as God had commanded, until the final pass around the city, when the trumpets blared and the walls of Jericho fell down. The people needed to pray and praise God before the battle ever commenced, a sword was raised, or a single arrow flew. The time of silence while circling the city was filled with meditation and prayers to God before God gave the Israelites victory.

OUR WARRIOR REDEEMER'S EXAMPLE

Christ, our Warrior Redeemer, would often withdraw from others to pray to His Father, and He is the Son of God. If He needed to pray, how much more do we! Not only did Jesus tell us how to pray in Matthew 6:9-15, He displayed it. Jesus perfectly showed what prayer should look like and how fellowship with our Lord can occur as a result of fervent prayer. Before He was tempted and battled Satan, the Scriptures tell us He had fasted forty days and nights (Matt. 4:2). I am sure that during that time He was in constant communication with God the Father through prayer.

First Thessalonians 5:17 instructs us to pray without ceasing. I cannot see a degree of separation between the manner we are instructed to pray and the necessity for it in spiritual combat. I cannot imagine doing any mission in the Marines without using verbal or non-verbal communication. Our need for communication in battles of the flesh underscores the importance of prayer in our walk with the

Lord and daily spiritual battles. Think of how dangerous a spiritual struggle can be when you are led to believe through a delusion of comfort that prayer is not that important, or that it does not need to be done all that fervently or all that long in duration. As Corrie ten Boom probingly asked, 'Is prayer your steering wheel or spare tire?'

Prior to embarking on a combat patrol, we Marines would conduct a series of checks we call PCCs and PCIs. These pre-combat checks and inspections are the vital process to double- and triple-check our gear before any move outside the wire is made. It included function checks of our weapons, having night vision goggles, gear silencing, topping off water, and ensuring that we had everything we needed to accomplish our mission on our combat load. Lastly, it consisted of a series of radio checks that consisted of multiple stations in case one was being used and/or compromised, as well as carrying extra batteries and forms of communication in case comm was lost. We even had our SOPs (Standard Operating Procedures) for when the multiple redundancies and layers to ensure constant communication failed. The bottom line was this: We would never go knowingly into a fight without the ability to communicate. Doing so would put us at a potential disadvantage, weaken us, and increase the probability of failure and significant losses.

Leaving Essential Equipment at Home

Why then do we as Christians constantly put ourselves at a disadvantage? This isn't just putting a chink in our armor. Rather, it is outright leaving our most important piece of equipment—prayer—at home. If we would only communicate with our Lord, we might have the wisdom to avoid certain battles altogether. The fast-paced society in which we live has hedged our lives with comfort while leaving us wide open to spiritual attacks, flanks, and maneuvers that can overwhelm our defenses, all because we don't pray. Spiritual warfare is likened to that of fire and maneuver warfare. Jesus Christ is offering overwhelming firepower and support by directing us where we need to be. We simply fail to ask (James 4:2-3) and communicate with Him.

We Christians have made the beach landing but remain exposed and vulnerable when we fail tenaciously to press the fight inland to the enemy. When we stay in one place, we come under suppressive fire; when we are suppressed by the enemy, we do not move. At this critical point a Christian warrior can do one of two things: he can hunker down and avoid the risks of loss and any hope of victory along with it or he can take up the full armor of God and use prayer, his most important piece of gear, to communicate with his greatest asset, his Commander, and his Leader, Jesus Christ.

We can illustrate the reasons why we do not pray. We can make excuses or rationalizations. But James 4:17 puts it simply and correctly, 'So whoever knows the right thing to do and fails to do it, for him it is sin.' When we know we are to be in prayer and are not, we are living in sin. When we do not pray, the principalities against which we battle bring us to our knees, although we should have begun our spiritual battle in this manner before God.

Prayer enables us to know when the enemy is coming, or at least, to stay in fellowship with our Lord when unexpected disaster strikes. It prevents us from some spiritual ambushes that could have been thwarted. Prayer should take on new meaning when we understand it as a piece of our spiritual armor. Let's remember and think of prayer differently as we read Paul's instructions and list of gear for spiritual preparation in battle.

NAVIGATING ALONE
Navigating the Christian life involves more than using Scripture and praying to God. We would be foolish to think that we can undertake the fight of faith alone. Of

course, we can't. That brings us back to our need as image bearers not to be alone and isolated in solitude. We need the fellowship of other believers. The reverse is true as well. We can't be in community with believers and then ignore the calls from Christ to bend our knees in submission to Him. If we want to get to God, we must go through His Son by the means that our map, Scripture, details. And if we want to be effective in fighting this fight of faith, we must be in constant communication with God. Knowing what Scripture says, knowing how our sin gets in the way, and knowing that we must be in communication with our Lord, are basic and necessary components to a fight of faith that won't enable us merely to survive—but to prevail.

18

FAITHFULNESS RESTORED

The United States has had troops in Afghanistan since 2002. That marked the first wave to leave home for what was to become a new chapter for the United States on the heels of September 11, 2001. The attacks on the World Trade Center, the Pentagon, and another plane, believed to be headed for the White House, triggered a pivot for the United States' war doctrine and foreign policy towards global terrorism. The War on Terror has had troops in a perpetual cycle of deployment, return, training, and re-deployment since the first boots stepped on the ground in Afghanistan in 2002. Although the United States military has always had troops moving, training, and doing exercises in parts of the world, or involved in some sort of conflict, this new chapter, coupled with the proliferation of social media, has raised awareness that those who are deploying are normal people. They are moms, dads, sons, and daughters, caught up in a call to service that tears them, not just away from their home soil, but from their most basic and beloved relationships.

COMING HOME
It's common on Facebook to see videos circulate of troops coming home. It doesn't matter if it's active duty or reservist,

married or unmarried, male or female, Army, Navy, Marine Corps, or Air Force. The act of coming home uniformly affects the armed forces. The videos often draw the water works of tears too. Not that they're sad, for they are far from sad. Rather, they draw upon the emotion of sheer joy of coming home at last. The feeling of restoration after a long deployment away unites families, couples, and hearts in a beautiful way that touches the soul. The videos of troops coming home is a reflection, however distant, of glory.

Scripture says that creation itself groans in pains of childbirth as we await a kind of homecoming, the redemption of our bodies (Rom. 8:22-23). This groaning is a longing for the final consummation, for restoration, to at last be made whole, and finally forever to come home. The feeling of coming home is truly elating. I can vividly recall the happiness I experienced at every step of the journey home from Iraq: from walking off my post as I was replaced by the next unit, to packing my gear, to staging and waiting for the convoy to come pick us up. Already at this early stage, I was excited, even giddy. The enlivened feeling of pent-up anticipation was greater than all the Christmas mornings of my childhood put together.

Each subsequent leg of the journey built anticipation. First, we had a short trip to the company BP for a few days and then we moved on to Al Assad for a week or so. From Al Assad, we flew to Kuwait, where we were able to stow our flaks and packs below the plane and leave a military airline and hop on board an actual international 747 plane, stewardesses and all. On my first deployment, our trip home went through Germany, where we landed feeling jet-lagged, sleep deprived, and trying to find new rhythms. That German beer we drank probably wasn't great, but at the time, nothing could have tasted better! From Leipzig, we hopped over to Bangor, Maine. We weren't 'home,' but we were home. Veterans from the VFW greeted us in the airport shaking our hands, welcoming us back to home soil. This was a great honor, for WW2, Korean, and Vietnam Veterans, who, in our estimation, had given much and deserved more, met us with open arms, reminding us of the brotherhood of troops into which we had enlisted.

Each step of the journey peeled back another layer of excitement, until we were almost all overcome with a feeling of the surreal. *Are we really back?* The flight from Maine to Andrews Air Force Base in California was exciting, and just like waiting to open presents on Christmas, it seemed to take forever. We were a mix of rowdy and relaxed. We were close to respite and could feel a weight being lifted from an exhausting deployment and trip. For a brief period of time, stepping off that plane in March 2008, America never seemed so beautiful. The memory still brings tears to my eyes, and we weren't even back to see our families yet! We were just a short bus ride away from MCAGCC. There are only two times in my life that I have been excited to be back to Twentynine Palms, and both of those were coming home from Iraq.

It was a bright, sunny California day when we stepped off that bus ride back to base. Along the way, we were intermittently escorted by veterans on their bikes, families, and so on. As we approached the last turn into Twentynine Palms, the anticipation reached a climax. There is a couple-mile stretch just outside the main gate at the base where a chain link fence was filled with banners made by wives, girlfriends, and families for their loved ones. At the end of that stretch rests the main gate. As the busses approach, the PMO guards wait outside, knowing in advance Marines are returning home. Typically, there is only one guard outside screening vehicles, but for those returning home five or six guards stand ready. They all snap to attention, their bodies rigid and poised, and render a salute to the passing busses. This display of respect, typically reserved for officers, brings a strong sense of honor to all of us returning to base.

The next step of the journey was a bit painful that first trip home. Before we can go to Victory Field and meet the waiting families, everyone has to go to the armory to turn in their EDL (equipment density list, which refers to all pertinent equipment like NVGs, rifles, and so on). The counts all have to match up or no one is allowed to leave. On this day, of all days, the counts didn't match up. We sat there for a few hours, being literally only a quarter a mile away from everyone who was waiting, without permission to see them. It's difficult to put words to the pent-up anticipation and frustration. The emotions of everyone were ready to burst. We were impatient and vocal. It seemed like a near rebellion was ready to break out at any moment if the order was given to stay put for much longer. Much of the stress that we thought we had blown off was rebuilding along with anger.

I'll never forget the roar from the company when someone, maybe our CO, maybe our First Sergeant, finally shouted, 'Load up!' Those busses were attacked with an unusual intensity and sense of purpose. Rounding the corners of those few short blocks to pull up to Victory Field was a sight. The Marine Corps Band, known as *The President's Own*, had cued up its music and the impatient crowd of families pressed in around where the busses would pull up. A few high-ranking officers and enlisted personnel from the base (none of whom I knew) were there shaking hands as those folding doors tore open, and we poured out of the busses to find our loved ones.

Coming Home to Two Very Different Results

That first return home I didn't have anyone waiting for me and stepped off the bus connecting with Jones almost immediately. We both worked our way through the crowd, he looking for his father, and I don't know for whom I was looking. I guess I was looking for someone to relay my own sense of being home to. And then Jones's dad, Casey, located his son. I almost cried seeing him embrace Jones the way he did. Being a father now, I can relate to the bond a father has with his son. And in that moment, I saw a father embrace his son with joy that he was now finally home.

I'll admit, it was dissatisfying to arrive and have no one to come home to. It wasn't until my second return home, that was almost identical, that someone met me. The feelings, the jubilation, the anticipation were all the same. This time, though, my beautiful fiancée was waiting. I was a mix of emotions that day. I was scared that I wasn't the same person, that she might not love me anymore. I had a flashback coming home that second trip to the first one of my squad leader sitting next to me waiting for the plane in Al Assad. He was listening to his iPod and pulled out his earbuds and put them into my hands and said, 'Listen to this song.' I did. It was the song *For Reasons Unknown* by The Killers. The lines that stood out (and still stand out to me) were:

I pack my case, I check my face
I look a little bit older
I look a little bit colder
With one deep breath, and one big step
I move a little bit closer, I move a little bit closer
For reasons unknown

I caught my stride, I flew and flied
I know if destiny's kind, I've got the rest on my mind
Well, my heart—it don't beat, it don't beat the way it used to
And my eyes—they don't see you no more
And my lips—they don't kiss, they don't kiss the way they used to
And my eyes don't recognize you no more.[1]

I cannot explain the amount of pure joy I was feeling, but simultaneously a sense of dread and panic rushed over me. I began to doubt everything I thought I knew about who I was,

1. https://genius.com/The-killers-for-reasons-unknown-lyrics

realizing I was in the midst of a miniature existential crisis. I would likely not be deployed again, and I was returning a completely different man. I saw the world through a new lens and the world looked back at me with a different lens too. I not only wondered if my fiancée was someone who would still love me, but if I was someone who could be loved and love in return.

Returning to Victory Field brought so many overwhelming memories. Instead of the busses, we marched, turned in a company formation and screamed some motto stuff and then were released to find our loved ones. I remember standing next to McClendon who had his girlfriend waiting for him. We both looked at the crowd mobbing us, not seeing our respective girlfriends around, and shared a brief moment of enochlophobia (fear of crowds) and disappointment by not seeing our loved ones right away. 'Where is she? Maybe she isn't here. Maybe she left.' This sentiment, unfortunately, often becomes a nightmare come true for many Marines who expect their family and find them gone. And then the crowd parted and there stood the love of my life, my future wife.

I didn't realize how much I had detached in those short few hours of self-reflection. Her tears, though, told me I could be present. I didn't cry, but inside my chest I moved toward her with joy. I was distant, in a sense, but was running toward her in my heart. Even though my guard was high up, I was ready to be vulnerable with her.

COMING HOME TO GLORY *NOT* VALHALLA

The act of coming home is etched on every human heart. The reason that so many stories reflect this commonly held sentiment is because we are all created in the image of God, and as image bearers, we long for restoration. Consider all the movies, books, and songs we devour that hit this theme. Humans aren't just slightly interested in talking about coming home; we are enamored with it. Coming home resonates an eternal longing that endlessly and restlessly dwells in every human heart. Things aren't set right until we can make it home. The slogan for the USO for years was 'Until everyone comes home.' When we see those videos of veterans returning from deployment separated from their loved ones, among the floods of tears, joy, and laughter, we are witnessing a glimpse of the final consummation of all things.

This final, great act in that narrative is the restoration of faithfulness. According to His faithful character, God created all things. Against His faithful character we rebelled. In Christ's redemptive act of dying on a cross that would pay for our unfaithfulness, He was faithful where we were not. And in this final chapter of the redemptive narrative, faithfulness will finally be fully restored. We live now in the in-between. We are after Christ's cross and resurrection, but before the final consummation. That means we live in a world still marred by sin, and even when we are no longer defined by our offenses, we still commit them. To come home to glory, though, means that we will be made right; we will be finally and permanently made as we are supposed to be. The last book of Scripture says this: 'He will wipe away every tear from their eyes, and death shall be no more, neither shall there be mourning, nor crying, nor pain anymore, for the former things have passed away' (Rev. 21:4). Death will no longer have a grip on this world. As the last enemy of Christ, it will be put under His feet. Isaiah 2:4 likewise reminds us of the fact that war, though necessary now, will not always be a reality we face. A day will come when we will no longer have to fight:

> He shall judge between the nations, and shall decide disputes for many peoples; and they shall beat their swords into plowshares, and their spears into pruning hooks; nation shall not lift up sword against nation, neither shall they learn war anymore (Isa. 2:4).

This is impossible to grasp for those who vehemently reject God. 'After death, there is nothing,' they reason. The tragedy of this is that there is an afterlife and glory awaiting God's people. After many of the men I knew died, a disconcerting way of memorializing them emerged on social media platforms like Facebook. Whether it was suicide or by a car accident, the place of 'Valhalla' would be cited as something along the lines of 'Until we meet again brother, until Valhalla.' I appreciate that my Marine buddies want to honor the memory of our fallen. I am encouraged that they would invoke an afterlife for them in light of their warrior profession. I sincerely want them to keep remembering their brothers, but I also have to press back and simply say, 'No.' There is no Valhalla.

The Viking afterlife may be very exciting, but it's also not real. Vikings may make an interesting parallel and connection to serving in the military, but it's definitely not the same. It likewise doesn't satisfy the necessary preconditions to intelligibly make sense of life, morality, our origin, meaning, and final destiny. It is almost 100% focused on the afterlife, but doesn't account for our need to fight, the need to end all wars, nor does it acknowledge our own brokenness, honor, and shame. It is simply an honorable but make-believe attempt to memorialize the fallen. But Scripture and the story we enter into have a much greater picture of going home.

Valhalla may be a place for Vikings, but going home to Christ is much greater, far better, and real. The blessings of Christ and being in His presence make the fiction of Valhalla or any other 'afterlife' look like story time. But what could compare to being in the presence of Christ, our warrior Redeemer? What could possibly hold its own against the weight of glory? For our faithfulness to be finally and completely restored means to be made whole and no longer struggle against the temptations, sufferings, and death of our loved ones. That ultimate consummation is what I long for. It's what every human heart, on some level, longs for. That final consummation is for us to come home and be greeted by Christ and hear those words, 'Well done, good and faithful servant. You have been faithful over a little; I will set you over much. Enter into the joy of your master' (Matt. 25:23).

The apostle Paul, knowing the blessedness of going home to glory and having his faithfulness restored, wrestled with two options: his desire to be with Christ and the necessary duty to be used in the Christian life, this great fight of faith. His words are very fitting on the longing to finally have our faithfulness restored: 'For to me to live is Christ, and to die is gain' (Phil. 1:21). That day *will* come, when our life has run its course, perhaps when we are old and gray, and there, awaiting on the other side of that last threshold is not hopelessness, but hope fulfilled. Awaiting after death for those who have bent the knee to God is not pain, but Christ. Awaiting after our last breath is our new life with God, forever. Our final gain is because of Christ and His faithfulness. What makes Jesus's work so grand is that He was faithful where we were not. Jesus was 'a merciful and faithful high priest in the service of God,' for He died to rescue all who put their faith in Him (Heb. 2:17). Paul writes of the greatness of heaven: 'What no eye has seen, nor ear heard, nor the heart of man imagined, what God has prepared for those who love him' (1 Cor. 2:9). And awaiting at the end of this fight of faith is the glory of Christ. Truly we can resonate and say in hope and anticipation of that day, 'for me, to live is Christ, and to die is gain.' *Semper Fidelis.*

CONCLUSION: NEXT STEPS

So, now what? I've included many applications throughout the book, including entering into one's story, listening long, growing in empathy, what to do when grieving, and more. But what do we do with the big picture? What do we do to 'solve' veteran suicide if the main points are correct: that veteran suicide is not primarily a problem born out of exposure to combat and then the inevitable diagnosis of PTSD? If the greatest challenges facing veterans are those complicated by a complex military culture, infused with honor and shame elements, what can veterans and those caring for them do? What follows is a succinct list that will assist in translating the message of the gospel, not just into military culture, but in relating to others as well.

1. FIND A HEALTHY CHURCH
Just because it says 'church' on the sign outside doesn't mean it has a healthy environment or is even a church. The best criteria to evaluate a church by is if it: 1) proclaims the Word of God and the gospel and 2) faithfully administers the sacraments of the Lord's Supper and baptism. These two marks are minimal expressions of what makes a church, but they are just that—minimal. After this, there are varying

degrees of church health. I would recommend reading a short book like *What Is a Healthy Church?* by Mark Dever that delves into many other indicators of a healthy church.

2. Join a Small Group/Community Outlet

Merely attending a service once a week is not sufficient to know God or to be known by others. Join one of the small groups the church offers for its community engagement (also known by names such as discipleship groups, life groups, or community groups). It is in these smaller more intimate settings that the on-ramps for relationship building are often found and where veterans (or anyone else) are able to share their stories. Only when people open up can others bear their burdens and care for them.

3. Identify Comfort 'Go-to's'

Knowing the mechanisms by which we worship and seek comfort and affirmation are vital. Identifying these are pro-active ways to ward off temptations to seek comfort outside of Christ. This is also a way in which to keep cycles of depression and substance abuse mitigated and at arm's length. The usual suspects, as were mentioned in previous chapters, rear their ugly heads in alcohol abuse, pain medication, overeating, and sexual exploits. Identifying these mechanisms is also insufficient. We need to be able to take our weaknesses and predispositions to another and say, 'Please bear this burden with me.' We all need someone to help carry our burdens just as much as others need you in their lives.

4. Root Yourself in God's Word

Without God's Word, the rest of this list is, at best, a secular self-help guide. The only place one can be nourished for a lifetime and be spiritually enriched is in the Bible. Charles Spurgeon said it well, 'Visit many books, but live in the Bible.' Obviously, I am making the assumption that someone who intends to read the Bible will set out to learn how to do so faithfully. In order to do this, one should join a healthy church where he or she can be discipled to do this very thing. People who read their Bibles apart from the community of the church can benefit greatly, but without someone to guide them, they might misunderstand what they read or give up on the endeavor entirely. I recommend *Spiritual Disciplines for the Christian Life* by Donald Whitney as a great primer for introducing the importance of reading, meditation, and prayer.

5. Consolidate Geographically

The lessons of chapter sixteen on community should be put to work here. Our lives are too disparate and spread out among segmented networks and relationships. As much as it is possible and reasonable, I suggest we disentangle our lives from those networks and consolidate ourselves geographically. Live closer to where you work. Shop, go to church, and find recreational things to do closer to where you call home. Many of us shop at multiple stores that take us out of our natural geographic community. Avoid this as the rule. If you can walk to these places, do so. The combined effect of all these consolidations is the increased likelihood of bumping into the same people. Bump into the same people enough over a small span of time, and this can begin to express a small but necessary feature of a community. The combined effect on a community level is that relationships can form where otherwise people would pass each other as strangers in a store. Someone who might be willing to hear others' stories and walk with them might already be in their life and bring them closer after this consolidation takes place.

6. Digitally Detox Your Life

For the majority of human history, people lived without the distractions of endless shows to stream or never-ending scrolls on devices glued to their faces that never turn off and never cease to distract. While there are many enjoyments to be had in this digital age, we largely don't need any of them. The effect of being connected to thousands of people on our phones is a neglect of the people living under our roof and next door. We are missing out on enriching relationships with people who could be part of the network and support system we need to bear our burdens, know us, and be known by us. I would start by deleting social media apps from your phone and restricting this kind of engagement to mornings or evenings. From there I would suggest unsubscribing from most cable, dish, and streaming platforms. No one needs to have the appetite for television at the level many of us have today. It should give us pause that today someone can consume seasons of a TV show in a few days that a previous generation took many years to enjoy. The time gained from spending less time with our phones and shows can be better spent cultivating relationships with flesh and blood human beings.

7. Meet Your Neighbor

I've heard varying reports that for some, it takes perhaps seven years to meet their neighbor! If this is true, it is tragic. The first person you should meet when you move into a new place is your neighbor. Let's just label the awkward and the obvious. I know how hard it can be to finally break the barrier and to go next door with a plate of cookies, or homemade hot sauce (one of my hobbies) and knock on their door. They answer. They've seen me before as I've pulled quickly into my garage making a minimal wave or nod to them (if I see them at all) and suddenly there I am in the flesh. Gasp! I know it's shocking. And I know it can feel awkward. 'Hi, I'm Josh, your neighbor next door, I've never actually had a chance to meet you, so I thought I would bring these cookies as a way to ease this ancient ritual.' Okay, it doesn't have to be this clunky, but we need to start somewhere. Scripture tells us over and over to love our neighbor. This includes our literal neighbor. Some of the most rewarding relationships of caring and being cared for come from the person next door.

8. Seek Specialization if Necessary

The main thrust of this book is not to create *more* niche ministries, non-profits and outreaches that cater specifically to veterans. The reverse is its goal: that we should create communities that need niche ministries less and less. While many of these ministries are noble and needed, it is the wrong impulse to think more out-sourcing is needed because it lends itself to the trend of being overly specialized. But I want to commend many of the ministries and non-profits out there. Many are doing great work. However, like many outreaches, the goal *should* be to work themselves out of a job when the problem has been alleviated.

Every ministry and outreach should be evaluated on its own merits (a few are listed in the appendices). But the main point is to avoid outsourcing a veteran whose struggles could be more naturally ministered to through his or her neighbor and in a local church setting. Many of the current non-profits for veterans are operating on the assumption that PTSD and combat exposure are the primary causes of veteran suicide. Given that they are not, such efforts can inadvertently invoke the dynamic of the haunt of honor while not addressing underlying issues. In fact, given the honor-shame culture of the military, wrongly assuming why someone struggles with depression can reinforce their unwillingness to open up. Why open up, they might think, when they seem to know my story already?

On the flip side, someone who is struggling with PTSD, for example, could greatly benefit from a ministry created for that specific need, especially if the local church finds itself ill-equipped to do so. The main diagnostic question to keep in mind is this: Is this ministry/outreach doing something we can do in our church? Secondly, is this ministry/outreach fracturing this individual communally? Just because a ministry is focused on veterans doesn't mean it is *the* thing that veteran needs in his or her life. This advice is a guideline, because it doesn't offer a hard 'yes' or 'no' but assumes that wisdom is needed in every situation.

If all of these little steps are taken in tandem, I would hope that we would have a different looking society. Even if we do just one, like canceling a streaming service or two, we would benefit ourselves. As you have noticed, not all of these suggestions are unique to the circumstances around veteran suicide. And as you have noted from reading the book, what is happening to veterans is really only an exasperated problem that is happening to everyone else.

Our ultimate and vertical reconciliation is with Christ. And our horizontal reconciliation is that which results from being made right with God. The effects are that the worst parts of our culture will be subverted, and the best parts will be redeemed. First, a redemption back to Christ, second, a redemption with each other that comes as a result of the first. This is what it means to Redeem Warriors.

APPENDIX

There is an abundance of resources for suicide prevention, coping with PTSD, addictions, support groups and more available for veterans. A resource book could be collated and devoted solely to this and would likely be hundreds of pages in length. Just in my rural corner of the state of Oklahoma, I have a document I've added to over time that is nearly fifteen pages long with only local resources for veterans. There is more than can or should be included in an appendix, so what is included are merely highlights of notable non-profits and ministries in the U.S. to veterans. Those caring for veterans will have to do some ground work to see what is available and appropriate to meet their needs where they live and work.

Many non-profits and ministries are good, but seeking out help should come with a sense of self-awareness and discernment. The situation and context will dictate what is best. Be mindful of the trends you see in yourself or that veteran you're assisting. As a society, we are already overly specialized, disparate, and disconnected from one another. I would approach these resources in the way I would a general practitioner in medicine. Whatever can be resolved through the avenues of community and your local church, prioritize them. Whatever is beyond their means to help you (such as dealing with combat related trauma) seek out specialized care. However, just as in medicine where an individual needing surgery doesn't fire their primary care physician for what they cannot provide, neither should we approach these non-profits as though they are the final substitute for community of long-term care. The two should go hand in hand as partners.

CHURCH FINDER

There are more theologically solid, gospel-proclaiming, churches out there than what can be found in the following links. These resources, in general, have a greater degree of quality control to infer their vitality and health. As such, they are good starting points, but it is not exhaustive nor an endorsement of every church that could be indexed under all of these directories.

9-Marks

At 9Marks, we help pastors, future pastors, and church members see what a biblical church looks like, and to take practical steps for becoming one. Our goal is to see churches characterized by nine biblical marks of a healthy church. Why these nine? Because sadly, they're too often assumed or ignored in evangelical churches.
https://www.9marks.org/church-search/

Acts 29

Acts 29 is a family of church-planting churches that stands in the tradition of historic evangelical confessionalism. While we believe it is vital that the Elders of each of our local churches determine where they stand on doctrines of second importance, we do wish to make known our convictions on the following five distinctive theological foundations.
https://www.acts29.com/find-churches/

Founders Ministries

Founders Ministries is committed to encouraging the recovery of the gospel and the biblical reformation of local churches. We believe that the biblical faith is inherently doctrinal, and we are therefore confessional in our convictions. We recognize the time-tested Second London Baptist Confession of Faith (1689) as a faithful summary of important biblical teachings and the abstract of that confession known as the Abstract of Principles.

https://founders.org/church-search/

The Gospel Coalition

We are a fellowship of evangelical churches in the Reformed tradition deeply committed to renewing our faith in the gospel of Christ and to reforming our ministry practices to conform fully to the Scriptures.

https://www.thegospelcoalition.org/churches/

The Presbyterian Church in America

We provide churches, presbyteries, and the Assembly with the expertise and action needed to keep its ministries moving forward. We don't set the agenda for the PCA. We just make sure its agenda is accomplished.

https://www.pcaac.org/church-directory/

MINISTRY & NON-PROFIT RESOURCES (descriptions are taken directly from the sites, respectively)

Code of Vets

We are bringing awareness and seeking practical solutions to the daily struggles and issues of our veteran community. Our mission is to take care of our own. One veteran at a time. We are coalescing our base to be a powerful voice speaking for the rights for veterans with dignity and respect.

https://www.codeofvets.com/

The Mighty Oaks Warrior Foundation

The Mighty Oaks Foundation is committed to serving the brokenhearted by providing intensive peer-based discipleship through a series of programs, outpost meetings, and speaking events. Our Mighty Oaks Warrior Programs host such Men, Women, and Marriage Advance Programs at multiple locations nationwide. The Warriors who attend are fully sponsored for training, meals, and lodging-needs to ensure that upon arrival to the ranch, each Warrior is focused solely on his or her recovery and identifying purpose moving forward.

https://www.mightyoaksprograms.org/

Operation: Heal Our Patriots

Operation Heal Our Patriots gives wounded veterans and their spouses the opportunity for spiritual refreshment, physical renewal, and marriage enrichment. Couples participate in Biblically based seminars that help strengthen their relationships with God and others and enjoy the beauty of God's creation with outdoor activities at our Alaskan wilderness lodge. We continue to support these men and women after their initial stay, keeping their spiritual needs and marriages a priority.

https://www.samaritanspurse.org/what-we-do/about-operation-heal-our-patriots/

Wounded Warriors Project

Every warrior has a next mission. We know that the transition to civilian life is a journey. And for every warrior, family member, and caregiver, that journey looks different. We are here for their first step, and each step that follows. Because we believe that every warrior should have a positive future to look forward to. There's always another goal to achieve, another mission to discover. We are their partner in that mission. Veterans and service members who incurred a physical or mental injury, illness, or wound while serving

in the military on or after September 11, 2001. You are our focus. You are our mission.
https://www.woundedwarriorproject.org/

PTSD Specific Resources

National Center for PTSD
The mission of the National Center for PTSD is to advance the clinical care and social welfare of America's Veterans and others who have experienced trauma, or who suffer from PTSD, through research, education, and training in the science, diagnosis, and treatment of PTSD and stress-related disorders.
https://www.ptsd.va.gov/

Immediate Suicide Prevention
Sometimes, life's challenges can feel overwhelming, like there's no way things can get better. When things feel unbearable, or if you're having thoughts of ending your life, support is available. VA offers a number of programs and resources for Veterans and their loved ones, friends, and health care providers. If you are a Veteran in crisis — or you're concerned about one — free, confidential support is available 24/7. Call the Veterans Crisis Line at 1-800-273-8255 and Press 1, send a text message to 838255, or chat online.
https://www.mentalhealth.va.gov/suicide_prevention/

Military Cultural Familiarization
There is no substitute for sitting down with a veteran face to face and getting to know them. The list below, however, can serve as a help to create on-ramps for becoming aware of the subcultures of America's military; in turn, they can also give light to blind spots many may have. The movies and TV shows are selected on the basis of historical accuracy. Many veterans possess a distaste for war movies. This could be for a variety of reasons. In part, the *faux pas* and vocational inaccuracies are painful to watch without a constant string

of criticism. For others, they can serve as painful reminders and triggers of traumatic events. The point of the list is not necessarily to have a talking point about a shared liking of a film (though that could happen) but to understand the contours of the culture, warts and all.

Films
1917 (2019)
Band of Brothers (2001)
Black Hawk Down (2001)
Dunkirk (2017)
Flags of Our Fathers (2006)
Generation Kill (2008)
Hacksaw Ridge (2016)
Jarhead (2005)
Letters from Iwo Jima (2006)
Lone Survivor (2013)
Midway (2019)
Pacific (2010)
Saving Private Ryan (1998)
Taking Chance (2009)
Unbroken (2014)
We Were Soldiers (2002)

Books
As far as books go, there are many great books that will assist in this area, far more than there are films. The Marine Corps University collates a list of books called 'The Commandant's Reading List' which is subdivided by levels according to rank. These books are the recommended (and sometimes required) reading list for the Marine Corps. Not all books possess the same quality, but they are formative to the culture and identity of many veterans.
https://grc-usmcu.libguides.com/usmc-reading-list/home

Support Plan for Addictions
This sample plan template is not a guarantee the one you love will always avoid the substance that triggers them. It is a help to think through some basic steps in caring for a veteran that needs to avoid certain substances. This plan can be amended and tailored to the specific needs of the veteran and with the input of any pastors, counselors or professionals involved in their care.

Example: John is a Marine vet. He is married with two kids and struggles with a pornography addiction.

1. Identify when the urge to look at porn peaks
Is it when he is alone? Is it after a stressful day? Is it after a fight with his wife?

2. Identify the desire behind the desire
Does he look at porn for comfort? Does he look at porn to numb some other feeling or disconnect? Why is porn the mechanism of comfort, at all?

3. Remove temptations
Remove any devices from the home that aren't being used anymore. Any computers or phones that are frequently used; be willing to install a software (I suggest *Covenant Eyes*) that monitors device activity and sends frequent reports to one or more accountability partner.

4. Have an accountability partner
An accountability partner is the one who will kick the person in the pants *and* care for them when they stumble. It should *not* be someone who also struggles with the same addiction (to avoid co-dependency and self-justification). It should be someone that loves, respects, and will have the tough love to walk with them in hard times, low-moments and failures.

5. Check-in regularly

Accountability check-ins should not be dependent upon merely receiving a clean report every week. It should be direct, face to face and specific. 'Are you staying pure? Have you looked at porn? Have you been tempted to?' This is far better than 'you doing, okay?' Which could elicit a vague and general response of 'I'm struggling with some lust.' Don't be content with this. Peel back the layers and get specific.

6. Rehearse your response to temptation

Something may happen when the temptation seizes a person and the will to fight shortens to a small window. What will that person do when that happens? The key is not to wait until the temptation comes to fight it. Decide now, what to do. This could go something like this scenario:

'I come home and find that my brother, who stayed over the weekend, left his laptop. I know he doesn't have any filtration or accountability software. My wife and kids are gone, and no one would know if I looked at porn just this once.'

This is a mine-field situation. It's unexpected, it's unplanned, and to some degree it's not the person's 'fault.' They are still responsible for their actions, but they didn't seek out the scenario. What will they do?

Here are the steps I recommend:

A. Remove yourself from the temptation—leave the room, the house even, if you can.

B. Call for help- This could be your accountability partner, wife, pastor or whoever. Call someone and don't hang up until the temptation ceases!

C. Pray—Cry out to the Lord to be freed from the temptation.

D. Meditate—Don't be content to simply wait out a temptation. Rather, be proactive in your prayer and focus on the goodness and sweetness of the Lord. Preach to yourself the truths of the gospel, of the glories, worthiness and satisfaction of Christ! Kill the desire for temptation with a greater desire.

E. Rehearse—Pornography trains the mind for an affair. It prepares the person to fall, and they will, even passively, when temptation comes. In a similar way, you should rehearse what you will do for victory against that addiction as often as it comes to mind. If you have the least impulse to think a lustful thought, walk through your plan in your head.

F. Share your plan—Take your plan to your accountability partner and spouse. Share with them the steps you are taking to fireproof your marriage and probe it for pitfalls or weaknesses that might not match your context.

With the exception of the filtration software, one can simply substitute pornography with another vice. Painkillers, alcohol abuse, overeating. It takes greater wisdom to know and identify abuse in these three other areas. There are proper times and places one can drink alcohol, take a painkiller or eat a meal. There is no proper place for pornography. Thus, consult with those that have a spiritual responsibility for you in how you can combat those vices.

GLOSSARY OF TERMS

1/7, 3/4—This is shorthand to refer to Marine infantry units. The first number designates the battalion, and the second designates the regiment. Someone will refer to a unit in this shorthand way by saying, 'one-seven' or 'three-four.' This is not to be confused with the common way one might read a fraction given it bears the same appearance. *See also* Organization of Units.

5-3-5s—Introduced by General Jim Mattis (the former Secretary of Defense). The 5-3-5s are composed of habits of action and thought that were carried on Marines' persons, usually printed on small laminated cards that could be neatly snugged into a breast pocket on a Marine's cammies. These habits served as a constant reminder to the attitudes and postures Marines were to adopt while in theater. They are:

Pre/Post Action
1. Pre-Combat Checks/Pre-Combat inspections
2. Rehearsals
3. Confirmation briefs
4. After-Actions Report
5. Debriefing

Habits of Action
1. Guardian Angel
2. Geometry of Fire
3. Unity of Command

Habits of Thought
1. Sturdy Professionalism
2. Make yourself hard to kill
3. No Better, No worse enemy
4. First, Do No Harm
5. The Iraqi people are not our enemy, but our enemy hides among them

Corollary 1: You have to look at these people as if they are trying to kill you, but you can't treat them that way.

Corollary 2: Be polite, be professional, have a plan to kill everyone you meet.

AWOL—Absent Without Leave. In previous eras of the U.S.'s military, this referred to a servicemember whose presence was unaccounted for. Presumably, the only reason one was permitted to be away from their duty station was because they had leave. *See also* Leave; UA.

AO—Area of Operations. An AO is literally the battle space or area in which a unit operates. AOs are organized, divided and subdivided in the same way units are. An AO can be assigned to a battalion and subdivided down to the most basic rifleman who has a small sector of fire while standing post.

BAS—Battalion Aid Station. The military equivalent of a clinic though organized slightly differently. In the Marine Corps, there are no medics, but have Navy Corpsmen attached to them who are trained and serve as the Navy's equivalent of a medic.

Battalion—*See* Organization of Units.

Blouse—The upper camouflage outer garment as part of a Marine's uniform.

Boat Space—Used to refer to the number of slots open in a particular MOS. This term is derived from the Navy terminology that refers to the number of people who can man a ship.

Bulkhead—A wall.

Cammies—The shorthand way to refer to camouflage fatigues or a uniform. The Marine Corps has two basic types: woodland and desert-patterned cammies.

CAS—Close Air Support. Actions taken by rotary or fixed wing aircraft to support friendly personnel and to attack enemies in an area.

CLIC—Company Level Intel Cell. This is composed of Marines who don't officially possess an intelligence MOS but operate in that capacity as assigned within a company.

COC—Company Operations Command. In essence, the command center or room for the company. It usually is composed of AO maps, monitors of cameras, a radio, radio log, and similar items. The COC is manned at all times, minimally by someone on radio watch.

COG—Corporal of the Guard. The head guard over the posts, watch, or stations. This is set up differently based on the context. While deployed, the COG is in charge of whoever is standing post at any given time. They brief and inspect those who are standing post before they begin and oversee the relief and change of command of those posts.

Company—*See* Organization of Units.

COP—Combat Out Post. Usually a smaller 'base' organized around a company or smaller unit. COPs can be as small as a squad-sized element with attachments.

Deck—A floor.

Division—*See* Organization of Units.

Drops—A drop is one who didn't make it through their respective class or training cycle. In basic training, a drop can be modified as a 'medical drop'. The collision of hundreds of people in a small, stressful space causes many illnesses to gallop through the platoons. Those that miss too much training are 'dropped' from their class into the next company so they get all their training in. In the Recon Training Platoon (RTP), a drop referred to those that quit the training. *See* RTP.

EGA—Eagle Globe and Anchor. The Marine Corps insignia given to recruits when they become Marines. Traditionally the EGA ceremony is on the Thursday before the Friday of graduation from basic training.

Fleet—Like other borrowed Navy terminology, this is used in the Marine Corps not to refer to a group of ships, but life beyond the basic steps of boot camp and MOS training when Marines arrive at their unit.

Grunt—Infantry Marines. Believed to be derived from either the abbreviation GRNT for 'ground unit' or to refer to the work that required one to 'grunt.' There are subtle distinctions within those who bear an infantry MOS designation. For example, although Recon Marines are technically in the infantry, they refer to non-Recon units as 'Grunts.' This is because their own status is more specialized, trained, and elite.

Head—A bathroom.

HESCO—The fillable barriers, usually topped with sand or soil, used for fortification of bases and COPS. The commonly recognizable HESCO style was a 4x4x6 foot box. Its exterior is a thin metal cage with a kind of burlap material inside that allows it to be fillable. Originally designed as a flood barrier that could be quickly erected, HESCOs are named for the company that developed them.

HOG—Hunter of Gunman. Refers to those Marine Corps Snipers who have finished Scout Sniper school. One step above a PIG. *See also* PIG.

Hooch—The sleeping quarters of a Marine. It could be a hole in the ground, or something more sophisticated like a small hut which houses bunk beds, which would be referred to as 'racks'. *See also* hut.

HQ—Head Quarters.

Hut—Any structure that is designed or re-appropriated to house Marines that is not technically the Barracks.

IED—Improvised Explosive Device. Often referred to as 'roadside bombs' in the media. IED warfare quickly became the choice weapon of insurgents in Iraq and Afghanistan because of its lower risk to avoid engaging coalition troops in a conventional battle and the higher payoff of inflicting damage.

Jersey Barrier—Also called a 'jersey wall.' They are modular concrete walls like those used on highway dividers often seen on interstates. They were used for fortification at most COPS in country and often used in a serpentine. *See also* COPS; Serpentine.

LCPL—*See* Ranks.

Leave—The allotted permissible time away from one's unit. After boot camp, the initial leave of a week or two is referred to as 'boot-leave.' Similarly, leave following a deployment is called 'post-deployment leave' and so on.

LZ—Landing zone. Most often used as the designated drop off and pick up points for helicopters.

MCAGCC—Marine Corps Air Ground Combat Center. The Marine Corps base located in Twentynine Palms, California.

MCRD—Marine Corps Recruit Depot. Also known as recruit training or boot camp.

MOUT Town—Mobile Operations of Urban Terrain Town. These modular, makeshift towns are designed for a host of different exercises. Most commonly used for patrolling urban style environments and practicing raiding homes.

MOS—Military Occupational Specialty. The official designation of a job represented by a four-digit code. A Marine Rifleman, for example, has the MOS code of 0311.

MSR—Main Supply Route. Used to refer to roads like 'MSR Bronze.' Used in conjunction with 'ASR' for Alternate Supply Route.

NCO—Non-Commissioned Officer. An enlisted person who has made it to a pay grade of E-4 or higher.

NJP—Non-Judicial Punishment. One of the forms of punishment the military uses for its system of military justice. *See also* UCMJ.

Organization of Units—From largest to smallest, the Marine Corps is composed of Divisions, of which there are four. The Divisions are broken down into three Regiments, which are composed of three Battalions. Three Companies make up a Battalion. Three (sometimes more) Platoons make up a Company. Three Squads make up a platoon, three teams make up a squad and four people make up a team. In all, the Marine Corps numbers approximately 186,000, making it the smallest of the primary branches in the U.S.

PFT—Physical Fitness Test. The Marine Corps standard conditioning test consisting of a max set of pullups, a 3-mile run, and a max set of sit-ups in two minutes.

PIG—Professionally Instructed Gunman. Refers to those Marines who are in a Scout Sniper Platoon (sometimes called 'STA' platoons [pronounced 'stay'; Surveillance and Target Acquisition] but have not gone through sniper school, yet). One step below a HOG. *See also* HOG.

Platoon—*See* Organization of Units.

POG—Personnel other than Grunts. Non-infantry MOSs in the Marine Corps. Usually used in a derogatory way. Among

Grunts, a sub-cultural designation was used to refer to pilots as the 'cool POGs.'

Police Call (Police)—The task of cleaning up an area on the ground. After a live fire range is completed, for example, Marines will get 'on line' forming long rows shoulder to shoulder with each other. They will then walk slowly forward to pick up every piece of expended brass casing. One of a junior Marine's basic morning routines is to police call the exterior grounds around a barracks. This includes trash and the thousands of cigarette butts that are discarded, usually by senior Marines who know they won't have to police call the trash in the morning.

QRF—Quick Reaction Force. QRFs are employed in a host of settings. The idea is to have a squad-sized element ready to rapidly deploy at a moment's notice. When someone is on QRF, they are required to remain dressed, and bloused. QRFs are sometimes alternated in layers so that one squad is on a one-minute trip warning and a second is on a five-minute trip warning. *See also* Blouse.

Ranks—The rank structure of the Marine Corps is similar to other militaries and other branches, but has its distinctives. It is divided among enlisted, officers, and warrant officers (warrant officers are not listed below, since they aren't mentioned in the book). In short, they are (with acronyms included):

E-1, Private, Pvt
E-2, Private First Class, PFC
E-3, Lance Corporal, LCpl

Noncommissioned Officers, or NCOs:
E-4, Corporal, Cpl
E-5, Sergeant, Sgt

Staff Noncommissioned Officers, or SNCOs:
E-6, Staff Sergeant, SSgt
E-7, Gunnery Sergeant, GySgt
E-8, Master Sergeant, MSgt First Sergeant, 1Sgt
E-9, Master Gunnery Sergeant, MGySgt, Sergeant Major, SgtMaj

Commissioned officers:
Company-grade officers
O-1, Second Lieutenant, 2ndLt
O-2, First Lieutenant, 1stLt
O-3, Captain, Capt

Field-grade officers
O-4, Major, Maj
O-5, Lieutenant Colonel, LtCol
O-6, Colonel, Col

Generals
O-7, Brigadier General, BGen
O-8, Major General, MajGen
O-9, Lieutenant General, LtGen
O-10, General, Gen

RBE/RBP—Remain Behind Element and Remain Behind Platoon. There are a variety of instances in which an RBE/RBP are formed. When a unit deploys, for example, and contains servicemembers that have too little time on their contract to make the deployment, an RBE or RBP stands up. Typically speaking there is minimal accountability or daily actions required of them since there is little motivation to incentivize someone who is about to finish their service.

Regiment—*See* Organization of Units.

Roper—The designation of those who have entered the Recon Training Platoon in hopes of becoming a Recon Marine. *See also* RTP.

RPG—Rocket Propelled Grenade.

RTP—Recon Training Platoon. The platoon class that is formed when the long and rigorous training to become a Recon Marine begins.

SAW—Squad Automatic Weapon. Applied to the M249 SAW, specifically. This belt-fed weapon is the fastest firing weapon in the fire team. It has been portrayed (with varying accuracy) in a host of video games, including Call of Duty.

School Circle—An organizational tool used for periods of instruction that happen in the often-unconventional pedagogical spaces in which Marines find themselves. The school circle can be formed on the fly in virtually any setting. Many units require their Marines to carry note-taking gear at all times so that they can be literally ready to take a 'hip pocket class' at the drop of a hat.

Scouts—When applied to Tank Scouts, they refer to the reconnaissance elements attached to Tank Companies to ensure a level of security and to determine the movement of the battalion. After the initial conventional warfare ceased in Iraq, Scouts assumed similar roles to other infantry units in COPS for maintaining security and standing post.

Serpentine—The intentional winding, zig zag entrance to COP entrances. The zig-zagging forces entering vehicles to slow down as they traverse around jersey barriers and other obstacles. This fortification precaution is especially necessary to guard against VBIEDs. *See also* COP; VBIED.

Skivvy Shirt—The olive-green undershirt that's part of a Marine's uniform.

SOI—School of Infantry. SOI is divided into two main parts, ITB and MCT. Those with specific infantry MOSs complete the longer ITB training while those with non-infantry MOSs first complete a reduced and simplified version of ITB before going onto their own respective MOS schools. *See also* ITB; MCT.

Squad—*See* Organization of Units.

TBS —The Basic School. TBS is for all Marine Corps Officers. Since Officers don't go through boot camp, this is a rough, more intensive equivalent. As its names implies, they cover all the basics, including coverage of all weapons systems and more attention to leading enlisted Marines.

Team—*See* Organization of Units.

UA—Unauthorized Absence. Not to be confused with the oft-used 'urine analysis' acronym in the civilian world. UA refers to what civilians know more familiarly as AWOL.

UCMJ—Uniform Code of Military Justice. The U.S.'s military justice system. It roughly resembles the broader U.S. justice system. The biggest difference is the sovereign control the military has over a person's life, even to their very job performance. A person who refuses to show up to work in the civilian world is fired. One who refuses to do their duty in the military is demoted and in extreme scenarios, discharged with something less than an honorable discharge.

VBIED—Vehicle Borne Improvised Explosive Device. As the name implies, this is a bomb that is detonated through the medium of a vehicle. A VBIED usually ends up being a volunteer suicide. *See also* IED.

Working Party—The group of Marines that is formed to work on any of the endless variety of tasks that require basic brawn and/or many hands. These vary from loading, unloading, cleaning, sorting, counting, police calling and so forth. A working party tends to consist entirely of junior Marines and is a temporary task. *See also* Police Call.

BIBLIOGRAPHY

Bialik, Kristen. '5 Facts about U.S. Veterans.' Pew Research Center. Pew Research Center, November 10, 2017. https://www.pewresearch.org/fact-tank/2017/11/10/the-changing-face-of-americas-veteran-population/.

Bossarte, Robert M. ed., Veteran Suicide: A Public Health Imperative (Washington, DC: American Public Health Association, 2013).

Crouch, Andy. The Tech-Wise Family: Everyday Steps for Putting Technology In Its Proper Place. Grand Rapids, MI: Baker Books, 2017.

Diagnostic and Statistical Manual of Mental Disorders: DSM-5. Arlington, VA: American Psychiatric Association, 2017.

Gradus, Jaimie L. 'PTSD and Death from Suicide.' *PTSD Research Quarterly* 28, no. 4 (2017). https://doi.org/https://www.ptsd.va.gov/publications/rq_docs/V28N4.pdf.

Hadhazy, Adam. 'Think Twice: How the Gut's "Second Brain" Influences Mood and Well-Being.' Scientific American.

Scientific American, February 12, 2010. https://www.scientificamerican.com/article/gut-second-brain/.

Handley, Lucy. 'Super Bowl Draws Lowest TV Audience in More than a Decade, Early Data Show.' CNBC. CNBC, February 5, 2019. https://www.cnbc.com/2019/02/05/super-bowl-draws-lowest-tv-audience-in-more-than-a-decade-nielsen.html.

Howley, Elaine K. 'Statistics on PTSD in Veterans.' U.S. News & World Report. U.S. News & World Report, June 28, 2019. https://health.usnews.com/conditions/mental-health/ptsd/articles/ptsd-veterans-statistics.

Junger, Sebastian. *Tribe: On Homecoming and Belonging.* New York, NY: Hatchet Book Group, 2017.

Kang, Han K., Tim A. Bullman, Derek J. Smolenski, Nancy A. Skopp, Gregory A. Gahm, and Mark A. Reger. 'Suicide Risk Among 1.3 Million Veterans Who Were on Active Duty During the Iraq and Afghanistan Wars.' *Annals of Epidemiology* 25, no. 2 (February 2015): 96-100. https://doi.org/10.1016/j.annepidem.2014.11.020.

Losey, Stephen. 'With Deaths By Suicide Rising, Air Force Orders Resiliency Stand-Down.' Air Force Times. Air Force Times, August 2, 2019. https://www.airforcetimes.com/news/your-air-force/2019/08/01/with-deaths-by-suicide-rising-air-force-orders-resiliency-stand-down/?utm_expid=.jFR93cgdTFyMrWXdYEtvgA.0&utm_referrer=.

Mohler, Albert. 'Homosexual "Marriage": A Tragic Oxymoron - Biblical and Cultural Reflections.' Desiring God, September 25, 2004. https://www.desiringgod.org/messages/

homosexual-marriage-a-tragic-oxymoron-biblical-and-cultural-reflections.

Pastor, Paul. 'One Hamburger, Hold the Depression, Please.' CT Pastors. Leadership Journal, September 4, 2014. https://www.christianitytoday.com/pastors/2014/fall/one-hamburger-hold-depression-please.html.

Piper, John. 'Prayer: The Work of Missions.' Desiring God. Desiring God, March 2, 2020. https://www.desiringgod.org/messages/prayer-the-work-of-missions.

'Posttraumatic Stress Disorder (PTSD).' Anxiety and Depression Association of America, ADAA. Accessed March 2, 2020. https://adaa.org/understanding-anxiety/posttraumatic-stress-disorder-ptsd.

Sanneh, Lamin O. *Translating the Message: The Missionary Impact on Culture.* Maryknoll, NY: Orbis Books, 2009.

Sledge, E. B. *With the Old Breed: At Peleliu and Okinawa.* New York, NY: Presidio Press, 2010.

Smith, Aaron. 'What People Like and Dislike about Facebook.' Pew Research Center. Pew Research Center, February 3, 2014. https://www.pewresearch.org/fact-tank/2014/02/03/what-people-like-dislike-about-facebook/.

'Suicide in America: Frequently Asked Questions.' National Institute of Mental Health. U.S. Department of Health and Human Services. Accessed March 2, 2020. https://www.nimh.nih.gov/health/publications/suicide-faq/index.shtml.

'Suicide Prevention - Mental Health.' Veterans Affairs. VA, September 3, 2008. https://www.mentalhealth.va.gov/suicide_prevention/.

'Suicide Rising across the US.' Centers for Disease Control and Prevention. Centers for Disease Control and Prevention, June 7, 2018. https://www.cdc.gov/vitalsigns/suicide/.

Swick, Gerald. 'What Percentage of the Population Served in WW2?' HistoryNet. HistoryNet, February 13, 2019. https://www.historynet.com/what-percentage-of-the-population-served-in-ww2.htm.

Wilcox, Holly C, Carla L Storr, and Naomi Breslau. 'Posttraumatic Stress Disorder and Suicide Attempts in a Community Sample of Urban American Young Adults.' *Archives of General Psychiatry* 66, no. 3 (March 2009): 305-11. https://doi.org/doi:10.1001/archgenpsychiatry.2008.557.

Zarembo, Alan. 'Detailed Study Confirms High Suicide Rate Among Recent Veterans.' Los Angeles Times. Los Angeles Times, January 14, 2015. https://www.latimes.com/nation/la-na-veteran-suicide-20150115-story.html.

SUBJECT INDEX

Christian Focus Publications

Our mission statement –

STAYING FAITHFUL

In dependence upon God we seek to impact the world through literature faithful to His infallible Word, the Bible. Our aim is to ensure that the Lord Jesus Christ is presented as the only hope to obtain forgiveness of sin, live a useful life and look forward to heaven with Him.

Our books are published in four imprints:

CHRISTIAN FOCUS

Popular works including biographies, commentaries, basic doctrine and Christian living.

CHRISTIAN HERITAGE

Books representing some of the best material from the rich heritage of the church.

MENTOR

Books written at a level suitable for Bible College and seminary students, pastors, and other serious readers. The imprint includes commentaries, doctrinal studies, examination of current issues and church history.

CF4•K

Children's books for quality Bible teaching and for all age groups: Sunday school curriculum, puzzle and activity books; personal and family devotional titles, biographies and inspirational stories – because you are never too young to know Jesus!

Christian Focus Publications Ltd,
Geanies House, Fearn, Ross-shire,
IV20 1TW, Scotland, United Kingdom.
www.christianfocus.com